Drupal 8 Development Cookbook

Second Edition

Harness the power of Drupal 8 with this recipe-based practical guide

Matt Glaman

BIRMINGHAM - MUMBAI

Drupal 8 Development Cookbook

Second Edition

First published: March 2016

Second edition: September 2017

Production reference: 1210917

Published by Packt Publishing Ltd.
Livery Place
35 Livery Street
Birmingham
B3 2PB, UK.

ISBN 978-1-78829-040-1

www.packtpub.com

Credits

Author
Matt Glaman

Reviewer
Tracy Charles Smith

Commissioning Editor
Amarabha Banerjee

Acquisition Editor
Nigel Fernandes

Content Development Editor
Mohammed Yusuf Imaratwale

Technical Editors
Ankur Ghiye
Murtaza Tinwala

Copy Editor
Dhanya Baburaj

Project Coordinator
Ritika Manoj

Proofreader
Safis Editing

Indexer
Rekha Nair

Graphics
Jason Monteiro

Production Coordinator
Shantanu Zagade

About the Author

Matt Glaman is a Senior Drupal Consultant at Commerce Guys and co-maintainer of Drupal Commerce. He is an open source developer who has been working with Drupal since 2013. Since then, he has contributed to over 60 community project.

I would like to thank, and I am grateful to, my beautiful and loving wife for putting up with the late nights split between work, spending time contributing to the Drupal community, and writing this book. I would also like to thank my two sons; thank you for giving up your playtime so that Daddy could write this book.

Thank you, Andy Giles, for helping me get to my first Drupal camp and kicking off my Drupal career. I would also like to thank my mentors Bojan Živanović, David Snopek, Ryan Szrama, and everyone else in the Drupal community!

About the Reviewer

Tracy Charles Smith began working with computers at the age of 10. His background includes network support, web development, customer service, project management, and financial management.

Tracy's entrepreneurial spirit is a key component to his success in interacting with clients and team members on business and user-experience related technology solutions. In fact, he used that passion to found his own technology-consulting firm called Alpha Geek Tech, LLC. He also served as Technology Director for Quiddities Dev., Inc., in Santa Cruz, CA, before moving back to the DC area to join Phase2 in 2010 as a Senior Programmer. Tracy now works as a Senior Project Manager at Phase2 supporting Growth & Support clients in government and private enterprise. His diverse development background complements his project management skills.

Tracy was also the lead programmer and architect for 12seconds.tv in 2007 (a video messaging platform), which leveraged Drupal. He also authored *Drupal Intranets with Open Atrium*. He earned a BS in Computer Information Systems and Business Administration from Wingate University.

www.PacktPub.com

For support files and downloads related to your book, please visit www.PacktPub.com.

Did you know that Packt offers eBook versions of every book published, with PDF and ePub files available? You can upgrade to the eBook version at www.PacktPub.com and as a print book customer, you are entitled to a discount on the eBook copy. Get in touch with us at service@packtpub.com for more details.

At www.PacktPub.com, you can also read a collection of free technical articles, sign up for a range of free newsletters and receive exclusive discounts and offers on Packt books and eBooks.

https://www.packtpub.com/mapt

Get the most in-demand software skills with Mapt. Mapt gives you full access to all Packt books and video courses, as well as industry-leading tools to help you plan your personal development and advance your career.

Why subscribe?

- Fully searchable across every book published by Packt
- Copy and paste, print, and bookmark content
- On demand and accessible via a web browser

Customer Feedback

Thanks for purchasing this Packt book. At Packt, quality is at the heart of our editorial process. To help us improve, please leave us an honest review on this book's Amazon page at https://www.amazon.com/dp/1788290402

If you'd like to join our team of regular reviewers, you can e-mail us at customerreviews@packtpub.com. We award our regular reviewers with free eBooks and videos in exchange for their valuable feedback. Help us be relentless in improving our products!

Table of Contents

Preface   1

Chapter 1: Up and Running with Drupal 8   7

Introduction   7
Installing Drupal   8
  Getting ready   8
  How to do it...   9
  How it works...   12
  There's more...   13
    Creating a database user and a database   13
    Database prefixes   14
    Downloading and installing with Drush   15
    Using Composer to create a Drupal site   15
    Security updates   16
  See also   16
Using a distribution with Drupal   17
  How to do it...   17
  How it works...   18
  There's more...   18
    Makefiles   18
    Installing with Drush   18
    Using Composer   19
  See also...   19
Installing modules and themes   20
  Getting ready   20
  How to do it...   21
  How it works...   23
    Discovering modules and themes   23
    Module installation   24
    Theme installation   24
  There's more...   24
    Installing a module or theme using Composer 24
    Installing a module with Drush   25
    Uninstalling a module   25
  See also   26
Using multisites in Drupal 8   26
  Getting ready   26
  How to do it...   27

How it works...   27
There's more...   28
    Security concerns   28
    Domain aliases   28
See also...   29
Tools for setting up an environment   29
Getting ready   29
How to do it...   29
How it works...   30
There's more...   31
    Acquia Dev Desktop   31
    XAMPP + Bitnami   31
    Kalabox   31
See also   32
Running tests - Simpletest and PHPUnit   32
Getting ready   32
How to do it...   33
How it works...   33
There's more...   34
    Is run-tests a shell script?   34
    Running tests without Drupal installed   35
    Running specific tests   35
    PhpStorm - Drupal Test Runner   35
    DrupalCI   36
See also...   36
Chapter 2: The Content Authoring Experience   37
Introduction   37
Configuring the WYSIWYG editor   38
Getting ready   38
How to do it...   38
How it works...   39
There's more...   40
    Filter module   40
    Improved links   41
    CKEditor plugins   42
See also   42
Adding and editing content   42
Getting ready   42
How to do it...   43
How it works...   44
There's more...   45

Save as draft	45
Pathauto	45
Bulk moderation	46
See also	46
Creating a menu and linking content	46
Getting ready	47
How to do it...	47
How it works...	49
There's more...	49
Managing a contents menu link from its form	49
Providing inline editing	49
How to do it...	50
How it works...	51
There's more...	52
The outside-in approach	52
Creating a custom content type	52
How to do it...	53
How it works...	55
Applying new Drupal 8 core field types	55
Getting ready	56
How to do it...	56
Link	56
The Email field	57
The Telephone field	57
The Date field	57
The Entity Reference field	58
How it works...	59
There's more...	60
Upcoming updates	60
Views and Entity Reference	60
See also	60
Customizing the form display of a node	60
How to do it...	61
How it works...	63
There's more...	64
Managing form display modes	64
Programmatically providing a default to hidden form items	64
See also	64
Customizing the display output of a node	64
How to do it...	65
How it works...	66
Chapter 3: Displaying Content through Views	67

Introduction   67
Listing content   68
  Getting ready   68
  How to do it...   68
  How it works...   70
  There's more...   71
    Views in Drupal core initiative   71
    Views and displays   71
    Format style plugins - style and row   72
    Using the Embed display   72
  See also   73
Editing the default admin interfaces   73
  How to do it...   73
  How it works...   75
  There's more...   76
    Exposed versus non-exposed   76
    Filter identifiers   76
    Overriding routes with Views   77
Creating a block from a View   77
  Getting ready   77
  How to do it...   77
  How it works...   80
  There's more...   80
    Exposed forms as blocks   80
  See also   81
Utilizing dynamic arguments   81
  How to do it...   81
  How it works...   83
  There's more...   83
    Previewing with contextual filters   83
    Displaying as a tab on the user page   83
    Altering the page title   84
    Validation   84
    Multiple and exclusion   85
Adding a relationship in a View   85
  How to do it...   85
  How it works...   88
  There's more...   88
    Relationships provided by entity reference fields   89
    Relationships provided through custom code 89
    Using aggregation and views.   90
Providing an Entity Reference result View   90

How to do it...	91
How it works...	93
See also	93

Chapter 4: Extending Drupal — 95

Introduction	95
Creating a module	96
How to do it...	96
How it works...	97
There's more...	98
Module namespaces	98
Module discovery locations	98
Defining a package group	99
Module dependencies	99
Specifying the module's version	100
See also...	101
Defining a custom page	101
Getting ready	101
How to do it...	101
How it works...	105
There's more...	105
Parameters in routes	105
Validating parameters in routes	106
Route requirements	107
Providing dynamic routes	107
Altering existing routes	109
See also	110
Defining permissions	110
Getting ready	110
How to do it...	111
How it works...	112
There's more...	113
Restrict access flag for permissions	113
Defining permissions programmatically	113
Checking whether a user has permissions	114
Providing the configuration on the installation or update	114
Getting ready	115
How to do it...	115
How it works...	117
There's more...	118
Configuration subdirectories	118
Modifying the existing configuration on installation	119

See also	119
Creating an event subscriber	120
How to do it...	120
How it works...	123
There's more...	123
Using dependency injection	123
See also	125
Using Features 3.0	125
How to do it...	126
How it works...	128
There's more...	128
Suggested feature modules	128
Features bundles	130
Managing the configuration state of Features	131
See also	131
Chapter 5: Frontend for the Win	133
Introduction	133
Creating a custom theme based on Classy	134
How to do it...	134
How it works...	136
There's more...	137
Theme screenshots	137
Themes, logos, and favicons	137
Base themes and shared resources	138
CKEditor style sheets	139
See also	139
Using the new asset management system	140
Getting ready	140
How to do it...	140
How it works...	143
There's more...	143
CSS groups	143
Library asset options	144
Library dependencies	144
Overriding and extending other libraries	145
Using a CDN or external resource as a library	146
Manipulating libraries from hooks	147
Placing JavaScript in the header	147
See also	148
Twig templating	148
Getting ready	148

How to do it...   149
How it works...   150
There's more...   151
   Security first   151
   Theme hook suggestions   151
   Debugging template file selection and hook suggestions   152
   The Twig logic and operators   152
See also   152
Using the Breakpoint module   153
Getting ready   153
How to do it...   153
How it works...   154
There's more...   155
   Caveat for providing breakpoints from themes   155
   Accessing breakpoints programmatically   155
   Multipliers   156
See also   156
Using the Responsive Image module   156
Getting ready   156
How to do it...   157
How it works...   159
There's more...   159
   Performance first delivery   159
   Removing picturefill polyfill   159
See also   160

Chapter 6: Creating Forms with the Form API   161

Introduction   161
Creating a form   162
Getting ready   162
How to do it...   162
How it works...   166
There's more...   167
   Form element definitions   167
   The form state   167
   The form cache   168
See also   168
Using new HTML5 elements   168
Getting ready   169
How to do it...   169
How it works...   171
There's more...   172

Specific element properties	172
Creating new elements	173
See also	173
Validating form data	**173**
Getting ready	173
How to do it...	173
How it works...	176
There's more...	176
Multiple validation handlers	176
Accessing multidimensional array values	177
Element validation methods	177
Processing submitted form data	**177**
Getting ready	178
How to do it...	178
How it works...	182
There's more...	183
Multiple submit handlers	183
See also	183
Altering other forms	**184**
Getting ready	184
How to do it...	184
How it works...	187
There's more...	187
Adding additional validate handlers	188
Adding additional submit handlers	188
Chapter 7: Plug and Play with Plugins	**189**
Introduction	**189**
Creating blocks using plugins	**190**
Getting ready	190
How to do it...	190
How it works...	194
There's more...	194
Altering blocks	194
Block settings forms	195
Defining access to a block	197
See also	198
Creating a custom field type	**198**
Getting ready	199
How to do it...	199
How it works...	203
There's more...	204

Altering field types	204
Defining whether a field is empty	204
See also	204
Creating a custom field widget	205
Getting ready	205
How to do it...	205
How it works...	209
There's more...	209
Field widget settings and summary	209
See also	210
Creating a custom field formatter	210
Getting ready	210
How to do it...	210
How it works...	213
There's more...	214
Formatter settings and summary	214
See also	214
Creating a custom plugin type	215
Getting ready	215
How to do it...	215
How it works...	221
There's more...	221
Specifying an alter hook	222
Using a cache backend	222
Accessing plugins through the manager	223
See also	223

Chapter 8: Multilingual and Internationalization — 225

Introduction	225
Translating administrative Interfaces	226
Getting ready	226
How to do it...	227
How it works...	228
There's more...	229
Manually installing language files	229
Checking translation status	231
Exporting translations	231
Interface translation permissions	231
Using interface translation to customize default English strings	232
Interface text language detection	232
Providing translations for a custom module	233
See also	233

Translating configuration 234
Getting ready 234
How to do it... 234
How it works... 236
There's more... 237
Altering configuration translation info definitions 237
Translating views 237
See also 237
Translating content 238
Getting ready 238
How to do it... 238
How it works 240
There's more... 241
Flagging translations as outdated 241
Translating content links 241
Defining translation handlers for entities 242
See also 242
Creating multilingual views 242
Getting ready 243
How to do it... 243
How it works... 245
There's more... 246
Translating exposed form items and filters 246
Translating display and row format items 247
Translating page display menu items 247
See also 248
Chapter 9: Configuration Management - Deploying in Drupal 8 249
Introduction 249
Importing and exporting configurations 250
Getting ready 250
How to do it... 250
How it works... 255
There's more... 255
Configuration dependencies 255
Saving to a YAML file for a module's configuration installation 256
Configuration schemas 256
See also 257
Synchronizing site configurations 257
Getting ready 258
How to do it... 258
How it works... 260

There's more...	260
Universally Unique Identifier	261
A synchronization folder	261
Installing a configuration from a new site	261
Using command-line workflow processes	262
Getting ready...	263
How to do it...	263
How it works...	264
There's more...	265
Drush config-pull	265
Using the Drupal Console	265
Editing the configuration from the command line	266
Exporting a single configuration item	267
Using version control and command-line workflow	267
See also	268
Updating and installing new module configurations	268
How to do it...	269
How it works...	271
There's more...	271
The Configuration Development module	271
See also	272
Chapter 10: The Entity API	273
Introduction	273
Creating a configuration entity type	274
Getting ready	274
How to do it...	275
How it works...	283
There's more...	284
Available data types for schema definitions	284
See also	285
Creating a content entity type	285
Getting ready	285
How to do it...	286
How it works...	294
There's more...	294
Using the AdminHtmlRouteProvider provider	294
Making the collection route a local task tab	294
See also	295
Creating a bundle for a content entity type	295
Getting ready	296
How to do it...	296

How it works...   303
There's more...   303
  Provide action links for adding new bundles   303
See also   304
Implementing custom access control for an entity   304
Getting ready   305
How to do it...   305
How it works...   308
There's more...   309
  Controlling access to entity fields   309
See also   310
Providing a custom storage handler   310
Getting ready   310
How to do it...   311
How it works...   312
There's more...   313
  Utilizing a different storage backend for an entity   313
See also   313
Creating a route provider   314
Getting ready   314
How to do it...   314
How it works...   315
There's more...   316
  The Entity API module provides additional providers   316
See also   317

Chapter 11: Off the Drupalicon Island   319

Introduction   319
Implementing and using a third-party JavaScript library   320
Getting ready   320
How to do it...   320
How it works...   324
There's more...   324
  Best practices for handling external libraries   325
See also   325
Implementing and using a third-party CSS library   326
Getting ready   326
How to do it...   326
How it works...   330
See also   331
Implementing and using a third-party PHP library   331

Getting ready	331
How to do it...	332
How it works...	334
See also	334

Chapter 12: Web Services — 335

Introduction	335
Enabling RESTful interfaces	336
Getting ready	337
How to do it...	337
How it works...	339
There's more...	340
Using _format instead of the Accept header	340
RestResource plugin to expose data through RESTful Web Services	341
Rate limiting your API	341
Using the HAL format	342
See also	343
Using POST to create data	343
Getting ready	343
How to do it...	344
How it works...	347
There's more...	348
Using HAL and understanding _links requirements	348
Working with images	349
Using Cross-Site Request Forgery tokens	349
See also	349
Using PATCH to update data	349
Getting ready	350
How to do it...	350
How it works...	354
Using Views to provide custom data sources	354
How to do it...	355
How it works	357
There's more...	357
Controlling the key name in JSON output	357
Controlling access to RESTful Views	358
Authentication	359
Getting ready	359
How to do it	359
How it works	362
There's more...	363
Authentication provider services	363

Page cache request policies and authenticated Web service requests	363
The IP Authentication provider	364
See also	365
Using JSON API	365
Getting ready	365
How to do it	366
How it works...	367
There's more...	367
Paginating, filtering, and sorting requests	367
Installing the JSON API Extras module	368
Changing the API path prefix	369
Disabling and enhancing returned entity fields	369
Contenta CMS	371
See also	371
Chapter 13: The Drupal CLI	373
Introduction	373
Rebuilding cache in Drupal Console or Drush	374
How to do it...	374
How it works...	375
See also	376
Using Drush to interact with the database	376
Getting ready	376
How to do it...	377
How it works...	378
There's more...	378
Using gzip with sql-dump	379
Using Console to interact with the database	379
Using Drush to manage users	380
How to do it...	380
How it works...	381
There's more...	382
Advanced user-login use cases	382
Using Drupal Console	382
Scaffolding code through Console	383
Getting ready	383
How to do it...	383
How it works...	387
Making a Drush command	388
Getting ready	388
How to do it...	388
How it works...	391

There's more… 392
  Specifying the level of Drupal's bootstrap 392
See also 392
Making a Console command 392
Getting ready 393
How to do it… 393
How it works… 397
There's more… 397
  Using a Console command to create entities 397
See also 397

Index 399

Preface

Drupal is a content management system used to build websites for small businesses, e-commerce, enterprise systems, and much more. Created by over 4,500 contributors, Drupal 8 provides many new features to Drupal. Whether you are new to Drupal, or an experienced Drupalista, *Drupal 8 Development Cookbook* contains recipes to dive into what Drupal 8 has to offer.

What this book covers

Chapter 1, *Up and Running with Drupal 8*, begins by covering the requirements for running Drupal 8 and going through the installation process and extending Drupal.

Chapter 2, *The Content Authoring Experience*, dives into the content management experience in Drupal, including working with the newly bundled CKEditor.

Chapter 3, *Displaying Content through Views*, explores how to use Views to create different ways to list and display your content in Drupal.

Chapter 4, *Extending Drupal*, introduces how to write a module for Drupal, the building blocks of functionality in Drupal.

Chapter 5, *Frontend for the Win*, covers how to create a theme, work with the new templating system Twig, and harness Drupal's responsive design features.

Chapter 6, *Creating Forms with the Form API*, explains how to work with Drupal's Form API to create custom forms for collecting data.

Chapter 7, *Plug and Play with Plugins*, introduces plugins, one of the newest components in Drupal. This chapter walks through developing the plugin system to work with fields.

Chapter 8, *Multilingual and Internationalization*, introduces the features provided by Drupal 8 to create an internationalized website, supporting multiple languages for content and administration.

Chapter 9, *Configuration Management - Deploying in Drupal 8*, explains the configuration management system, new to Drupal 8, and how to import and export site configurations.

Chapter 10, *The Entity API*, dives into the Entity API in Drupal, allowing you to create custom configuration and content entities.

Chapter 11, *Off the Drupalicon Island*, explains how Drupal allows embracing the mantra of "proudly built elsewhere" and including third-party libraries with your Drupal site.

Chapter 12, *Web Services*, shows how to turn your Drupal 8 site into a web services API provider through a RESTful interface.

Chapter 13, *The Drupal CLI*, explores working with Drupal 8 through two command-line tools created by the Drupal community: Drush and Drupal Console.

What you need for this book

In order to work with Drupal 8, and to run the code examples found in this book, the following software will be required:

Web server software stack:

- Web server: Apache (recommended), Nginx, or Microsoft IIS
- Database: MySQL 5.5 or MariaDB 5.5.20 or higher
- PHP: PHP 5.5.9 or higher

The first chapter details all of these requirements, and includes a recipe highlighting an out-of-the-box development server setup.

You will also need a text editor; the following is a suggestion of popular editors and IDEs:

- Atom.io editor, https://atom.io/
- Visual Code Studio, https://code.visualstudio.com/
- PHPStorm (specific Drupal integration), https://www.jetbrains.com/phpstorm/
- Vim with Drupal configuration, https://www.drupal.org/project/vimrc
- Your operating system's default text editor or command-line file editors

Who this book is for

This book is for those have been working with Drupal, such as site builders, backend and frontend developers, and who are eager to see what awaits them when they start using Drupal 8.

Sections

In this book, you will find several headings that appear frequently (Getting ready, How to do it, How it works, There's more, and See also).

To give clear instructions on how to complete a recipe, we use these sections as follows:

Getting ready

This section tells you what to expect in the recipe, and describes how to set up any software or any preliminary settings required for the recipe.

How to do it...

This section contains the steps required to follow the recipe.

How it works...

This section usually consists of a detailed explanation of what happened in the previous section.

There's more...

This section consists of additional information about the recipe in order to make the reader more knowledgeable about the recipe.

See also

This section provides helpful links to other useful information for the recipe.

Conventions

In this book, you will find a number of text styles that distinguish between different kinds of information. Here are some examples of these styles and an explanation of their meaning.

Code words in text, database table names, folder names, filenames, file extensions, pathnames, dummy URLs, user input, and Twitter handles are shown as follows: "You will see `drupal-org.make` and `drupal-org-core.make`."

A block of code is set as follows:

```
public function alterRoutes(RouteCollection $collection) {
    // Change path of mymodule.mypage to use a hyphen
    if ($route = $collection->get('mymodule.mypage'))
```

Any command-line input or output is written as follows:

```
$ CREATE USER username@localhost IDENTIFIED BY 'password';
```

New terms and **important words** are shown in bold. Words that you see on the screen, for example, in menus or dialog boxes, appear in the text like this: "Check the checkbox and click on **Install**."

Warnings or important notes appear in a box like this.

Tips and tricks appear like this.

Reader feedback

Feedback from our readers is always welcome. Let us know what you think about this book-what you liked or disliked. Reader feedback is important for us as it helps us develop titles that you will really get the most out of.

To send us general feedback, simply e-mail feedback@packtpub.com, and mention the book's title in the subject of your message.

If there is a topic that you have expertise in and you are interested in either writing or contributing to a book, see our author guide at www.packtpub.com/authors .

Customer support

Now that you are the proud owner of a Packt book, we have a number of things to help you to get the most from your purchase.

Downloading the example code

You can download the example code files for this book from your account at `http://www.packtpub.com`. If you purchased this book elsewhere, you can visit `http://www.packtpub.com/support` and register to have the files e-mailed directly to you.

You can download the code files by following these steps:

1. Log in or register to our website using your e-mail address and password.
2. Hover the mouse pointer on the **SUPPORT** tab at the top.
3. Click on **Code Downloads & Errata**.
4. Enter the name of the book in the **Search** box.
5. Select the book for which you're looking to download the code files.
6. Choose from the drop-down menu where you purchased this book from.
7. Click on **Code Download**.

You can also download the code files by clicking on the **Code Files** button on the book's webpage at the Packt Publishing website. This page can be accessed by entering the book's name in the **Search** box. Please note that you need to be logged in to your Packt account.

Once the file is downloaded, please make sure that you unzip or extract the folder using the latest version of:

- WinRAR / 7-Zip for Windows
- Zipeg / iZip / UnRarX for Mac
- 7-Zip / PeaZip for Linux

The code bundle for the book is also hosted on GitHub at `https://github.com/PacktPublishing/Drupal-8-Development-Cookbook-Second-Edition`. We also have other code bundles from our rich catalog of books and videos available at `https://github.com/PacktPublishing/`. Check them out!

Errata

Although we have taken every care to ensure the accuracy of our content, mistakes do happen. If you find a mistake in one of our books-maybe a mistake in the text or the code-we would be grateful if you could report this to us. By doing so, you can save other readers from frustration and help us improve subsequent versions of this book. If you find any errata, please report them by visiting http://www.packtpub.com/submit-errata, selecting your book, clicking on the **Errata Submission Form** link, and entering the details of your errata. Once your errata are verified, your submission will be accepted and the errata will be uploaded to our website or added to any list of existing errata under the Errata section of that title.

To view the previously submitted errata, go to https://www.packtpub.com/books/content/support and enter the name of the book in the search field. The required information will appear under the **Errata** section.

Piracy

Piracy of copyrighted material on the Internet is an ongoing problem across all media. At Packt, we take the protection of our copyright and licenses very seriously. If you come across any illegal copies of our works in any form on the Internet, please provide us with the location address or website name immediately so that we can pursue a remedy.

Please contact us at copyright@packtpub.com with a link to the suspected pirated material.

We appreciate your help in protecting our authors and our ability to bring you valuable content.

Questions

If you have a problem with any aspect of this book, you can contact us at questions@packtpub.com, and we will do our best to address the problem.

1
Up and Running with Drupal 8

In this chapter, we will get introduced to Drupal 8 and cover the following recipes:

- Installing Drupal
- Using a distribution with Drupal
- Installing modules and themes
- Using multisites in Drupal 8
- Tools for setting up an environment
- Running tests: Simpletest and PHPUnit

Introduction

This chapter will kick off with an introduction to installing a Drupal 8 site. We will walk through Drupal's interactive installer. We will cover installing Drupal using a command-line tool called Drush. Drupal provides two installation types: standard and minimal. Throughout this book, we will use the standard installation.

Once we have installed our Drupal 8 site, we will cover the basics of extending Drupal. We will discuss using distributions and installing contributed projects, such as modules and themes. We will also include uninstalling modules, as the process for uninstalling modules has changed in Drupal 8.

This book will involve a hands-on example for working with Drupal 8, and this chapter will provide information on setting up a local development environment. This chapter will also provide recipes on how to set up a Multisite installation in Drupal 8 and run the available test suites.

Before we get started, you should install Composer. Composer is the de facto package management tool for PHP. In case you are unfamiliar with Composer, it is just like using Gems for Ruby, npm for Node.js, and Bower for frontend libraries. Go to the Composer documentation to learn how to install Composer globally on your system:

- Linux / Unix / macOS:
  `https://getcomposer.org/doc/00-intro.md#installation-linux-unix-osx`
- **Windows:** `https://getcomposer.org/doc/00-intro.md#installation-windows`

Installing Drupal

There are many different methods to download Drupal and install it. In this recipe, we will focus on downloading Drupal from `https://www.drupal.org/` and setting it up on a basic Linux, Apache, MySQL, or PHP (LAMP) server.

In this recipe, we will set up the files for Drupal 8 and step through the installation process.

Getting ready

Before we start, you will need a development environment that meets the new system requirements for Drupal 8:

- Apache 2.0 (or higher) or Nginx 1.1 (or higher) web server
- PHP 5.5.9 or higher, but PHP 5.6 or PHP 7 is recommended, as PHP 5.5 has reached its end-of-life support
- MySQL 5.5 or MariaDB 5.5.20 for your database

 You will need a user with privileges to create databases or a created database with a user who has privileges to make tables in that database.

- Access to upload or move files to the server
- While a default installation of PHP will work with Drupal, it does require certain PHP extensions, such as mbstring. Check out `https://www.drupal.org/requirements/php` for up-to-date requirement information.

Drupal 8 ships with Symfony (`https://symfony.com/`) components. One of the new dependencies in Drupal 8, to support the Symfony routing system, is the Drupal `Clean URL` functionality. If the server is using Apache, ensure that `mod_rewrite` is enabled. If the server is using Nginx, the `ngx_http_rewrite_module` must be enabled.

We will download Drupal 8 and place its files in your web server's document root. This is the `/var/www` folder. If you used a tool, such as XAMPP, WAMP, or MAPP, consult the proper documentation to know your document root.

For full system requirements for Drupal 8, check out `https://www.drupal.org/docs/8/system-requirements/`. The Drupal.org documentation is currently being migrated. Also, review the Drupal 7 requirements page on `https://www.drupal.org/docs/7/system-requirements/overview`, which highlights Drupal 8 items, as well.

How to do it...

We need to follow these steps to install Drupal 8:

1. First, we will need to navigate to `https://www.drupal.org/download` and download the latest release of Drupal 8.x. You can find the most recent and recommended release on the `https://www.drupal.org/project/drupal` page for Drupal 8 (8.3.1, 8.4.0, and so on). Extract the archive and place the files in your document root as the `drupal8` folder :

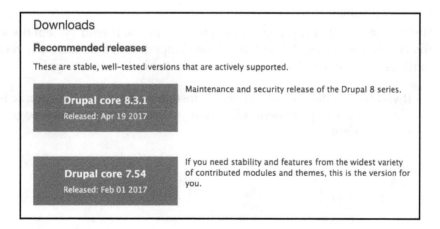

2. Open your browser and visit your web server, for example, `http://localhost/drupal8`, which will then take you to the Drupal installation wizard. You will land on the new multilingual options install screen. Select your language and click on **Save and continue**:

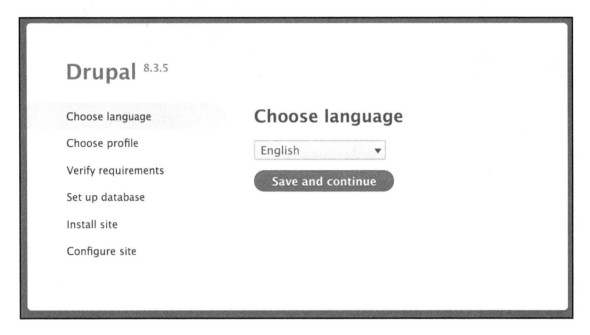

3. On the next screen, select the default **Standard** option for the installation profile. This will provide us with a standard configuration with the most commonly used modules installed.

4. The next step will verify your system requirements. If your system does not have any reportable issues, the screen will be skipped. If you do have any requirement conflicts, you can resolve them and click on the button to try again.

 If you have requirement issues, the installer will report the specific issues. Nearly every requirement will link to a Drupal.org handbook page with solution steps.

5. Enter the database information for Drupal. In most cases, you will only need to supply the username, password, and database name and leave others as defaults. If your database does not exist, the installer will attempt to create the database:

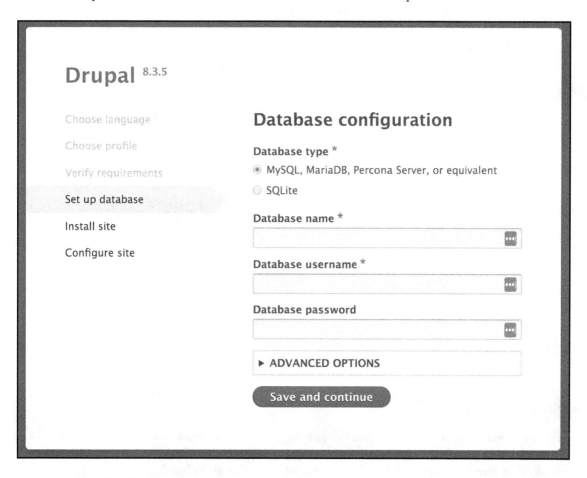

 See the *There's more...* section of this recipe for information on setting up your database.

6. Your Drupal 8 site will begin installing. When it is done installing the base modules, you will be taken to a site configuration screen.

7. The configure site form provides the base configuration for your Drupal site. Enter your site name and the email address for the site. The site email will be used to send administrative notifications and has the originating email for outgoing emails from the Drupal site. This form allows you to set regional information regarding the country and time zone of the site. Setting the timezone ensures that time values display correctly.

8. Fill in the site maintenance account information, also known as user 1, which acts in a similar way to the root on Unix-based systems. The site maintenance account is crucial. As stated, this acts as the first user and is given the user ID of 1. In Drupal, the user with the user ID of 1 often can bypass permission checks automatically and have global access.

9. Enter the site's regional information, and check whether the site should check for updates available for modules enabled and Drupal itself. By checking for updates automatically, your site will report anonymous usage statistics to Drupal along with providing a summary of your version status. You have the option to also opt-in for the site to email you notifications of new releases, including security releases.

10. When the information is satisfied, click on **Save and continue**, and congratulations, you installed Drupal! The next screen will provide you a link to your installed Drupal site.

How it works...

The Drupal installation process will provide a Drupal installation for the selected language and install modules and configuration based on the installation profile (standard or minimal in this recipe.)

When you visit the installer, it reads the language code from the browser. With this language code, it will then select a supported language. If you choose a non-English installation, the translation files will be automatically downloaded from `https://localize.drupal.org/`. Previous versions of Drupal did not support automated multilingual installs. More on multilingual will be covered in *Chapter 8, Multilingual and Internationalization*.

The installation profile instructs Drupal what modules to install by default. Contributed install profiles are termed distributions; we will discuss this more in the next recipe.

When verifying requirements, Drupal checks application versions and PHP configurations. For example, if your server has the PHP Xdebug (`https://xdebug.org`) extension installed, the minimum `max_nesting_level` must be 256 or else Drupal will not be installed (`https://www.drupal.org/node/2393531`).

There's more...

The Drupal installation process is straightforward, but there are a few things worth discussing.

Creating a database user and a database

As mentioned earlier, to install Drupal, you will need to have access to a database server (or the ability to create one) and an existing database (or the ability to create one). This process will depend on your environment setup.

If you are working with a hosting provider, there is more than likely a web-based control panel. This should allow you to create databases and users. Refer to your hosting provider's documentation for more information on this topic.

If you are using **phpMyAdmin** (`https://www.phpmyadmin.net/`) on your server, often installed by MAMP, WAMP, and XAMPP, and have root access, you can create your databases and users by following these steps:

1. Sign in to phpMyAdmin as the root user.
2. Click on **Add a new User** from the bottom of the privileges page.
3. Fill in the user's information.
4. Select to create a database for the user with all privileges granted.
5. You can now use that user's information to connect Drupal to your database.

If you do not have a user interface but have a command-line access, you can set up your database and user using the MySQL command line. These instructions can be found in the `core/INSTALL.mysql.txt` file. From the command line of your site, perform the following:

1. Log in to MySQL:

```
$ mysql -u username -p
```

2. Create the database; you will use the following command to create the `my_database` database:

```
$ CREATE DATABASE my_database CHARACTER SET utf8 COLLATE
utf8_general_ci;
```

3. Create a new user to access the database:

```
$ CREATE USER username@localhost IDENTIFIED BY 'password';
```

4. Grant the new user permissions on the database, as follows:

```
$ GRANT SELECT, INSERT, UPDATE, DELETE, CREATE, DROP, INDEX, ALTER,
CREATE TEMPORARY TABLES ON databasename.* TO 'username'@'localhost'
IDENTIFIED BY 'password';
```

 If you are installing Drupal with a PostgreSQL or SQLite database, check out the appropriate installation instructions, either `INSTALL.pgsql.txt` or `INSTALL.sqlite.txt`.

Database prefixes

Drupal, like other content management systems, allows you to prefix its database tables from the database set-up form. This prefix will be placed before table names to help make them unique. Although it is not recommended, this would allow multiple installations to share one database. Utilizing table prefixes can, however, provide some level of security through obscurity since the tables will not be their default names:

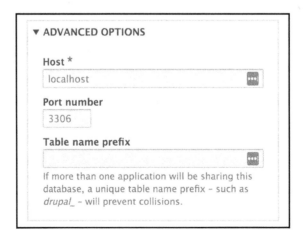

Downloading and installing with Drush

You may also install Drupal using the PHP command-line tool, Drush. Drush is a command-line tool created by the Drupal community and must be installed if you wish to use it. Drush is covered in *Chapter 13*, *The Drupal CLI*.

 As of Drush 9, which supports Drupal 8.3+, this section is deprecated. Using Drush to download Drupal core or contributed modules will throw a warning to use Composer instead.

The `pm-download` command will download packages from Drupal.org. The `site-install` command will allow you to specify an installation profile and other options to install a Drupal site. The installation steps in this recipe could be run through Drush, as follows:

```
$ cd /path/to/web
$ drush pm-download drupal-8 drupal8
$ cd drupal8
$ drush site-install standard -locale=en-US --account-name=admin --account-
pass=admin -account-email=demo@example.com -db-
url=mysql://user:pass@localhost/database
```

We used Drush to download the latest Drupal 8 and place it in a folder named `drupal8`. Then, the `site-install` command instructs Drush to use the standard install profile, configure the maintenance account, and provide a database URI string so that Drupal can connect to its database.

Using Composer to create a Drupal site

You can download Drupal using Composer, the de facto PHP package manager. The preferred method is to use the Drupal Composer project template provided by the community.

To build your Drupal 8 site, run the following commands:

```
$ cd /path/to/document/root
$ composer create-project drupal-composer/drupal-project drupal8 --
stability dev
```

Wait for the commands to finish--it may take some time, as it downloads all the required dependencies. You can feel free to grab a coffee (the first time takes a while; it primes caches. Have faith, it will be much faster the next time.)

When finished, you will find a different directory structure inside your `drupal8` directory. The `vendor` directory contains all third-party PHP libraries, and the `web` directory contains your Drupal 8 site. You will need to modify your web server to use the `web` directory as the new docroot within your `drupal8` directory.

The project and its details can be found at `https://github.com/drupal-composer/drupal-project`, along with its full documentation.

Security updates

If you choose to disable the update options, you will have to check manually for module upgrades. While most upgrades are for bug fixes or features, some are for security updates. It is highly recommended that you subscribe to the Drupal security team's updates. These updates are available on Twitter at `@drupalsecurity` (`https://twitter.com/drupalsecurity`) or the feeds on `https://www.drupal.org/security`.

See also

- For more on multilingual, check out `Chapter 8`, *Multilingual and Internationalization*
- For more on using the command line and Drupal, check out `Chapter 13`, *The Drupal CLI*
- Check out the Drupal.org handbook on installing Drupal at `https://www.drupal.org/documentation/install`
- Check out the Drupal.org handbook that discusses Drupal 8 and Composer at `https://www.drupal.org/docs/develop/using-composer/using-composer-with-drupal`
- Check out more information on Drush site install at `https://drushcommands.com/drush-8x/core/site-install/`

Using a distribution with Drupal

Why would you want to use a distribution? A distribution is a contributed installation profile that is not provided by Drupal core. Distributions provide a specialized version of Drupal with specific installed modules and themes along with specific configurations (content types, and blocks.) On Drupal.org, when you download an installation profile, it not only includes the profile and its modules but a version of Drupal core, hence the name distribution. You can find a list of all Drupal distributions at https://www.drupal.org/project/project_distribution.

How to do it...

We will follow these steps to download a distribution to use as a customized version of Drupal 8:

1. Download a distribution from Drupal.org. For this recipe, let's use the Demo Framework provided by Acquia at https://www.drupal.org/project/df.

2. Select the recommended version for the 8.x branch.

3. Extract the folder contents to your web server's document root--you'll note that there is Drupal core; within the profiles folder, there's the installation profile's folder--df.

4. Due to current Drupal.org packaging limitations, there is a manual step that you will need to run in order to install additional dependencies. Run the following command using your terminal inside of the extracted contents:

```
$ composer require "commerceguys/intl: ~0.7"
"commerceguys/addressing: ~1.0" "commerceguys/zone: ~1.0"
"embed/embed: ~2.2
```

5. Install Drupal as you would normally, by navigating to your Drupal site in your browser.

6. Follow the installation instructions in the site to install the distribution.

How it works...

Installation profiles work by including additional modules that are part of the contributed project realm or custom modules. The profile will then define them as dependencies to be installed with Drupal. When you select an installation profile, you are instructing Drupal to install a set of modules on installation.

Demo Framework declares itself as an exclusive installation profile. Distributions that declare this are automatically selected and assumed to be the default installation option. The exclusive flag was added with Drupal 7.22 to improve the experience of using a Drupal distribution (`http://drupal.org/node/1961012`).

There's more...

Distributions provide a specialized version of Drupal with specific feature sets, but there are a few items worth discussing.

Makefiles

The current standard for generating a built distribution is the utilization of Drush and makefiles. Makefiles allow a user to define a specific version of Drupal core and other projects (such as themes, modules, and third-party libraries) that will make up a Drupal code base. It is not a dependency management workflow, like Composer, but is a build tool.

If you take a look at the Demo Framework's `profile` folder, you will see `drupal-org.make` and `drupal-org-core.make`. These are parsed by the Drupal.org packager to compile the code base and package it as a `.zip` or `.tar.gz`, like the one you downloaded.

Installing with Drush

As discussed in the first recipe's *There's more...* section, you can install a Drupal site through the Drush command-line tool. You can instruct Drush to use a specific installation profile by providing it as the first argument.

 As of Drush 9, which supports Drupal 8.3+, this section is deprecated. Using Drush to download Drupal core or contributed modules will throw a warning to use Composer instead.

The following command would install the Drupal 8 site using the Demo Framework:

```
$ cd /path/to/drupal8
$ drush pm-download df
$ drush site-install df –db-url=mysql://user:pass@localhost/database
```

Using Composer

Currently, Drupal.org does not package distributions using Composer, which is why there was an extra step to add dependencies when installing the distribution. Many distributions provide project templates to make scaffolding projects simpler.

For example, the following command will set up a Demo Framework site with `docroot` as the directory for the web server document root, which contains Drupal 8:

```
$ composer create-project acquia/df-project df
```

The project template is available on Acqua's GitHub at `https://github.com/acquia/df-project/`.

Another distribution, Open Social, provides a template of its own:

```
$ composer create-project goalgorilla/social_template
```

The project template is available at `https://github.com/goalgorilla/social_template`.

See also...

- Refer to `Chapter 13`, *The Drupal CLI*, for information on makefiles.
- Refer to Distribution documentation on Drupal at `https://www.drupal.org/documentation/build/distributions`.
- Refer to *Managing Your Drupal Project with Composer* at `https://glamanate.com/blog/managing-your-drupal-project-composer`.
- Refer to Managing your Drupal platform with Drush at `https://glamanate.com/blog/managing-your-drupal-platform-drush`.

Installing modules and themes

Drupal 8 provides more functionality out-of-the-box than previous versions of Drupal, allowing you to do more with less. However, one of the more appealing aspects of Drupal is the ability to extend and customize.

In this recipe, we will download and enable the Honeypot module (`https://www.drupal.org/project/honeypot`) and tell Drupal to use the Bootstrap theme (`https://www.drupal.org/project/bootstrap`). The Honeypot module provides Honeypot and timestamps antispam measures on Drupal sites. This module helps protect forms from spam submissions. The Bootstrap theme implements the Bootstrap frontend framework and supports using Bootswatch styles to theme your Drupal site.

 This chapter's recipe will use the standard way of installing modules, by downloading archives available on Drupal.org. As of Drupal 8.2.0, installing modules through Composer has been possible and is the required method for some modules. Installing modules and themes using Composer is covered in the *There's more...* section of this recipe and is highly recommended.

Getting ready

If you have used Drupal before, note that the folder structure has changed. Modules, themes, and profiles are now placed in their respective folders in the `root` directory and no longer under `sites/all`. For more information about the developer experience change, refer to `https://www.drupal.org/node/22336`.

 Downloading the example code: You can download the example code files for all Packt books you have purchased from your account at `http://www.packtpub.com`. If you have purchased this book from elsewhere, you can go to `http://www.packtpub.com/support` and register yourself to have the files emailed directly to you.

How to do it...

Let's install modules and themes:

1. Visit `https://www.drupal.org/project/honeypot` and download the latest 8.x release for Honeypot.

2. Extract the archive and place the `honeypot` folder inside the `modules` folder, which is inside of your Drupal core installation:

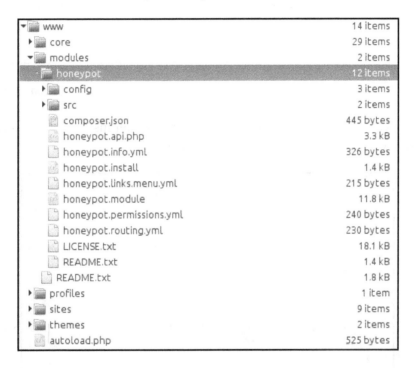

▼ www	14 items
▶ core	29 items
▼ modules	2 items
· honeypot	12 items
▶ config	3 items
▶ src	2 items
composer.json	445 bytes
honeypot.api.php	3.3 kB
honeypot.info.yml	326 bytes
honeypot.install	1.4 kB
honeypot.links.menu.yml	215 bytes
honeypot.module	11.8 kB
honeypot.permissions.yml	240 bytes
honeypot.routing.yml	230 bytes
LICENSE.txt	18.1 kB
README.txt	1.4 kB
README.txt	1.8 kB
▶ profiles	1 item
▶ sites	9 items
▶ themes	2 items
autoload.php	525 bytes

3. In Drupal, log in and select the **Extend** option to access the list of available modules.

4. Using the search text field, type in `Honeypot`. Check the checkbox and click on **Install**.

5. Once enabled, search for it again. Clicking on the module's description will expand the row and expose links to configure permissions and module settings:

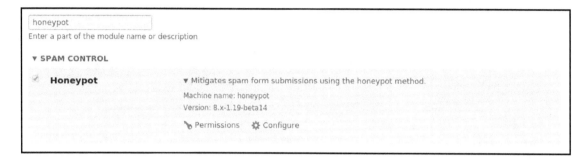

6. Visit `https://www.drupal.org/project/bootstrap` and download the latest 8.x release for Bootstrap.

7. Extract the archive and place the `bootstrap` folder inside the `themes` folder, which is inside your Drupal core installation:

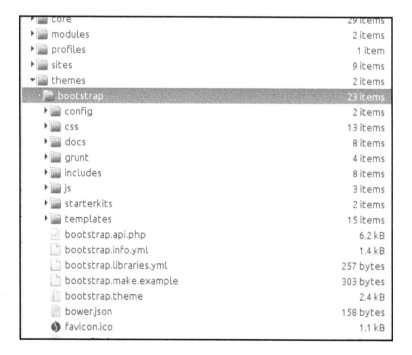

8. In Drupal, select the **Appearance** option to manage your Drupal themes.
9. Scroll down the page and click on **Install and set as default** under **Bootstrap** to enable and set the theme as default:

How it works...

The following sections outline the procedure for installing a module or theme and how Drupal discovers these extensions.

Discovering modules and themes

Drupal scans specific folder locations to identify modules and themes defined by the `.info.yml` file in their directory. The following is the order in which projects will be discovered:

- Their respective core folders (modules, or themes)
- The currently installed profile
- The root `modules` or `themes` folder
- The current site directory (default or current domain)

Module installation

By placing the module inside the root `modules` folder, we are allowing Drupal to discover the module and allow it to be installed. When a module is installed, Drupal will register its code with the system through the `module_installer` service. The service will check for required dependencies and prompt them to be enabled if required. The configuration system will run any configuration definitions provided by the module on installation. If there are conflicting configuration items, the module *will not be installed*.

Theme installation

A theme is installed through the `theme_installer` service and sets any default configuration by the theme along with rebuilding the theme registry. Setting a theme to default is a configuration change in `system.theme.default` to the theme's machine name (in the recipe, it would be `bootstrap`).

There's more...

The following section outlines the procedure for installing a module or theme and includes some additional information for installing.

Installing a module or theme using Composer

Although it is not the required way to install an extension, this should become your default method. Why? Because each module is a dependency in your project, and each of those may have its own dependencies. Composer can manage dependencies for you, or you can manage them manually. Your time and capabilities probably will not grow to scale as well as Composer will. Not to mention, it also provides a standard way for PHP projects to interoperate and load classes.

You can get the Honeypot module and Bootstrap using the following two commands:

```
$ cd /path/to/drupal8
$ composer require drupal/honeypot
$ composer require drupal/bootstrap
```

Here is an example of contributed projects, which require Composer for installation, because they leverage existing libraries in the PHP community at large:

- Drupal Commerce
- GeoIP
- Search API Solr
- Entity Print

As more and more modules integrate existing SDK libraries, the requirement to use Composer will increase.

Installing a module with Drush

Modules can be downloaded and enabled through the command line using `drush`. The command to replicate the recipe would resemble the following:

```
$ drush pm-download honeypot
$ drush pm-enable honeypot
```

 As of Drush 9, which supports Drupal 8.3+, this section is deprecated. Using Drush to download Drupal core or contributed modules will throw a warning to use Composer instead.

It will prompt you to confirm your action. If there were dependencies for the module, it would ask whether you will like to enable those, too.

 Drush simply downloads the archive available from Drupal.org. If the module or theme requires third-party PHP library dependencies, these will not be downloaded or be available in Drupal's class autoloading process.

Uninstalling a module

One of the substantial changes in Drupal 8 is the module disable and uninstall process. Previously, modules were first disabled and then uninstalled once disabled. This created a confusing process, which would disable its features, but not clean up any database schema changes. In Drupal 8, modules cannot just be disabled but must be uninstalled. This ensures that when a module is uninstalled it can safely be removed from the code base.

A module can only be uninstalled if it is not a dependency of another module or does not have a configuration item in use--such as a field type--which could disrupt the installation's integrity.

 With a standard installation, the Comment module cannot be uninstalled until you delete all the Comment fields on the article content type. This is because the field type is in use.

See also

- Refer to Chapter 4, *Extending Drupal*, to learn about setting defaults on enabling a module.
- Refer to Chapter 9, *Configuration Management - Deploying in Drupal 8*.

Using multisites in Drupal 8

Drupal provides the ability to run multiple sites from one single Drupal code base instance. This feature is referred to as multisite. Each site has a separate database; however, extensions stored in *modules*, *profiles*, and *themes* can be installed by all of the sites. Site folders can also contain their own modules and themes. When provided, these can only be used by that one site.

The default folder is the default folder used if there is no matching domain name.

Getting ready

If you are going to work with multisite functionality, you should have an understanding of how to set up virtual host configurations with your web server. In this recipe, we will use two subdomains under localhost, called dev1 and dev2.

How to do it...

We will use multisites in Drupal 8 by two subdomains under localhost:

1. Copy `sites/example.sites.php` to `sites/sites.php`.
2. Create a `dev1.localhost` and `dev2.localhost` folder inside the `sites` folder.
3. Copy the `sites/default/default.settings.php` file into `dev1.localhost` and `dev2.localhost` as `settings.php` in their respective folder:

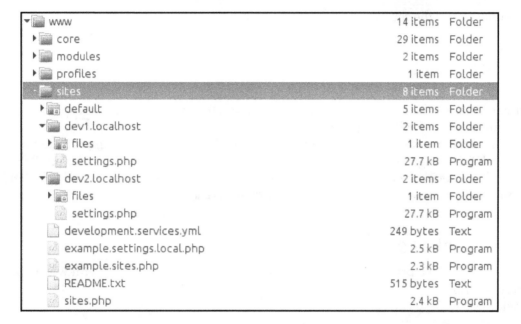

▼ 🗀 www	14 items	Folder
▶ 🗀 core	29 items	Folder
▶ 🗀 modules	2 items	Folder
▶ 🗀 profiles	1 item	Folder
▾ 🗀 sites	8 items	Folder
▶ 🗀 default	5 items	Folder
▾ 🗀 dev1.localhost	2 items	Folder
▶ 🗀 files	1 item	Folder
🗎 settings.php	27.7 kB	Program
▾ 🗀 dev2.localhost	2 items	Folder
▶ 🗀 files	1 item	Folder
🗎 settings.php	27.7 kB	Program
🗎 development.services.yml	249 bytes	Text
🗎 example.settings.local.php	2.5 kB	Program
🗎 example.sites.php	2.3 kB	Program
🗎 README.txt	515 bytes	Text
🗎 sites.php	2.4 kB	Program

4. Got to `dev1.localhost` and run the installation wizard.
5. Got to `dev2.localhost` and verify that you still have the option to install a site!

How it works...

The `sites.php` must exist for the multisite functionality to work. By default, you do not need to modify its contents. The `sites.php` file provides a way to map aliases to specific site folders. The file contains the documentation for using aliases.

The `DrupalKernel` class provides `findSitePath` and `getSitePath` methods to discover the site folder path. On Drupal's Bootstrap, this is initiated and reads the incoming HTTP host to load the proper `settings.php` file from the appropriate folder. The `settings.php` file is then loaded and parsed into a `\Drupal\Core\Site\Settings` instance. This allows Drupal to connect to the appropriate database.

There's more...

Let's understand the security concerns of using multisite.

Security concerns

There can be cause for concern if you are using multisite. Arbitrary PHP code executed on a Drupal site might be able to affect other sites sharing the same code base. Drupal 8 marked the removal of the PHP filter (https://www.drupal.org/docs/8/modules/php/overview) module that allowed site administrators to use PHP code in the administrative interface. Although this mitigates the various ways an administrator had easy access to run PHP through an interface, it does not mitigate the risk wholesale. For example, the PHP filter module is now a contributed project and could be installed.

Domain aliases

The `sites.php` file provides a way to add domain aliases. This can be useful when you use a multisite functionality and need to develop it locally. A simple example would be providing a `local.alias` to each site.

If you had `example.com` and `mycompany.com` as different site directories, the following mapping would allow `local.example.com` and `local.mycompany.com` to map to those directories:

```php
<?php
$sites['example.com'] = 'example.com';
$sites['local.example.com'] = 'example.com';
$sites['mycompany.com'] = 'mycompany.com';
$sites['local.mycompany.com'] = 'mycompany.com';
```

See also...

- Refer to Multisite documentation on Drupal
  at `https://www.drupal.org/documentation/install/multi-site`.

Tools for setting up an environment

One of the initial hurdles to getting started with Drupal is a local development environment. This recipe will cover how to set up the DrupalVM project by Jeff Geerling. DrupalVM is a VirtualBox virtual machine run through Vagrant, provisioned and configured with Ansible. It will set up all of your services and build a Drupal installation for you.

Luckily, you will only need to have VirtualBox and Vagrant installed on your machine, and DrupalVM works on Windows, macOS X, and Linux.

Getting ready

To get started, you will need to install the two dependencies required for DrupalVM:

- **VirtualBox**: `https://www.virtualbox.org/wiki/Downloads`
- **Vagrant**: `http://www.vagrantup.com/downloads.html`

How to do it...

Let's set up the DrupalVM project by Jeff Geerling by following these steps:

1. Download the DrupalVM archive from
   `https://github.com/geerlingguy/drupal-vm/archive/master.zip`.
2. Extract the archive and place the project in the directory of your choice.
3. Copy `example.drupal.make.yml` to `drupal.make.yml`.
4. Copy `default.config.yml` to `config.yml`.

5. Edit `config.yml` and modify the `local_path` setting to be the directory where you've placed the DrupalVM project. This will be synchronized into the virtual machine:

```
vagrant_synced_folders:
local_path: /path/to/drupalvm
destination: /var/www
type: nfs
create: true
```

6. Open a terminal and navigate to the directory where you have placed the DrupalVM project.
7. Enter the `vagrant up` command to tell Vagrant to build the virtual machine and begin the provisioning process.
8. While this process is ongoing, modify your host file to provide easy access to the development site. Add the `192.168.88.88 drupalvm.dev` line to your host file.
9. Open your browser and access `http://www.drupalvm.com/`.
10. Log in to your Drupal site with the username `admin` and password `admin`.

How it works...

DrupalVM is a development project that utilizes the Vagrant tool to create a VirtualBox virtual machine. Vagrant is configured through the project's `Vagrantfile`. Vagrant then uses Ansible--an open source IT automation platform--to install Apache, PHP, MySQL, and other services on the virtual machine.

The `config.yml` file has been set up to provide a simple way to customize variables for the virtual machine and provisioning process. It also uses Drush to create and install a Drupal 8 site, or whatever components are specified in `drupal.make.yml`. This file is a Drush `make` file, which contains a definition for Drupal core by default and can be modified to include other contributed projects.

The `vagrant up` command tells Vagrant to either launch an existing virtual machine or create one anew in a headless manner. When Vagrant creates a new virtual machine, it triggers the provisioning process. In this instance, Ansible will read the `provisioning/playbook.yml` file and follow each step to create the final virtual machine. The only files that need to be modified, however, are the `config.yml` and `drupal.make.yml` files.

There's more...

The topic of automating and streamlining a local environment is quite popular right now with quite a few different options. If you are not comfortable with using Vagrant, there are a few other options that provide a server installation and Drupal.

Acquia Dev Desktop

Acquia Dev Desktop is developed by Acquia and can be found at `https://docs.acquia.com/dev-desktop2`. It is an automated environment installer for Windows and Mac. It is a xAMP stack (or DAMP stack) installer that provides a full Drupal-specific stack that includes Apache, MySQL, and PHP. The Dev Desktop application allows you to create a regular Drupal installation or select from a distribution.

XAMPP + Bitnami

XAMPP - Apache + MySQL + PHP + Perl - is a cross-platform environment installation. XAMPP is an open source project from Apache Friends. XAMPP has partnered with Bitnami (`https://bitnami.com/`) to provide free all-in-one installations for common applications, including Drupal 8. You can download XAMPP at `https://www.apachefriends.org/download.html`.

Kalabox

Kalabox is developed by the Kalamuna group and intends to be a robust workflow solution for Drupal development. Kalabox is cross-platform compatible, allowing you to easily work on Windows machines. It is based on the command line and provides application binaries for you to install. You can learn more about Kalabox at `http://www.kalamuna.com/products/kalabox/`.

See also

- Refer to *Chapter 13*, *The Drupal CLI*, for information on makefiles.
- DrupalVM documentation http://docs.drupalvm.com/en/latest/.
- Refer to Drupal.org community documentation on local environment setup at https://www.drupal.org/node/157602.

Running tests - Simpletest and PHPUnit

Drupal 8 ships with two testing suites. Previously, Drupal only supported Simpletest. Now, there are PHPUnit tests as well. In the official change record, PHPUnit was added to provide testing without requiring a full Drupal Bootstrap, which occurs with each Simpletest test. You can read the change record at https://www.drupal.org/node/2012184.

There is currently a PHPUnit initiative active in Drupal core development. The goal is to fully remove the Simpletest framework by Drupal 9. No new Simpletest tests are being written, at least since 8.2. All current tests are currently being converted by contributors. More about the initiative can be found in this issue, https://www.drupal.org/node/2807237, where it is being coordinated.

We will be running tests using the run-tests.sh test runner. This is a test runner provided by Drupal that supports concurrency and running all of the various test suites. Running tests directly with PHPUnit will be covered in the following *There's more...* section.

Getting ready

Drupal 8.1.0 introduced the ability to perform JavaScript browser tests. This is powered using PhantomJS (http://phantomjs.org/), which uses a browser emulator powered by the Mink PHP library (http://mink.behat.org/). In order to run the FunctionalJavascript test suite, you must have PhantomJS running.

To install PhantomJS, refer to the official installation instructions at http://phantomjs.org/download.html.

How to do it...

1. First, install the `Simpletest` module. Even though you might only want to run PHPUnit, this is a soft dependency for running the test runner script.
2. Open a command-line terminal and navigate to your Drupal installation directory.
3. Next, we will run the test runner script. We will pass it a `url` option so that the Functional tests can run the browser emulator properly. We will also specify the test suites to run. This allows us to skip FunctionalJavascript tests due to PhantomJS not handling concurrency properly in the test runner:

```
$ php core/scripts/run-tests.sh --url http://localhost--types
Simpletest,PHPUnit-Unit,PHPUnit-Kernel,PHPUnit-Functional --
concurrency 20 --all
```

4. Running `FunctionalJavascripts` tests require PhantomJS to be running. Since PhantomJS prints output to the terminal, open a new tab or terminal and run the following command:

```
phantomjs --ssl-protocol=any --ignore-ssl-errors=true
vendor/jcalderonzumba/gastonjs/src/Client/main.js 8510 1024 768
```

5. With PhantomJS running, we can now execute the FunctionalJavascript test suite:

```
php core/scripts/run-tests.sh --url http://localhost--types
PHPUnit-FunctionalJavascript --concurrency 1 --all
```

6. Review test output from each test suite run.

How it works...

The `run-tests.sh` script has been shipped with Drupal since 2008, then named `run-functional-tests.php`. This command interacts with the test suites in Drupal to run all or specific tests and sets up other configuration items.

There are several different test suites that operate in specific ways:

- **Simpletest**: The deprecated test system, full bootstraps and installs Drupal and uses its own browser emulator pattern using curl and XPath.
- **PHPUnit-Unit**: Unit tests backed by PHPUnit. These are intended to test specific classes and not interact with the database.

- **PHPUnit-Kernel**: Integration-level tests backed by PHPUnit. It is a test that has the ability to install schema and configuration to the database, minimally bootstrapping Drupal for basic integration testing.
- **PHPUnit-Functional**: Functional tests are tests that require a fully bootstrapped Drupal and provide browser emulation via Mink. These can be considered a direct replacement of Simpletest tests but leveraging third-party testing libraries.
- **PHPUnit-FunctionalJavascript**: Functional tests that have the ability to interact with PhantomJS in order to test JavaScript, such as AJAX operations and specific user interface interactions.

The following are some of the useful options:

- `--help`: This displays the items covered in the following bullets
- `--list`: This displays the available test groups that can be run
- `--url`: This is required unless the Drupal site is accessible through `http://localhost:80`
- `--sqlite`: This allows you to run tests without having Drupal installed
- `--concurrency`: This allows you to define how many tests run in parallel

There's more...

We will now discuss more techniques and information for running Drupal's test suites.

Is run-tests a shell script?

The `run-tests.sh` isn't actually a shell script. It is a PHP script--which is why you must execute it with PHP. In fact, within `core/scripts`, each file is a PHP script file meant to be executed using the command line. These scripts are not intended to be run through a web server, which is one of the reasons for the `.sh` extension.

There can be issues with PHP across platforms that prevent providing a shebang line to allow executing the file as a normal `bash` or `bat` script. For more information, refer to this Drupal.org issue at `https://www.drupal.org/node/655178`.

Running tests without Drupal installed

With Drupal 8, tests can also be run from SQLlite and no longer requires an installed database. This can be accomplished by passing the `sqlite` and `dburl` options to the `run-tests.sh` script. This requires the PHP SQLite extension to be installed.

Here is an example adapted from the DrupalCI test runner for Drupal core. DrupalCI is the continuous integration service, which runs on Drupal.org for all submitted patches and commits:

```
php core/scripts/run-tests.sh --sqlite /tmp/.ht.sqlite --die-on-fail --
dburl sqlite://tmp/.ht.sqlite --all
```

Combined with the built-in PHP web server for debugging, you can run test suites without a full-fledged environment.

Running specific tests

Each example so far has used the `all` option to run every `Simpletest` available. There are various ways to run specific tests:

- `--module`: This allows you to run all the tests of a specific module
- `--class`: This runs a specific path, identified by a full namespace path
- `--file`: This runs tests from a specified file
- `--directory`: This run tests within a specified directory

Previously in Drupal, tests were grouped inside the `module.test` files, which is where the file option derives from. Drupal 8 utilizes the `PSR-4` `autoloading` method and requires one class per file.

PhpStorm - Drupal Test Runner

Drupal 8 has seen a surge in test coverage for both Drupal core and contributed projects, most likely due to PHPUnit adoption. In response to this, the author has written a PhpStorm plugin called Drupal Test Runner that simplifies executing the `run-tests.sh` script runner.

The plugin's page can be found at
`https://plugins.jetbrains.com/plugin/8384-drupal-test-runner`, and it's public source
code can be found at `https://github.com/mglaman/intellij-drupal-run-tests`.

DrupalCI

With Drupal 8 came a new initiative to upgrade the testing infrastructure on Drupal.org.
The outcome was DrupalCI. DrupalCI is open source and can be downloaded and run
locally. The project page for DrupalCI is `https://www.drupal.org/project/drupalci`.

The test bot utilizes Docker and can be downloaded locally to run tests. The project ships
with a Vagrant file that allows it to be run within a virtual machine or locally. Learn more
on the testbot's project page at `https://www.drupal.org/project/drupalci_testbot`.

See also...

- Refer to the PHPUnit manual
  at `https://phpunit.de/manual/4.8/en/writing-tests-for-phpunit.html`.
- Refer to the Drupal PHPUnit handbook at `https://drupal.org/phpunit`.
- Refer to Running tests from the command line
  at `https://www.drupal.org/node/645286`.

- Refer to Commerce 2.x: Unit, Kernel, and Functional Tests Oh My! Authors blog
  post and tutorial for running tests in Drupal 8 for Drupal Commerce
  at `https://drupalcommerce.org/blog/45322/commerce-2x-unit-kernel-and-fu`
  `nctional-tests-oh-my`.

2
The Content Authoring Experience

In this chapter, we will explore what Drupal 8 brings to the content authoring experience:

- Configuring the WYSIWYG editor
- Adding and editing content
- Creating a menu and linking content
- Providing inline editing
- Creating a custom content type
- Applying new Drupal 8 core field types
- Customizing the form display of a node
- Customizing the display output of a node

Introduction

In this chapter, we'll cover the Drupal 8 content authoring experience. We will show you how to configure text formats and set up the bundled CKEditor that ships with Drupal 8. We will take a look at how to add and manage content and utilize menus to link to content. Drupal 8 ships with inline editing for per-field modifications from the frontend.

This chapter dives into *creating custom content types* and harnessing different fields to create advanced content. We'll cover the five new fields added to Drupal 8 core and how to use them, along with configuring new field types through contributed projects. We will go through customizing the content's display and modifying the new form display added in Drupal 8.

Configuring the WYSIWYG editor

Drupal 8 saw the collaboration between the Drupal development community and the CKEditor development community. Because of this, Drupal now ships with CKEditor out of the box as the default **What You See Is What You Get** (**WYSIWYG**) editor. The new Editor module provides an API to integrate WYSIWYG editors. Although CKEditor is provided out of the box, contributed modules can provide integrations with other WYSIWYG editors.

Text formats control the formatting of content and WYSIWYG editor configuration for content authors. The standard Drupal installation profile provides a fully configured text format with the enabled CKEditor. We will walk through the steps of recreating this text format.

In this recipe, we will create a new text format with a custom CKEditor WYSIWYG configuration.

Getting ready

Before starting, make sure that the CKEditor module is enabled, which also requires Editor as a dependency. **Editor** is the module that provides an API to integrate WYSIWYG editors with text formats.

How to do it...

Let's create a new text format with a custom CKEditor WYSIWYG configuration:

1. Visit **Configuration** from the administrative toolbar and head to **Text formats and editors** under the **CONTENT AUTHORING** heading.
2. Click on **Add text format** to begin creating the new text format:

Text formats and editors ☆

Home » Administration » Configuration » Content authoring

Text formats define how text is filtered for output and how HTML tags and other text is displayed, replaced, or removed. **Improper text format configuration is a security risk.** Learn more on the Filter module help page.

Text formats are presented on content editing pages in the order defined on this page. The first format available to a user will be selected by default.

(+ Add text format)

---

3. Enter a name for the text format, such as **editor format**.

4. Select which roles have access to this format--this allows you to have granular control over what users can use when authoring content.

5. Select **CKEditor** from the **Text editor** select list. The configuration form for CKEditor will then be loaded.

6. You may now use an in-place editor to drag buttons onto the provided toolbar to configure your CKEditor toolbar:

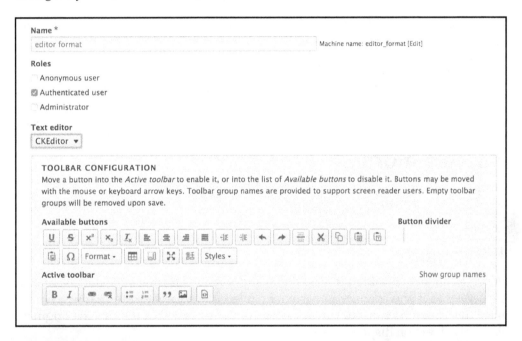

7. Select any of the **Enabled** filters you would like, except for **Display any HTML as Plain text**. That would be counter-intuitive to using a WYSIWYG editor!

8. When satisfied, click on **Save Configuration** to save your configuration and create the text filter.

How it works...

The Filter modules provide text formats that control over how rich text fields are presented to the user. Drupal will render rich text saved in a text area based on the defined text format for the field. Text fields with "formatted" in their title will respect text format settings; others will render in plain text.

The text formats and editors screen warns of a security risk due to improper configuration. This is because you could grant an anonymous user access to a text format that allows full HTML or allows image sources to be from remote URLs.

The Editor module provides a bridge to WYSIWYG editors and text formats. It alters the text format form and rendering to allow the integration of WYSIWYG editor libraries. This allows each text format to have its own configuration for its WYSIWYG editor.

Out of the box, the Editor module alone does not provide an editor. The CKEditor module works with the Editor API to enable the usage of the WYSIWYG editor.

Drupal can support other WYSWIG editors, such as markItUp (`http://markitup.jaysalvat.com/home/`) or TinyMCE (`https://www.tinymce.com/`) through contributed modules.

There's more...

Drupal provides granular control of how rich text is rendered, and extensible ways, which we will discuss further.

Filter module

When string data is added to a field that supports text formats, the data is saved and preserved as it was originally entered. Enabled filters for a text format will not be applied until the content is viewed. Drupal works in such a way that it saves the original content and only filters on display.

With the Filter module enabled, you gain the ability to specify how text is rendered based on the roles of the user who created the text. It is important to understand the filters applied to a text format that uses a WYSIWYG editor. For example, if you selected the **Display any HTML as plain text** option, the formatting done by the WYSIWYG editor would be stripped out when viewed.

Improved links

A major component of WYSIWYG editing is the ability to insert links to other pieces of content or external sites. The default link button integrated with CKEditor allows for basic link embedding. This means that your content editors must know their internal content URLs ahead of time to link to them. A solution to this issue is the Linkit module at `https://www.drupal.org/project/linkit`.

The module can be installed using Composer by running the following command:

```
$ cd /path/to/drupal8
$ composer require drupal/linkit
```

The **Linkit** module provides a drop-in replacement for the default link functionality. It adds auto-complete search for internal content and adds additional options for displaying the field. **Linkit** works by creating different profiles that allow you to control what content can be referenced, what attributes can be managed, and which users and roles can use a Linkit profile.

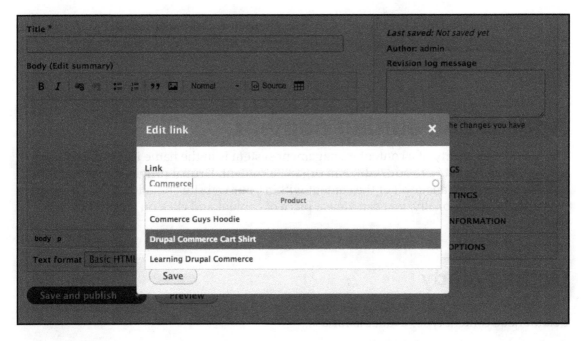

CKEditor plugins

The CKEditor module provides a plugin type called CKEditorPlugin. Plugins are small pieces of swappable functionality within Drupal 8. Plugins and plugin development are covered in *Chapter 7*, *Plug and Play with Plugins*. This type provides integration between CKEditor and Drupal 8.

The image and link capabilities are plugins defined within the CKEditor module. Additional plugins can be provided through contributed projects or custom development.

Refer to the \Drupal\ckeditor\Annotation\CKEditorPlugin class for the plugin definition and the suggested \Drupal\ckeditor\Plugin\CKEditorPlugin\DrupalImage class as a working example.

See also

- The official blog post from CKEditor about how Drupal adopted it as the official WYSIWYG editor at http://ckeditor.com/blog/CKEditor-Joins-Drupal.
- Refer to *Chapter 7*, *Plug and Play with Plugins*.

Adding and editing content

The main functionality of a content management system is in the name itself--the ability to manage content; that is, to add, edit, and organize content. Drupal provides a central form that allows you to manage all of the content within your website and allows you to create new content. Additionally, you can view a piece of content and click on an edit link when viewing it.

Getting ready

This recipe assumes that you have installed the standard installation profile and have the default node content types available for use.

How to do it...

Let's manage the content by adding, editing, and organizing the content:

1. Go to **Content** to view the content management overview from.
2. Click on **Add content** to view the list of available content types.
3. Click on **Article** as the piece of content you would like to make.
4. Provide a title for the piece of content. Titles are always required for content. Fill in the body text for the article:

 You may change the text format to customize what kind of text is allowed. If the user only has one format available, there will be no select box, but the **About text formats** link will still be present.

5. Once you have added your text, click on **Save and publish** at the bottom of the form. You will then be redirected to view the newly created piece of content.
6. Note that the URL for the piece of content is /node/#. This is the default path for content and can be changed by editing the content.
7. Click on **Edit** tab from the tabs right above the content.

8. From the right sidebar, click on **URL PATH SETTINGS** to expand the section and enter a custom alias, for example `/awesome-article` (note the required `/` symbol):

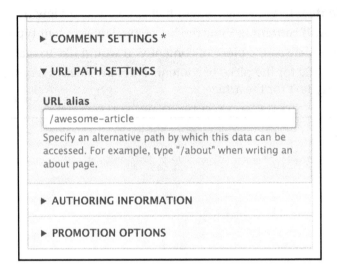

9. Save the content, and note that the URL for your article is `/awesome-article`.
10. You could also edit this article from the **Content** table by clicking on **Edit** there, instead of from viewing the content.

How it works...

The **Content** page is a **View**, which will be discussed in `Chapter 3`, *Displaying Content Through Views*. This creates a table of all the content on your site that can be searched and filtered. From here, you can view, edit, or delete any single piece of content.

In Drupal, there are content entities that provide a method of creation, editing, deletion, and viewing. Nodes are a form of a content entity. When you create a node, it will build the proper form that allows you to fill in the piece of content's data. The same process follows for editing content.

When you save the content, Drupal writes the node's content to the database along with all of its respective field data.

There's more...

Drupal 8's content management system provides many features; we will cover some extra information.

Save as draft

New to Drupal 8 is the ability to easily save a piece of content as a draft instead of directly publishing it. Instead of clicking on **Save and publish**, click on the arrow next to it to expand the **Save as unpublished** option:

The aforementioned button has several usability and user experience reviews and will be changing, for the better, in future versions of Drupal. One of the issues to follow is located at https://www.drupal.org/node/1899236. The issue highlights different proposed fixes following consistent user experience patterns defined in existing frontend libraries.

Pathauto

There is a contributed project called Pathauto that simplifies the process of providing URL aliases. It allows you to define patterns that will automatically create URL aliases for content. This module utilizes tokens to allow for very robust paths for content.

The Pathauto project can be found at https://www.drupal.org/project/pathauto.

There is a proposed issue to provide the functionality of Pathauto in Drupal core, and it can be followed at https://www.drupal.org/node/229568.

Bulk moderation

You also have the capability to perform bulk actions on content. This is available on the **Content management** screen. The table that lists the site content provides checkboxes at the beginning of each row. For each selected item, you can choose an item from **With selection** to make bulk changes, such as deleting, publishing, and unpublishing content:

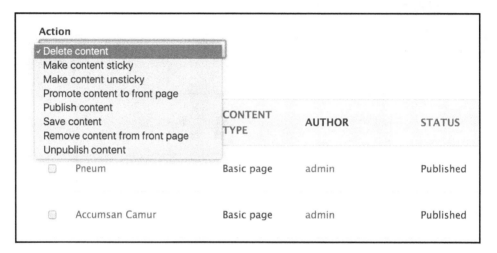

See also

- Refer to the *Customizing the form display of a node* recipe of this chapter.

Creating a menu and linking content

Drupal provides a way to link content being authored to a specified menu on the website, generally the main menu. You can, however, create a custom menu to provide links to content. In this recipe, we will show you how to create a custom menu and link content to it. We will then place the menu as a block on the page, in the sidebar.

Getting ready

This recipe assumes that you have installed the standard installation profile and have the default node content types available for use. You should have some content created to create a link.

How to do it...

1. Visit **Structure** and click on **Menus**.
2. Click on **Add menu**.
3. Provide the title **Sidebar** and optional summary and then click on **Save**.
4. Once the menu is saved, click on the **Add link** button.
5. Enter a link title and then type the title for a piece of content. The form will provide autocomplete suggestions for linkable content:

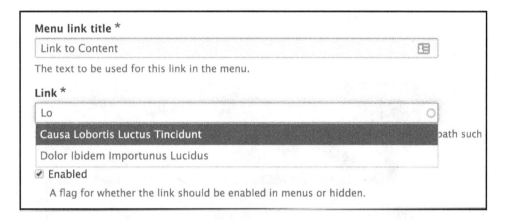

6. Click on **Save** to save the menu link.
7. With the menu link saved, go to **Structure**, and then **Block layout**.

8. Click on **Place block** next to **Sidebar first**. In the modal, search for the **Sidebar** menu and click on **Place block**:

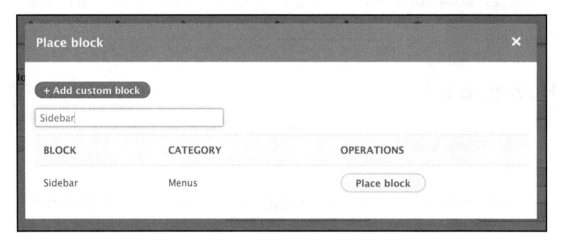

9. In the following form, click on **Save block**.
10. View your Drupal site by clicking on **Home** in the administration menu, and you will see the following menu:

How it works...

Menus and links are part of Drupal core. The ability to make custom menus and menu links is provided through the **Menu UI** module. This module is enabled on the standard installation profile, but may not be in others.

The **Link** input of the menu link form allows you to begin typing node titles and easily linking them to existing content. This was a piece of functionality not available in previous versions of Drupal. It will automatically convert the title into the internal path for you. Link input also accepts a regular path, such as /node/1 or an external path.

 You must have a valid path; you cannot add empty links to a menu. There is work being done to allow adding empty or ID selector link paths--refer to https://www.drupal.org/node/1543750.

There's more...

Links can be managed through the content edit form itself, which will be covered next.

Managing a contents menu link from its form

A piece of content can be linked to a menu from the **add** or **edit** form. The **menu settings** section allows you to toggle the availability of a menu link. The menu link title will reflect the content's title by default.

The parent item allows you to decide which menu and which item it will appear under. By default, content types only have the main menu allowed. Editing a content type can allow for multiple menus or only choose a custom menu.

This allows you to populate the main menu or complimentary menu without having to visit the menu management screens.

Providing inline editing

A touted feature of Drupal 8 is the ability to provide inline editing. Inline editing is enabled by default with the standard installation profile through the **Quick Edit** module. The Quick Edit module allows editing individual fields while viewing a piece of content, and integrates it with the Editor module for WYSIWYG editors!

How to do it...

Let's provide inline editing:

1. Go to a piece of created content.
2. In order to enable inline editing, you must toggle contextual links on the page by clicking on **Edit** in the upper right of the administrative toolbar:

3. This will toggle the contextual links available on the page. Click on the context link next to the content and select **Quick edit**:

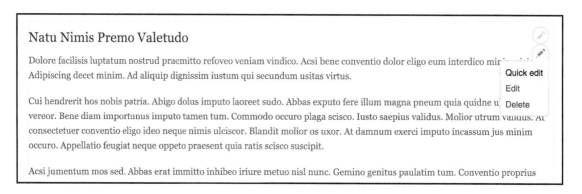

4. Hover over the body text and click on **Edit**. You can now edit the text with a minimal version of the WYSIWYG editor toolbar:

5. Once you have changed the text, click on **Save**.
6. The changes will be saved immediately.

How it works...

The **Contextual links** module provides privileged users with shortcut links to modify blocks or content. The contextual links are toggled by clicking on **Edit** in the toolbar. The **Edit** link toggles the visibility of contextual links on the page. Previously, in Drupal 7, contextual links appeared as cogs when a specific region was hovered over.

The Quick Edit module builds on the contextual links features. It allows field formatters, which display field data, to describe how they will interact. By default, Quick Edit sets this to a form. Clicking on an element will use JavaScript to load a form and save data via AJAX calls.

Quick Edit will not work on administrative pages.

There's more...

With each minor release of Drupal 8, there are more improvements to the inline editing experience.

The outside-in approach

There is an experimental module in Drupal 8.2 that allows you to editing blocks and other site configuration from the frontend of the website, just like Quick Edit for content. To enable this, install the **Settings Tray** module.

When you browse the Drupal site, you will note a new **Edit** button in the left of the toolbar. Clicking on this will allow you to edit blocks and the site configuration.

For more information, review the Drupal.org handbook for this feature at `https://www.drupal.org/docs/8/core/modules/outside-in/overview`.

Creating a custom content type

Drupal excels in the realm of content management by allowing different types of content. In this recipe, we will walk you through creating a custom content type. We will create a **Services** type that has some basic fields and would be used in a scenario that brings attention to a company's provided services.

You will also learn how to add fields to a content type in this recipe, which generally goes hand in hand with making a new content type on a Drupal site.

How to do it...

1. Go to **Structure** and then **Content types**. Click on **Add content type** to begin creating a new content type.
2. Enter **Services** as the name, and an optional description.
3. Select **Display settings** and uncheck the **Display author and date information** checkbox. This will hide the author and submitted time from services pages:

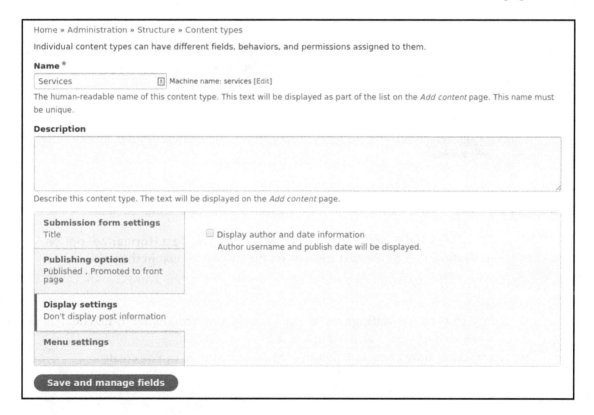

4. Click on the **Save and manage fields** button to save the new content type and manage its fields.

5. By default, new content types have a **Body** field automatically added to them. We will keep this field in place.

6. We will add a field that will provide a way to enter a marketing headline for the service. Click on **Add field**.

7. Select **Text (plain)** from the dropdown and enter **Marketing headline** as the label:

 The **Text (plain)** option is a regular text field. The **Text (formatted)** option will allow you to use text formats on the displayed text in the field.

8. Click on **Save field settings** on the next form. On the following form, click on **Save settings** to finish adding the field.

9. The field has now been added, and content of this type can be created:

How it works...

In Drupal, there are entities that have bundles. A bundle is just a type of entity that can have specific configurations and fields attached. When working with nodes, a bundle is generally referred to as a content type.

Content types can be created as long as the Node module is enabled. When a content type is created through the user interface, it invokes the `node_add_body_field()` function. This function adds the default body field for content types.

Fields can only be managed or added if the Field UI module is enabled. The Field UI module exposes the **Manage Fields**, **Manage Form Display**, and **Manage Display** for entities, such as nodes and blocks.

Applying new Drupal 8 core field types

The field system is what makes creating content in Drupal so robust. With Drupal 8, some of the most used contributed field types have been merged into Drupal core as their own module. In fact, Entity Reference is no longer a module but part of the main Field API now.

This recipe is actually a collection of mini-recipes to highlight the new fields provided by Drupal 8 core: `Link`, `Email`, `Telephone`, `Date`, and `Entity reference`.

Getting ready

The standard installation profile does not enable all of the modules that provide these field types by default. For this recipe, you will need to manually enable select modules so that you can create the field. The module that provides the field type and its installation status in the standard profile will be highlighted.

Each recipe will start off expecting that you have enabled the module, if needed, and that you are at the **Manage fields** form of a content type and have clicked on **Add field** and provided a field label. The recipes here cover the settings for each field.

How to do it...

This section contains a series of mini recipes that show how to use each of the new core field types.

Link

The Link field is provided by the Link module. It is *installed by default with the standard installation profile*. It is a dependency of the **Menu UI**, **Custom Menu Links**, and **Shortcut module**.

1. The Link field type does not have any additional field level settings that are used across all bundles.
2. Click on **Save field settings** to customize the field for this specific bundle.
3. Using the **Allowed link type** setting, you can control whether provided URLs can be external, internal, or both. Selecting **Internal or Both** will allow linking to content by autocompleting the title.
4. The **Allow link** text defines whether a user must provide text to go along with the link. If no text is provided, then the URL itself is displayed.
5. The field formatter for a **Link** field allows you to specify `rel="nofollow"` or whether the link should open in a new window.

The Email field

The **Email** field is provided by Drupal core and is available without installing additional modules:

1. The **Email** field type does not have any additional field level settings that are used across all bundles.
2. Click on **Save field settings** to customize the field for this specific bundle.
3. There are no further settings for an **Email** field instance. This field uses the HTML5 email input, which will leverage browser input validation.
4. The field formatter for an **Email** field allows you to display the email as a plain text or a `mailto:` link.

The Telephone field

The **Telephone** field is provided by the Telephone module. It is not installed by default with the standard installation profile, and must be installed through the Extend form.

1. The **Telephone** field type does not have any additional field level settings that are used across all bundles.
2. Click on **Save field settings** to customize the field for this specific bundle.
3. There are no further settings for a **Telephone** field instance. This field uses the HTML5 telephone input, which will leverage browser input validation.
4. The field formatter for a **Telephone** field allows you to display the telephone number as a plain text item, or use the `tel:link` with an optional replacement title for the link.

The Date field

The **Date** field is provided by the Datetime module. It is enabled by default with the standard installation profile.

1. The Date module has a setting that defines what kind of data it will be storing: date and time, or date only. This setting cannot be changed once the field data has been saved.
2. Click on **Save field settings** to customize the field for this specific bundle.

3. The **Date** field has two ways of providing a default value. It can either be the current date or a relative date using PHP's date time modifier syntax.
4. By default, **Date** fields use the HTML5 date and time inputs, resulting in a native date and time picker provided by the browser.
5. Additionally, **Date** fields can be configured to use a select list for each date and time component:

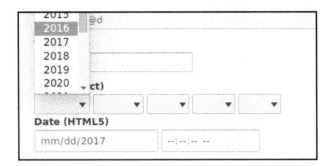

6. The default date field formatter display uses Drupal's time formats to render the time format. These are configured under **Configuration** and **Regional and language** in the **Date and time formats** form.
7. Dates and times can be displayed as **Time ago** to provide a semantic display of how far in the future or past a time is. The formats for both are customizable in the display settings.
8. Finally, dates and times can be displayed using a custom format, as specified by the PHP date formats.

The Entity Reference field

The **Entity Reference** field is part of Drupal core and is available without enabling additional modules. Unlike other fields, Entity Reference appears as a grouping of specific items when adding a field. This is because you must pick a type of entity to reference. Follow these steps:

1. The interface allows you to select a **Content**, **File**, **Image**, **Taxonomy term**, **User**, or **Other**. Selecting one of the predefined options will preconfigure the field's target entity type.
2. When creating an Entity Reference field using the **Other** choice, you must specify the type of item to reference. This option cannot be changed once your data is saved.

You will note that there are two groups: **content** and **configuration**. Drupal uses configuration entities. Even though configuration is an option, you may not benefit from referencing those entity types. Only content entities have a way to be viewed. Referencing configuration entities would fall under an advanced use case implementation.

3. Click on **Save field settings** to customize the field for this specific bundle.
4. The Entity Reference field has two different methods to allow users to search for content: using the default autocomplete or a view.
5. Depending on the type of entity you are referencing, there will be different entity properties that you may sort the results based on.
6. The default field widget for an Entity Reference field is autocomplete, however, there is the option to use a select list or checkboxes for the available options.
7. The values of an Entity Reference field can display the referenced entity's label or the rendered output. When rendering a label, it can be optionally linked to the entity itself. When displaying a rendered entity, you may choose a specific view mode.

How it works...

When working with fields in Drupal 8, there are two steps that should be noted. When you first create a field, you are defining a base field to be saved. This configuration is a base that specifies how many values a field can support and whether any additional settings are defined by the field type. When you attach a field to a bundle, it is considered a field storage and contains configuration unique to that specific bundle. If you have the same **Link** field on the **Article** and **Page** content type, the label, link type, and link text settings are for each instance.

Each field type provides a method for storing and presents a specific type of data. The benefit of using these fields comes from validation and data manipulation. It also allows you to utilize HTML5 form inputs. Using HTML5 for telephone, email, and date, the authoring experience uses the tools provided by the browser instead of additional third-party libraries. This also provides a more native experience when authoring with mobile devices.

There's more...

Having Drupal 8 released with new fields was a significant improvement in integrating widely used contributed modules into Drupal core. In the following sections, we will cover additional improvements and some additional topics.

Upcoming updates

Each of the recipes covers a field type that was once part of the contributed project space. These projects provided more configuration options than those found in Drupal core at the time of writing this book. Over time, more and more features will be brought into Drupal core from their source projects.

For instance, the Datetime module is based on the contributed Date project. However, not all of the contributed project's features have made it to Drupal core. Each minor release of Drupal 8 sees more features moved to core. An example is the Datetime range module, which is an experimental module slated to be near stable for Drupal 8.4. This module adds support to start and end dates for Datetime fields. Documentation for the Datetime range module can be found at `https://www.drupal.org/docs/8/core/modules/datetime-range`.

Views and Entity Reference

Using a View with an Entity Reference field is covered in `Chapter 3`, *Displaying Content Through Views*. Using a View, you can customize the way results are fetched for a reference field.

See also

- Refer to the *Providing an entity reference result view* recipe in `Chapter 3`, *Displaying Content through Views*.

Customizing the form display of a node

The latest in Drupal 8 is the availability of form display modes. Form modes allow a site administrator to configure different field configurations for each content entity bundle edit form. In the case of nodes, you have the ability to rearrange and alter the display of fields and properties on the node edit form.

In this recipe, we'll modify the default form for creating the **Article** content type that comes with the standard installation profile:

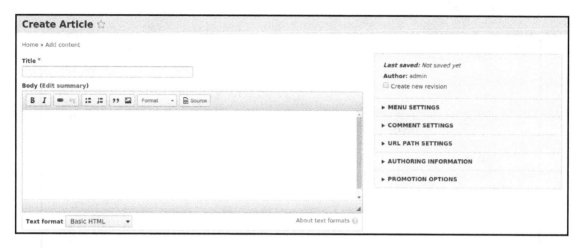

How to do it...

1. To customize the form display mode, go to **Structure** and then **Content Types**.
2. We will modify the **Article** content type's form. Click on the expand the **OPERATIONS** dropdown and select **Manage form display**.

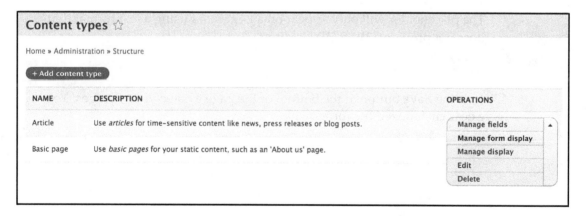

3. First, we will modify the **Comments** field. Click on the drag icon to the left and drag the row into the **Disabled** section. Follow the same steps for the **sticky at top of lists** field:

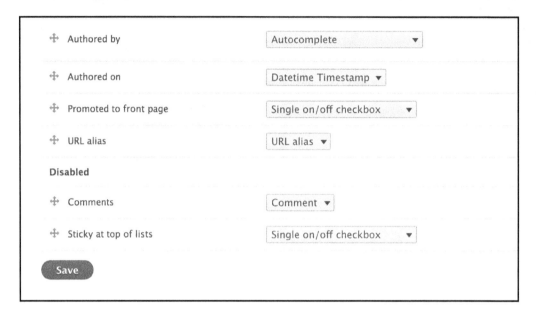

4. Click on the settings cog for the **Body** field. Enter in a placeholder for the field, such as Enter your article text here. Click on **Update**.

  The placeholder will only appear on a textarea using a text format that does not provide a WYSIWYG editor.

5. Click on the **Save** button at the bottom of the page to save your changes. You have now customized the form display.

6. Go to **Content** | **Add Content** and then to **Article**. Note that the comment settings are no longer displayed nor are the sticky options under promotion options:

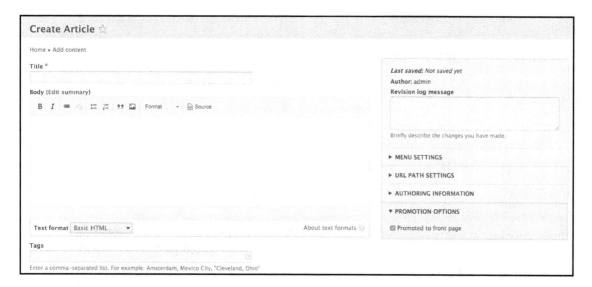

How it works...

Entities in Drupal have various view modes for each bundle. In Drupal 7, there were only display view modes, which are covered in the next recipe. Drupal 8 brings in new form modes to allow for more control of how an entity edit form is displayed.

Form display modes are configuration entities. Form display modes dictate how the `\Drupal\Core\EntityContentEntityForm` class will build a form when an entity is edited. This will always be set to default unless changed or specified to a different mode programmatically.

Since form display modes are configuration entities, they can be exported using configuration management.

Hidden field properties will have no value unless there is a provided default value. For example, if you hide the authoring information without providing code to set a default value, the content will be authored by anonymous (no user).

There's more...

We will discuss more items for managing the form of a content entity in the following section.

Managing form display modes

Form display modes for all entities are managed under one area and are enabled for each bundle type. You must first create a display mode, and then it can be configured through the bundle manage interface.

Programmatically providing a default to hidden form items

In *Chapter 6, Creating Forms with the Form API*, we will have a recipe that details with altering forms. In order to provide a default value for an entity property hidden on the form display, you will need to alter the form and provide a default value. The Field API provides a way to set a default value when fields are created.

See also

- Refer to *Chapter 10, The Entity API*.
- Refer to *Chapter 6, Creating Forms with the Form API*.

Customizing the display output of a node

Drupal provides display view modes that allow for customization of the fields and other properties attached to an entity. In this recipe, we will adjust the teaser display mode of an Article. Each field or property has a control for displaying the label, the format to display the information in, and additional settings for the format.

Harnessing view displays allows you to have full control over how content is viewed on your Drupal site.

How to do it...

1. Now, it is time to customize the form display mode by navigating to **Structure** and then **Content Types**.
2. We will modify the **Article** content type's display. Click on the dropdown button arrow and select **Manage display**.
3. Click on the **Teaser** view mode option to modify it. The teaser view mode is used in node listings, such as the default homepage:

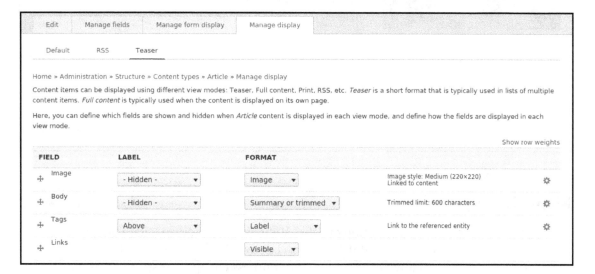

4. Change the format for **Tags** to be **Hidden**. Additionally, this can be accomplished by dragging it to the hidden section. The tags on an article will no longer be displayed when viewing a teaser view mode.
5. Click on the settings cog for the **Body** field to adjust the trimmed limit. The trim limit is a fallback for **Summary or trimmed** when the summary of a textarea field is not provided. Modify this from 600 to 300.
6. Click on **Save** to save all of the changes that you have made.

7. View the homepage and take a the at your changes that have taken effect.

Fusce bibendum finibus risus

Submitted by admin on Sun, 10/04/2015 - 13:16

Lorem ipsum dolor sit amet, consectetur adipiscing elit. Morbi eu dolor vehicula, ullamcorper quam sed, bibendum diam. Proin cursus euismod nisi sit amet ultricies. Suspendisse tincidunt vitae sem nec facilisis. Sed hendrerit risus eros, quis fringilla ligula cursus et.

Read more   Add new comment

How it works...

View display modes are configuration entities. View display modes dictate how the `\Drupal\Core\EntityContentEntityForm` class will build a view display when an entity is viewed. This will always be set to default unless changed or specified as a different mode programmatically.

Since view display modes are configuration entities, they can be exported using configuration management.

3
Displaying Content through Views

This chapter will cover the Views module and how to use a variety of its major features. In this chapter, we will cover the following recipes:

- Listing content
- Editing the default admin interfaces
- Creating a block from a View
- Utilizing dynamic arguments
- Adding a relationship in a View
- Providing an Entity Reference result View

Introduction

For those who have used Drupal previously, Views is in core for Drupal 8. If you are new to Drupal, note that Views has been one of the most used contributed projects for Drupal 6 and Drupal 7.

Briefly described, Views is a visual query builder that allows you to pull content from the database and render it in multiple formats. Select administrative areas and content listings provided out of the box by Drupal are all powered by Views. We'll dive into how to use Views to customize the administrative interface, customize ways to display your content, and interact with the entity reference field.

Listing content

Views does one thing, and it does it well--listing content. The power behind the Views module is the amount of configurable power it gives the end user to display content in various forms.

This recipe will cover creating a content listing and linking it in the main menu. We will use the `Article` content type provided by the standard installation and make an article's landing page.

Getting ready

The **Views UI** module must be installed to manipulate Views from the user interface. By default, this is enabled with the standard installation profile.

How to do it...

Let's list the Views listing content:

1. Go to **Structure** and then **Views**, as shown in the following screenshot; this will bring you to the administrative overview of all the views that have been created:

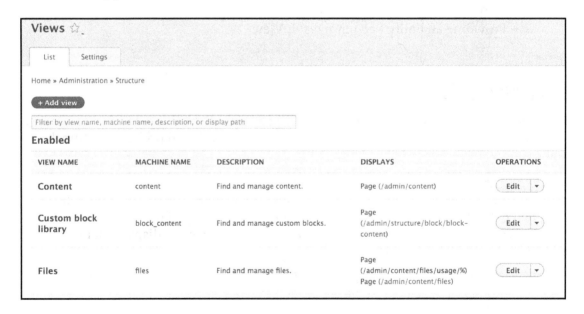

2. Click on **Add view** to create a new view.

3. The first step is to provide the **View name** of articles, which will serve as the administrative and (by default) displayed title.

4. Next, we will modify the **VIEW SETTINGS**. We want to display **Content** of the type `Article` and leave the **tagged with** field empty. This will force the view to only show content of the `Article` content type.

5. Check the **Create a page** option. The **Page title** and **Path** will be autopopulated based on the view name and can be modified as desired. For now, leave the display and other settings at their default values:

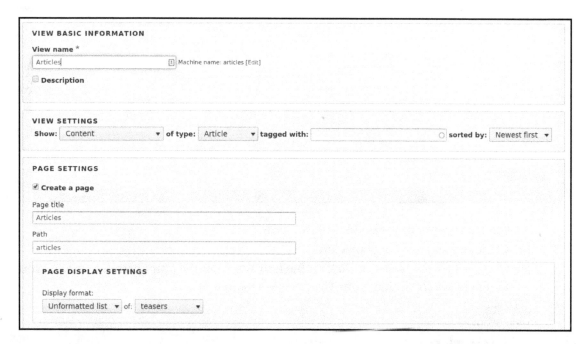

6. Click on **Save and edit** to continue modifying your new view.

7. In the middle column, under the **PAGE SETTINGS** section, we will change the **Menu item** settings. Click on **No menu** to change the default.

8. Select **Normal menu entry**. Provide a menu link title and an optional description. Set **Parent** to **<Main Navigation>**:

9. Click on **Apply** at the bottom of the form.
10. Click on **Save** to save your view.
11. Once your view is saved, click on **Back to site** from the administrative menu. You will now see the link in your Drupal site's main menu.

How it works...

The first step to create a view involves selecting the type of data you will be displaying. This is referred to as the base table, which can be any type of entity or data specifically exposed to Views.

Nodes are labeled as **Content** in Views, and you will find this interchanged terminology throughout Drupal.

When creating a Views page, we add a menu path that can be accessed. It tells Drupal to invoke Views to render the page, which will load the view you create and render it.

There are display `style` and `row` plugins that format the data to be rendered. Our recipe used the unformatted list style to wrap each row in a simple `div` element. We could have changed this to a table for a formatted list. The row display controls how each row is outputted.

There's more...

The Views module has been one of the must-use modules since it first debuted, to the point that almost every Drupal 7 site used this module. In the following section, we will dive further into Views.

Views in Drupal core initiative

The Views module has been a contributed module up until Drupal 8. In fact, it was one of the most used modules. Although the module is now part of Drupal core, it still has many improvements that are needed, and are being committed.

Through their 8.1, 8.2, and 8.3 releases, there have been many improvements. We will continue to see this pattern with each future minor release.

Views and displays

When working with Views, you will see some different terminologies. One of the key items to be grasped is what a display is. A view can contain multiple displays. Each display is of a certain type. Views comes with the following display types:

- **Attachment**: This is a display that becomes attached to another display in the same view
- **Block**: This allows you to place the view as a block
- **Embed**: The display is meant to be embedded programmatically
- **Entity Reference**: This allows Views to provide results for an entity reference field
- **Feed**: This display returns a XML-based feed and can be attached to another display to render a feed icon
- **Page**: This allows you to display the view from a specific route

Each display can have its own configuration, too. However, each display will share the same base table (content, files, and so on). This allows you to take the same data and represent it in different ways.

Format style plugins - style and row

Within Views, there are two types of style plugins that represent how your data is displayed: style and row:

- The **style** plugin represents the overall format
- The **row** plugin represents each result row's format

For example, the `grid` style will output multiple `div` elements with specified classes to create a responsive `grid`. At the same time, the `table` style creates a tabular output with labels used as table headings.

Row plugins define how to render the row. The default content will render the entity as defined by its selected display mode. If you choose **Fields**, you can manually select which fields to include in your view.

Each format style plugin has a corresponding `Twig` file that the theme layer uses. Refer to the *Twig templating* recipe of *Chapter 5, Frontend for the Win* to learn more about Twig in Drupal 8.

You can define new plugins in custom modules or use contributed modules to access different options.

Using the Embed display

Each of the available display types has a method to expose itself through the user interface, except for Embed. Often, contributed and custom modules use Views to render displays instead of manually writing queries and rendering the output. Drupal 8 provides a special display type to simplify this.

If we were to add an Embed display to the view created in the recipe, we could pass the following render array to output our view programmatically:

```
$view_render = [
  '#type' => 'view',
  '#name' => 'articles',
  '#display_id' => 'embed_1',
];
```

When rendered, the `#type` key tells Drupal that this is a view element. We then point it to our new display `embed_1`. The Embed display type has no special functionality, in fact, it is a simplistic display plugin. The benefit is that it does not have additional operations conducted for the sake of performance.

Using an Embed display is beneficial when you want to use a View in a custom page, block, or even form. For example, Drupal Commerce uses this pattern for its shopping cart block and the order summary in the checkout. A view is used to display the order information within a custom block and form.

See also

- Refer to the VDC initiative at `https://www.drupal.org/community-initiatives/drupal-core/vdc`.
- Refer to `Chapter 7`, *Plug and Play with Plugins*, to learn more about plugins.

Editing the default admin interfaces

With the addition of Views in Drupal core, many of the administrative interfaces are powered by Views. This allows customization of default admin interfaces to enhance site management and content authoring experiences.

> In Drupal 6 and 7, there was the Administrative Views contributed module, which provided a way to override administrative pages with Views. This module is no longer required, as the functionality comes with Drupal core out of the box.

In this recipe, we will modify the default content overview form that is used to find and edit content. We will add the ability to filter content by the user who authored it.

How to do it...

1. Go to **Structure** and then **Views**. This will bring you to the administrative overview of all existing views.
2. From the **Enabled** section, select the **Edit** option from the operations column for the **Content** view. This is the view displayed on `/admin/content` when managing content.

3. To filter by the content author, we must add a **FILTER CRITERIA** to our view, where we will expose the following for users to modify:

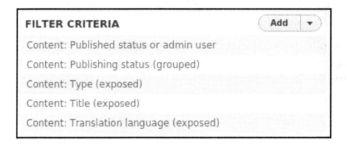

4. Click on **Add** in the **FILTER CRITERIA** section to add a new filter. In the search textbox, type **Authored by** to search the available options. Select **Authored by** for the **Content** category. Click on **Add and configure filter criteria**:

5. Check the **Expose this filter to visitors to allow them to change it** checkbox. This will allow users to modify the data for the filter.

6. You may modify the **Label** and add a **Description** to improve the usability of the filter option for your use case.

7. Click on **Apply** once more to finish configuring the filter. It will now show up in the list of filter criteria. You will also see the new filter in the preview below the form.

8. Click on **Save** to commit all changes to the view.

9. Take a look at `/admin/content`, and you will have your filter. Content editors will be able to search for content authored by a user through autocompleted username searches:

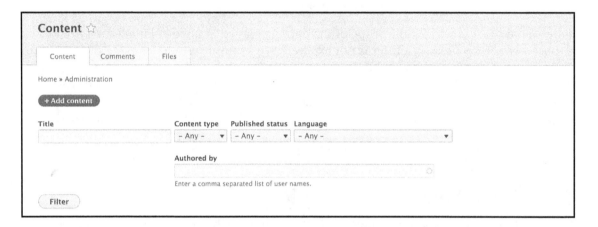

How it works...

When a view is created that has a path matching an existing route, it will override it and present itself. That is how the `/admin/content` and other administrative pages are able to be powered by Views.

 If you were to disable the Views module, you can still manage content and users. The default forms are tables that do not provide filters or other extra features.

Drupal uses the overridden route and uses Views to render the page. From that point on, the page is handled like any other Views page would be rendered.

There's more...

We will dive into additional features available through Views that can enhance the way you use Views and present them on your Drupal site.

Exposed versus non-exposed

Filters allow you to narrow the scope of the data displayed in a view. Filters can either be exposed or not; by default, a filter is not exposed. An example would be using the **Content: Publishing status** set to **Yes (published)** to ensure that a view always contains published content. This is an item you would configure to display content to site visitors. However, if it were for an administrative display, you may want to expose that filter. This way, content editors can view, easily, what content has not been published yet or been unpublished.

All filter and sort criteria can be marked as exposed.

Filter identifiers

Exposed filters work by parsing query parameters in the URL. For instance, on the content management form, changing the `Type` filter will add `type=Article`, among others to the current URL.

With this recipe, the author filter would show up as **uid** in the URL. Exposed filters have a **Filter identifier** option that can change the URL component:

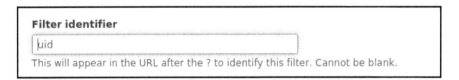

This could be changed to `author` or some other value to enhance the user experience behind the URL, or mask the Drupal-ness of it.

Overriding routes with Views

Views can replace administrative pages with enhanced versions due to the way the route and module system works in Drupal. Modules are executed in order of the module's weight or alphabetical order if weights are the same. Naturally, in the English alphabet, the letter *V* comes toward the end of the alphabet. That means any route that Views provides will be added toward the end of the route discovery cycle.

If a view is created and it provides a route path, it will override any that exist on that path. There is no collision checking mechanism (and there was not one present in Views before merging into Drupal core) that prevents this.

This allows you to easily customize most existing routes, but, beware that you could easily have conflicting routes, and Views will normally override the other.

Creating a block from a View

Previous recipes have shown how to create and manipulate a page created by a view. Views provides different display types that can be created, such as a block. In this recipe, we will create a block powered by Views. The Views block will list all Tag taxonomy terms that have been added to the `Article` content type.

Getting ready

This recipe assumes that you have installed the standard installation profile and have the default node content types available for use.

How to do it...

1. Go to **Structure** and then **Views**. This will bring you to the administrative overview of all the views that are created.
2. Click on **Add view** to create a new view.
3. The first step is to provide the View name of **Tags**, which will serve as the administrative and (by default) displayed title.

4. Next, we will modify the **VIEW SETTINGS**. We want to display **Taxonomy terms** of the type **Tags**. This will make the view default to only displaying taxonomy terms created under the **Tags** vocabulary.

5. Check the **Create a block** checkbox in the **BLOCK SETTINGS** section.

6. Select the **HTML List** option from the **Display format** choices. Leave the style as **Fields**:

7. Click on **Save and edit** to create the view.

8. We want to display all the available tags. Under the **PAGER** section, click on the field next to **Use Pager** and select **Display all items** and click on **Apply**.

9. Next, we will sort the view by tag name instead of order of creation. Click on **Add** on the **SORT CRITERIA** section.Select the checkbox where **Name** : **Taxonomy term** and click on **Add and configure sort criteria** to use the default, that is, ascending. Click on **Apply**:

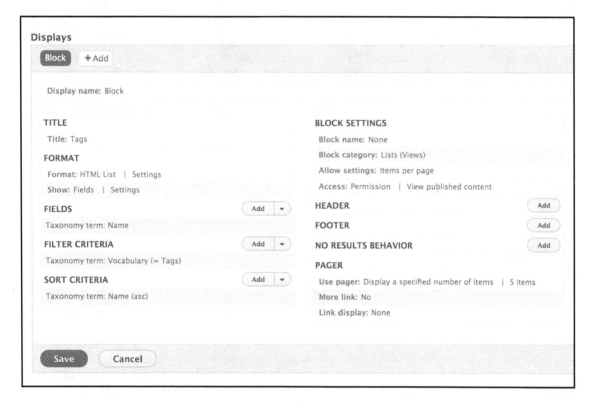

10. Click on **Save** to save the view.
11. Go to **Structure** and **Block layout** to place the block on your Drupal site. Click on **Place block** for the **Sidebar first** region in the **Bartik** theme.
12. Filter the list by typing your view's name (Tags). Click on **Place block** to add your view's block to the block layout.
13. Finally, click on **Save block** to commit your changes.

How it works...

In the Drupal 8 plugin system, there is a concept called Derivatives. Plugins are small pieces of swappable functionality within Drupal 8. Plugins and plugin development are covered in *Chapter 7, Plug and Play with Plugins*. A derivative allows a module to present multiple variations of a plugin dynamically. In the case of Views, it allows the module to provide variations of a `ViewsBlock` plugin for each view that has a block display. Views implements the `\Drupal\views\Plugin\Block\ViewsBlock\ViewsBlock` class, providing the base for the dynamic availability of these blocks. Each derived block is an instance of this class.

When Drupal initiates the block, Views passes the proper configuration required. The view is then executed and the display is rendered whenever the block is displayed.

There's more...

We will now explore some of the other ways in which Views interacts with blocks.

Exposed forms as blocks

If your view utilizes exposed filters, you have the option to place the exposed form in a block. With this option enabled, you may place the block anywhere on the page, even pages not for your view.

An example of using an exposed form in a block is for a search result view. You will add an exposed filter for keywords that control the search results. With the exposed filters in a block, you can easily place it in your site's header. When an exposed filter block is submitted, it will direct users to your view's display.

To enable the exposed filters as a block, you must first expand the **Advanced** section on the right side of the Views edit form. Click on the **Exposed form in block** option from the **Advanced** section. In the options modal that opens, select the **Yes** radio button, and click on **Apply**. You can then place the block from the **Block layout** form:

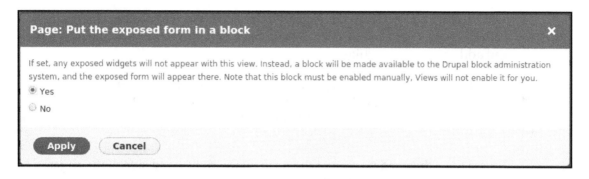

See also

- Refer to `Chapter 7`, *Plug and Play with Plugins*, to learn more about derivatives

Utilizing dynamic arguments

Views can be configured to accept **contextual filters**. Contextual filters allow you to provide a dynamic argument that modifies the view's output. The value is expected to be passed from the URL; however, if it is not present, there are ways to provide a default value.

In this recipe, we will create a new page called `My Content`, which will display a user's authored content on the `/user/%/content` route.

How to do it...

1. Go to **Structure** and then **Views**. This will bring you to the administrative overview of all the views created. Click on **Add view** to create a new view.
2. Set the **View name** to **My Content**.
3. Next, we will modify the **View** settings. We want to display **Content of the type All** and leave the **Tagged** with empty. This will allow all content to be displayed.

4. Select **Create a page**. Keep the page title the same. We will need to change the path to user/%user/content. Click on **Save and edit** to move to the next screen and add the contextual filter.

 When building a views page, adding a percent sign to the path identifies a route variable. By adding an entity type's name, Drupal will match the input as an identifier to an entity of that type.

5. Toggle the **Advanced** portion of the form on the right-hand side of the page. Click on **Add** in the **Contextual filters** section.
6. Select **Authored by: Content** and then click on **Add and configure contextual filters**.
7. Change the default value of **WHEN THE FILTER VALUE IS *NOT* IN THE URL** to **Display "Access Denied"** to prevent all content from being displayed with a bad route value:

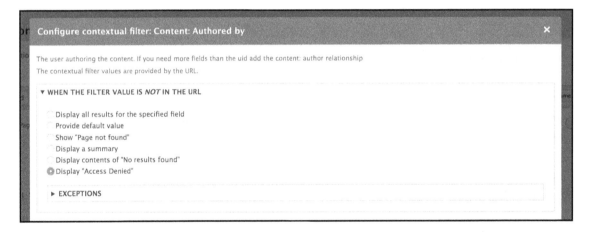

8. Click on **Apply** and then click on **Save** to save the view.
9. Go to /user/1/content, and you will see content created by the first user.

How it works...

Contextual filters mimic the route variables found in the Drupal routing system. Variables are represented by percentage signs as placeholders in the view's path. Views will match up each placeholder with contextual filters by order of their placement. This allows you to have multiple contextual filters; you just need to ensure that they are ordered properly.

The Views module is aware of how to handle the placeholder because the type of data is selected when you add the filter. Once the contextual filter is added, there are extra options available for handling the route variable.

There's more...

We will now explore the extra options available when using contextual filters.

Previewing with contextual filters

You are still able to preview a view from the edit form. You simply add the contextual filter values to the text form concatenated by a forward slash (/). In this recipe, you could replace navigating to `/user/1/content` with simply inputting `1` into the preview form and updating the preview.

Displaying as a tab on the user page

Even though the view created in the recipe follows a route under `/user`, it will not show up as a local task tab until it has a menu entry defined.

Go back and edit the **My Content** view. From the **Page settings** section, you will need to change **No menu** from the **Menu** option. Clicking on that link will open the menu link settings dialog.

Select **Menu tab** and provide a **Menu link title**, such as **My Content**. Select **<User account menu>** for the **Parent**. Click on **Apply** and save your view. When you go to the `/user` page again, it will have the **My Content** page available.

 You may need to rebuild Drupal's caches in order for the routing system to be rebuilt, making Drupal aware of the menu tab.

Altering the page title

With contextual filters, you have the ability to manipulate the current page's title. When adding or editing a contextual filter, you can modify the page title. You may check the **Override title** option in **When the filter value is present in the URL or a default is provided** section.

This textbox allows you to enter in a new title that will be displayed. Additionally, you can use the information passed from the route context using the format of %#, where # is the argument order.

Validation

Contextual filters can have validation attached. Without specifying extra validation, Views will take the expected argument and try to make it *just work*. You can add validation to help limit this scope and filter out invalid route variables.

You can enable validation by checking **Specify validation criteria** from the **When the filter value is present in the URL or a default is provided** section. The default is set to **Basic Validation**, which allows you to specify how the view should react if the data is invalid; based on our recipe, this would be if the user is not found.

The list of **Validator** options is not filtered by the contextual filter item you selected, so some may not apply. For our recipe, one might want **User ID** and select the **Validate user has access to the** *User*. This validator would make sure that the current user is able to view the route's user's profile. Additionally, it can be restricted further based on its role:

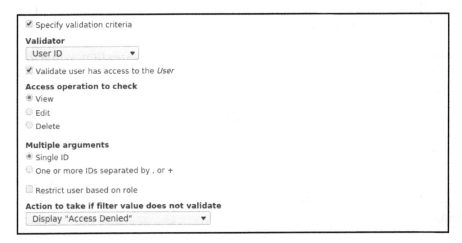

This gives you more granular control over how the view operates when using contextual filters for route arguments.

Multiple and exclusion

You may also configure the contextual filter to allow AND or OR operations along with exclusion. These options are under the **More** section when adding or editing a contextual filter.

The **Allow multiple values** option can be checked to enable AND or OR operations. If the contextual filter argument contains a series of values concatenated by plus (+) signs, it acts as an OR operation. If the values are concatenated by commas (,) it acts as an AND operation.

When the **Exclude** option is checked, the value will be excluded from the results rather than the view being limited by it.

Adding a relationship in a View

As stated at the beginning of the chapter, Views is a visual query builder. When you first create a view, a base table is specified from which to pull data. Views automatically knows how to join tables for field data, such as body text or custom-attached fields.

When using an entity reference field, you can display the value as the raw identifier, the referenced entity's label, or the entire rendered entity. However, if you add a relationship based on a reference field, you will have access to display any of that entity's available fields.

In this recipe, we will update the Files view, used for administering files, to display the username of the user who uploaded the file.

How to do it...

1. Got to **Structure** and then **Views**. This will bring you to the administrative overview of all the views that have been created
2. Find the **Files** view and click on **Edit**.

3. Click on **Advanced** to expand the section and then click on **Add** that is next to **Relationships**.

4. Search for **user**. Select the **User who uploaded** relationship option and click on **Apply (this display):**

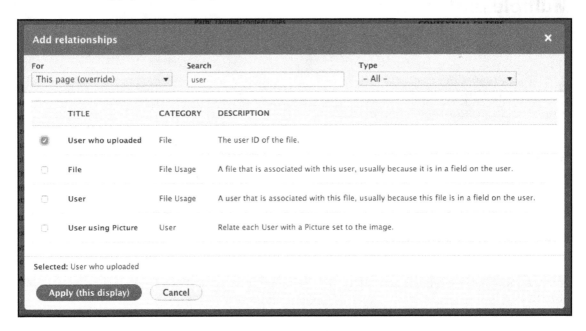

5. Next, we will be presented with a configuration form for the relationship. Click on **Apply (this display)** to use the defaults.

6. Add a new field by clicking on **Add** in the **Fields** section.

7. Search for **name** and select the **Name: User** field and, click on **Apply (all display)**.

8. This view uses aggregation, which presents a new configuration form when you first add a field. Click on **Apply and continue** to use the defaults.

We will discuss Views and aggregation in the *There's more...* section of this recipe.

9. We will use the default field settings that will provide the label **Name** and format it as the username and link to the user's profile. Click on **Apply (this display).**

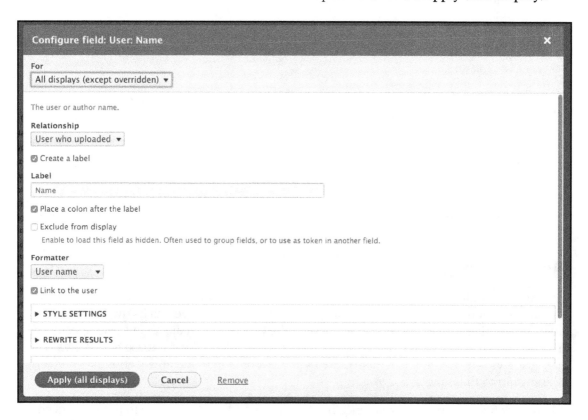

10. Click on **Save** to finish editing the view and commit your changes.

11. When viewing the **Files** list in `/admin/content/files`, the username that uploaded the file will now be displayed:

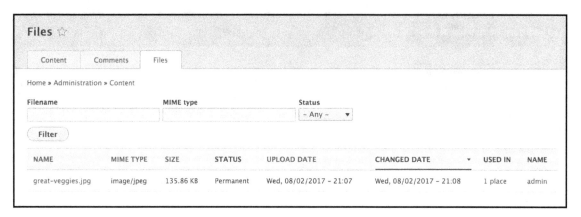

How it works...

Drupal stores data in a normalized format. Database normalization, in short, involves the organization of data in specifically related tables. Each entity type has its own database table, and all fields have their own database table. When you create a view and specify what kind of data will be shown, you are specifying a base table in the database that Views will query. Views will automatically associate fields that belong to the entity and it's relationship to those tables for you.

When an entity has an entity reference field, you can add a relationship to the referenced entity type's table. This is an explicit definition, whereas fields are implicit. When the relationship is explicitly defined, all the referenced entity type's fields come into scope. The fields on the referenced entity type can then be displayed, filtered, and sorted.

There's more...

Using relationships in Views allows you to create some powerful displays. We will discuss aggregation and additional information about relationships.

Relationships provided by entity reference fields

The Views module uses a series of hooks to retrieve data that it then uses to represent ways to interact with the database. One of these is the `hook_field_views_data` hook, which processes a field storage configuration entity and registers its data with Views. The Views module implements this on behalf of the Drupal core to add relationships and reverse relationship, for Entity reference fields.

Since Entity reference fields have set schema information, Views can dynamically generate these relationships by understanding the field's table name, destination entity's table name, and the destination entity's identifier column.

Relationships provided through custom code

There are times where you will need to define a relation on your own with custom code. Typically, when working with custom data in Drupal, you would more than likely create a new entity type; this topic is covered in *Chapter 9, Configuration Management - Deploying in Drupal 8*. This is not always the case, however, and you may just need a simple method of storing data. An example can be found in the Database Logging module. The Database Logging module defines a schema for a database table and then uses `hook_views_data` to expose its database table to Views.

The `dblog_schema` hook implementation returns a `uid` column on the watchdog database table created by the module. That column is then exposed to Views using the following definition:

```
$data['watchdog']['uid'] = array(
  'title' => t('UID'),
  'help' => t('The user ID of the user on which the log entry
    was written..'),
  'field' => array(
    'id' => 'numeric',
  ),
  'filter' => array(
    'id' => 'numeric',
  ),
  'argument' => array(
    'id' => 'numeric',
  ),
  'relationship' => array(
    'title' => t('User'),
    'help' => t('The user on which the log entry as written.'),
    'base' => 'users',
    'base field' => 'uid',
```

```
        'id' => 'standard',
    ),
  );
```

This array tells Views that the `watchdog` table has a column named `uid`. It is numeric in nature for its display, filtering capabilities, and sorting capabilities. The `relationship` key is an array of information that instructs Views how to use this to provide a relationship (`LEFT JOIN`) on the `users` table. The `User` entity uses the `users` table and has the primary key of `uid`.

Using aggregation and views.

There is a view setting under the **Advanced** section that allows you to enable aggregation. This feature allows you to enable the usage of SQL aggregate functions, such as `MIN`, `MAX`, `SUM`, `AVG`, and `COUNT`. In this recipe, the Files view uses aggregation to sum the usage counts of each file on the Drupal site.

Aggregation settings are set for each field, and when enabled, they have their own link to configure these settings:

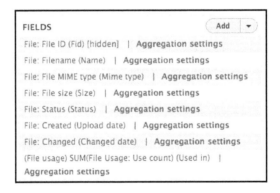

Providing an Entity Reference result View

The Entity reference field, covered in *Chapter 2, The Content Authoring Experience*, can utilize a custom view for providing the available field values. The default entity reference field will display all available entities of the type it can reference. The only available filter is based on the entity bundle, such as only returning `Article` nodes. Using an entity reference view, you can provide more filters, such as only returning the content that your user has authored.

In this recipe, we will create an entity reference view that filters content by the author. We will add the field to the user account form, allowing users to select their favorite contributed content.

How to do it...

1. Go to **Structure** and then **Views**. This will bring you to the administrative overview of all the views that have been created. Click on **Add view** to create a new view.

2. Set the **View name** to **My Content Reference View**, and retain the current **View settings** configuration.

3. Do not choose to create a page or block. Click on **Save and edit** to continue working on your view.

4. Click on the **Add** button to create a new display. Select the **Entity Reference** option to create the display:

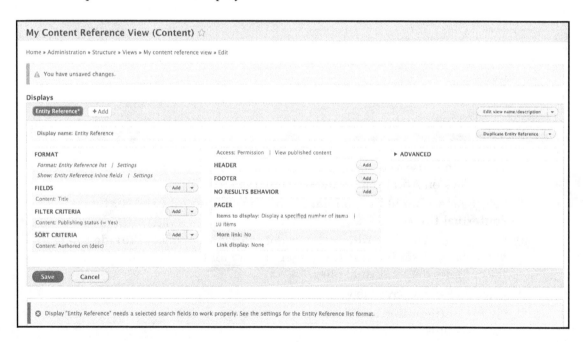

5. The **Format** will be automatically set to **Entity Reference List**, which utilizes fields. Click on **Settings** next to it to modify the style format.

6. For **Search Fields**, check the **Content: Title** option and then click on **Apply**. This is what the field will perform the autocomplete search on.

7. You will need to modify the **Content: Title** field to stop it from wrapping the result as a link. Click on the field label and uncheck **Link to the Content**. Click on **Apply** to save the field settings:

8. We will then use a contextual filter to limit the results to the currently loggedin user. Click on **Add** from **Contextual Filters** in the **Advanced** section.

9. Select the **Authored by: Content** option and click on **Add and configure contextual filters**.

10. Change the **When the filter value is not available** setting to **Provide a default value**. Select **User ID from the logged in user** for the type value. Click on **Apply** to configure the contextual filter.

11. Click on **Save** to save the view.

12. Go to **Configuration** and then **Account settings** to be able to manage fields on user accounts.

13. Add a new **Entity Reference** field that references **Content**, call it Highlighted Contributions, and allow it to have unlimited values. Click on the **Save field settings** button.

14. Change the **Reference type** method to use **View: Filter by an entity reference view** and select the view we have just created:

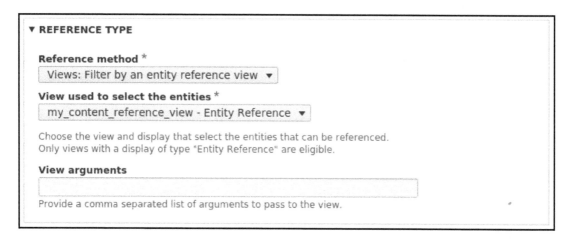

15. Now, when a user edits their account, they can reference only content that they have created in this reference field.

How it works...

The entity reference field definition provides selection plugins. The Views module provides an entity reference selection plugin. This allows entity reference to gather data into a view to receive available results.

The display type for Views requires you to select which fields will be used to search against when using the autocomplete widget. If you are not using the autocomplete widget and instead use the select list or checkboxes and radio buttons, then it will return the view's entire results.

See also

- Refer to `Chapter 7`, *Plug and Play with Plugins*, to learn more about plugins

4
Extending Drupal

This chapter dives into extending Drupal using a custom module:

- Creating a module
- Defining a custom page
- Defining permissions
- Providing the configuration on installation or update
- Creating an event subscriber
- Using Features 3.0

Introduction

A feature of Drupal that makes it desirable is the ability to customize it through modules. Whether custom or contributed, modules extend the functionalities and capabilities of Drupal. Modules can be used to not only extend Drupal, but also to create a way to provide configuration and reusable features.

This chapter will discuss how to create a module and allow Drupal to discover it, allowing it to be installed from the extend page. Permissions, custom pages, and default configurations all come from modules. We will explore how to provide these through a custom module.

In addition to creating a module, we will discuss the Features module that provides a set of tools to generate a module and export its configuration.

Creating a module

The first step to extend Drupal is to create a custom module. Although the task sounds daunting, it can be accomplished in a few simple steps. Modules can provide functionalities and customizations to functionalities provided by other modules, or they can be used as a way to contain the configuration and a site's state.

In this recipe, we will create a module by defining an `info.yml` file, a file containing information that Drupal uses to discover extensions, and enabling the module.

How to do it...

1. Create a folder named `mymodule` in the `modules` folder in the base directory of your Drupal site. This will be your module's directory.
2. Create a `mymodule.info.yml` file in your module's directory. This contains metadata that identifies the module to Drupal.
3. Add a line to the `name` key to provide a name for the module:

    ```
    name: My Module!
    ```

4. We will need to provide the `type` key to define the type of extension. We provide the `module` value:

    ```
    type: module
    ```

5. The `description` key allows you to provide extra information about your module, which will be displayed on the module's list page:

    ```
    description: This is an example module from the Drupal 8 Cookbook!
    ```

6. All modules need to define the `core` key in order to specify a major release compatibility:

    ```
    core: 8.x
    ```

7. Save the `mymodule.info.yml` file, which resembles the following code:

    ```
    name: My Module!
    type: module
    description: This is an example module from the Drupal 8 Cookbook!
    core: 8.x
    ```

8. Log in to your Drupal site and go to **Extend** from the administrative toolbar.
9. Search for **My Module** to filter the list of options.
10. Check the checkbox and click on **Install** to enable your module:

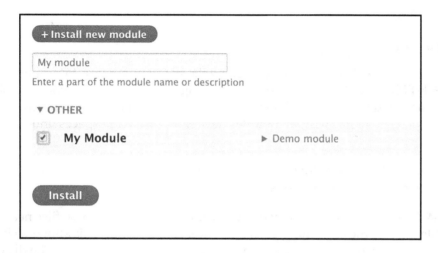

How it works...

Drupal utilizes info.yml files to define extensions. Drupal has a discovery system that locates these files and parses them to discover modules. The info_parser service, provided by the \Drupal\Core\Extension\InfoParser class, reads the info.yml file. The parser guarantees that the required type, core, and name keys are present.

When a module is installed, it is added to the core.extension configuration object, which contains a list of installed modules and themes. The collection of modules in the core.extension module array will be installed, and will have PHP namespaces resolved, services loaded, and hooks registered.

When Drupal prepares to execute a hook or register services, it will iterate through the values in the module key in core.extension.

There's more...

There are more details about Drupal modules and the module `info.yml` files that we can explore.

Module namespaces

Drupal 8 uses the PSR-4 standard developed by the **PHP Framework Interoperability Group (PHP-FIG)**. The PSR-4 standard is for package-based PHP namespace autoloading. It defines a standard to understand how to automatically include classes based on a namespace and class name. Drupal modules have their own namespaces under the Drupal root namespace.

Using the module from the recipe, our PHP namespace will be `Drupal\mymodule`, which represents the `modules/mymodule/src` folder.

With PSR-4, files need to contain only one class, interface, or trait. These files need to have the same filename as the containing class, interface, or trait name. This allows a class loader to resolve a namespace as a directory path and know the class's filename. The file can then be automatically loaded when it is used in a file.

Module discovery locations

Drupal supports multiple module discovery locations. Modules can be placed in the following directories and discovered:

- `/profiles/CURRENT PROFILE/modules`
- `/sites/all/modules`
- `/modules`
- `/sites/default/modules`
- `/sites/example.com/modules`

The `\Drupal\Core\Extension\ExtensionDiscovery` class handles the discovery of extensions by type. It will iteratively scan each location and discover modules that are available. The discovery order is important. If the same module is placed in `/modules`, but also in the `sites/default/modules` directory, the latter will take precedence.

Defining a package group

Modules can define a `package` key to group modules on the module list page:

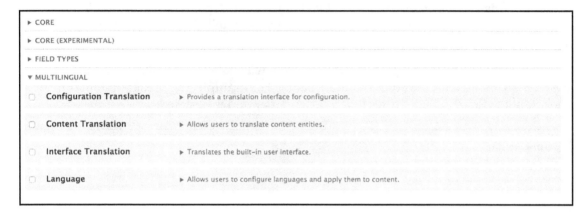

Projects that include multiple submodules, such as Drupal Commerce, specify packages to normalize the modules' list form. Contributed modules for the Drupal Commerce project utilize a package name, `Commerce (contrib)`, to group them on the module list page.

Module dependencies

Modules can define dependencies to ensure that those modules are enabled before your module can be enabled.

Here is the `info.yml` for the `Responsive Image` module:

```
name: Responsive Image
type: module
description: 'Provides an image formatter and breakpoint mappings to output
responsive images using the HTML5 picture tag.'
package: Core
version: VERSION
core: 8.x
dependencies:
  - breakpoint
  - image
```

The `dependencies` key specifies that the `breakpoint` and `image` modules need to be enabled first before the `Responsive Image` module can be enabled. When enabling a module that requires dependencies that are disabled, the installation form will provide a prompt asking you whether you would like to install the dependencies as well. If a dependency module is missing, the module cannot be installed. The dependency will show a status of (**missing**).

A module that is a dependency of another module will state the information in its description, along with the other module's status. For example, the Breakpoint module will show that the Re module requires it as a dependency and is disabled:

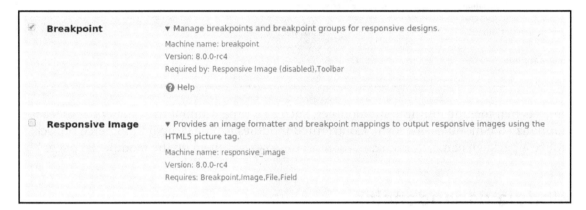

Specifying the module's version

There is a `version` key that defines the current module's version. Projects on Drupal.org do not specify this directly, as the Drupal.org extension packager adds it when a release is created. However, this key can be important for private modules to track the release information.

Versions are expected to be single strings, such as `1.0-alpha1` and `2.0.1`. You can also pass `VERSION`, which will resolve to the current version of Drupal core.

Drupal.org does not currently support semantic versioning for contributed projects. There is a, now postponed, policy discussion in the issue queue, which can be found at `https://www.drupal.org/node/1612910`.

See also...

- Refer to the PSR-4: Autoloader specification at `http://www.php-fig.org/psr/psr-4/`
- Refer to the Drupal.org documentation for creating a module at `https://www.drupal.org/docs/8/creating-custom-modules`

Defining a custom page

In Drupal, there are routes that represent URL paths that Drupal interprets to return content. Modules can define routes and methods that return data to be rendered and then displayed to the end user.

In this recipe, we will define a controller that provides an output and a route. The route provides a URL path that Drupal will associate with our controller to display the output.

Getting ready

Create a new module like the one in the first recipe. We will refer to the module as `mymodule` throughout the recipe. Use your module's name as appropriate.

How to do it...

1. Firstly, we'll set up the controller. Create a `src` folder in your module's base directory and another folder named `Controller` inside it.

2. Create `MyPageController.php` that will hold the route's controller class:

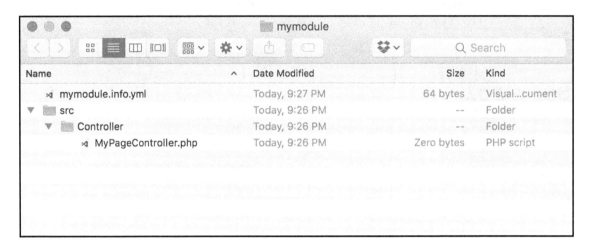

3. The PSR-4 standard states that filenames match the class names they hold, so we will create a `MyPageController` class:

```php
<?php

namespace Drupal\mymodule\Controller;

use Drupal\Core\Controller\ControllerBase;

/**
 * Returns responses for My Module module.
 */
class MyPageController extends ControllerBase {

}
```

This creates the `MyPageController` class, which extends the `\Drupal\Core\Controller\ControllerBase` class. This base class provides a handful of utilities for interacting with the container.

The `Drupal\mymodule\Controller` namespace allows Drupal to automatically load the file from `/modules/mymodule/src/Controller`.

4. Next, we will create a method that returns a string of text in our class. Add the following method to our `MyPageController` class:

```
/**
 * Returns markup for our custom page.
 */
public function customPage() {
  return [
    '#markup' => t('Welcome to my custom page!'),
  ];
}
```

The `customPage` method returns a render array that the Drupal theming layer can parse. The `#markup` key denotes a value that does not have any additional rendering or theming processes.

5. Create a `mymodule.routing.yml` file in the base directory of your module so that a route can be added to this controller and method.

6. The first step is to define the route's internal name for the route to be referenced by:

```
mymodule.mypage:
```

7. Give the route a path (`mypage`):

```
mymodule.mypage:
  path: '/mypage'
```

8. The `defaults` key allows us to provide the controller with a fully qualified class name, the method to use, and the page's title:

```
mymodule.mypage:
  path: '/mypage'
  defaults:
    _controller:
'\Drupal\mymodule\Controller\MyPageController::customPage'
    _title: 'My custom page'
```

You need to provide the initial \ when providing the fully qualified class name.

Remember that Drupal uses PSR-4 autoloading. Drupal is able to determine that a class with the namespace of `\Drupal\mymodule\Controller` is in the `/path/to/drupal/modules/mymodule/src/Controller` directory.

9. Lastly, define a `requirements` key to set the access callback:

```
mymodule.mypage:
  path: '/mypage'
  defaults:
  _controller:
'\Drupal\mymodule\Controller\MyPageController::customPage'
  _title: 'My custom page'
requirements:
  _permission: 'access content'
```

10. Go to **Configuration**, and then **Performance** in the **DEVEOLOPMENT** section, and click on **Clear all caches** button to rebuild Drupal's routes.

11. Go to `/mypage` on your Drupal site and view your custom page:

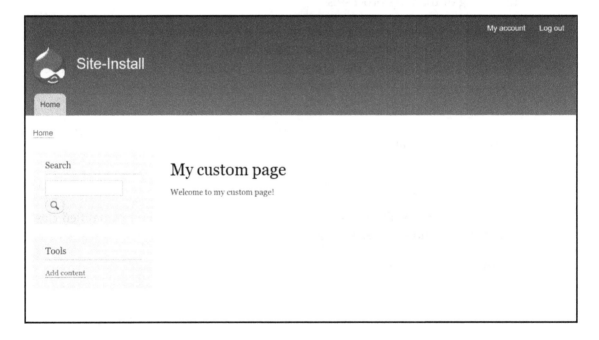

How it works...

Drupal uses routes, which define a path, that returns content. Each route has a method in a controller class that generates the content, in the form of a render array, to be delivered to the user. When a request comes to Drupal, the system tries to match the path to known routes. If the route is found, the route's definition is used to deliver the page. If the route cannot be found, the 404 page is displayed.

The HTTP kernel takes the request and loads the route. It will invoke the defined controller method or procedural function. The result of the invoked method or function is then handed to the presentation layer of Drupal to be rendered into the content that can be delivered to the user.

Drupal 8 builds on top of the Symfony HTTP kernel to provide the underlying functionality of its route system. It has added the ability to provide access requirements, cast placeholders into loaded objects, and provide partial page responses.

There's more...

Routes have extra capabilities that can be configured; we will explore those in the next section.

Parameters in routes

Routes can accept dynamic arguments that can be passed to the route controller's method. Placeholder elements can be defined in the route using curly brackets in the URL that denote dynamic values.

The following example code shows what a route might look like:

```
mymodule.cats:
  path: '/cat/{name}'
  defaults:
    _controller: '\Drupal\mymodule\Controller\MyPageController::cats'
  requirements:
    _permission: 'access content'
```

This route specifies the /cat/{name} path. The {name} placeholder will accept dynamic values and pass them to the controller's method:

```
class MyPageController {
  // ...
  public function cats($name) {
```

```
    return [
      '#markup' => t('My cats name is: @name', [
        '@name' => $name,
      ]),
    ];
  }
}
```

This method accepts the `name` variable from the route and substitutes it into the render array to display it as a text.

Drupal's routing system provides a method of upcasting a variable into a loaded object. In Drupal, upcasting is the process of taking a route parameter and converting it into a richer piece of data. This includes taking an entity ID and providing the loaded entity to the system. There are a set of parameter converter classes under the `\Drupal\Core\ParamConverter` namespace. The `EntityConverter` class will read options defined in the route and replace a placeholder value with a loaded entity object.

If we have an entity type called **cat**, we can turn the `name` placeholder into a method that will be provided with the loaded `cat` object in our controller's method:

```
mymodule.cats:
  path: '/cat/{name}'
  defaults:
    _controller: '\Drupal\mymodule\Controller\MyPageController::cats'
  requirements:
    _permission: 'access content'
  options:
    parameters:
      name:
        type: entity:cat
```

 This is not required for entities as the defined entity route handler can automatically generate this. Entities are covered in *Chapter 10*, *The Entity API*.

Validating parameters in routes

Drupal provides regular expression validation against route parameters. If the parameter fails the regular expression validation, a 404 page will be returned. Using an example route, we can add the validation to ensure that only alphabetical characters are used in the route parameter:

```
mymodule.cats:
```

```
path: '/cat/{name}'
defaults:
  _controller: '\Drupal\mymodule\Controller\MyPageController::cats'
requirements:
  _permission: 'access content'
  name: '[a-zA-z]+'
```

Under the `requirements` key, you can add a new value that matches the name of the placeholder. You can then set it to have the value of the regular expression you would like to use. This would prevent `c@ts` or `cat!` from being valid parameters.

Route requirements

Routes can define different access requirements through the `requirements` key. Multiple validators can be added. However, there must be one that provides a true result, or else the route will return **403, access denied**. This is true if the route defines no requirement validators.

Route requirement validators are defined by implementing `\Drupal\Core\Routing\Access\AccessInterface`. Here are some of the common requirement validators defined throughout Drupal core:

- `_access: TRUE`: Always grants access to the route
- `_entity_access`: Validates that the current user has the ability to perform `entity_type.operation`, such as `node.view`
- `_permission`: Checks whether the current user has the provided permission
- `_user_is_logged_in`: Validates that the current user is logged in, which is defined with a Boolean value in the `routing.yml` file

Providing dynamic routes

The routing system allows modules to define routes programmatically. This can be accomplished by providing a `routing_callbacks` key that defines a class and method that will return an array of the `\Symfony\Component\Routing\Route` objects.

 If you are working with entities, refer to *Chapter 10, The Entity API* to learn about overriding the default route handler to create dynamic routes.

In the module's `routing.yml`, you will define the routing callbacks key and related class:

```
route_callbacks:
  - '\Drupal\mymodule\Routing\CustomRoutes::routes'
```

The `\Drupal\mymodule\Routing\CustomRoutes` class will then have a method named routes, which returns an array of Symfony route objects:

```php
<?php

namespace Drupal\mymodule\Routing;
use Symfony\Component\Routing\Route;

class CustomRoutes {
  public function routes() {
    $routes = [];
    // Create mypage route programmatically
    $routes['mymodule.mypage'] = new Route(
        // Path definition
        'mypage',
        // Route defaults
        [
          '_controller' =>
'\Drupal\mymodule\Controller\MyPageController::customPage',
          '_title' => 'My custom page',
        ],
        // Route requirements
        [
          '_permission' => 'access content',
        ]
    );
    return $routes;
  }
}
```

If a module provides a class that interacts with routes, the best practice is to place it in the routing portion of the module's namespace. This helps you identify its purpose.

The invoked method is expected to return an array of initiated route objects. The route class takes the following arguments:

- `Path`: This represents the route
- `Defaults`: This is an array of default values
- `Requirements`: This is an array of required validators
- `Options`: This is an array that can be passed and used optionally

Altering existing routes

When Drupal's route system is rebuilt because of a module being enabled or caches being rebuilt, an event is fired that allows modules to alter routes defined statically in YAML or dynamically. This involves implementing an event subscriber by extending `\Drupal\Core\Routing\RouteSubscribeBase`, which subscribes the `RoutingEvents::ALTER` event.

Create a `src/Routing/RouteSubscriber.php` file in your module. It will hold the route subscriber class:

```php
<?php

namespace Drupal\mymodule\Routing;

use Drupal\Core\Routing\RouteSubscriberBase;
use Symfony\Component\Routing\RouteCollection;

class RouteSubscriber extends RouteSubscriberBase {

  /**
   * {@inheritdoc}
   */
  public function alterRoutes(RouteCollection $collection) {
    // Change path of mymodule.mypage to use a hyphen
    if ($route = $collection->get('mymodule.mypage')) {
      $route->setPath('/my-page');
    }
  }

}
```

The preceding code extends `RouteSubscribeBase` and implements the `alterRoutes()` method. We make an attempt to load the `mymodule.mypage` route, and, if it exists, we change its path to `my-page`. Since objects are always passed by reference, we do not need to return a value.

For Drupal to recognize the subscriber, we will need to describe it in the module's `services.yml` file. In the base directory of your module, create a `mymodule.services.yml` file and add the following code:

```
services:
  mymodule.route_subscriber:
    class: Drupal\mymodule\Routing\RouteSubscriber
    tags:
      - { name: event_subscriber }
```

This registers our route subscriber class as a service to the container so that Drupal can execute it when the event is fired.

 The *Creating an event subscriber* recipe later in this chapter will cover more about event dispatching and subscribing.

See also

- Refer to the Symfony routing documentation at http://symfony.com/doc/current/book/routing.html
- Refer to *Chapter 10*, *The Entity API*
- Refer to the access checking on routes community documentation at https://www.drupal.org/node/2122195

Defining permissions

In Drupal, there are roles and permissions used to define robust access control lists for users. Modules use permissions to check whether the current user has access to perform an action, view specific items, or do other operations. Modules then define the permissions that are used so that Drupal is aware of them. Developers can then construct roles, which are made up of enabled permissions.

In this recipe, we will define a new permission to view custom pages defined in a module. The permission will be added to a custom route and will restrict access to the route path to users who have a role containing the permission.

Getting ready

Create a new module like the one in the first recipe. We will refer to the module as `mymodule` throughout the recipe. Use your module's name in the following recipe as appropriate.

This recipe also modifies a route defined in the module. We will refer to this route as `mymodule.mypage`. Modify the appropriate path in your module's `routing.yml` file.

How to do it...

1. Permissions are stored in a `permissions.yml` file. Add a `mymodule.permissions.yml` to the base directory of your module.

2. First, we will need to define the internal string used to identify this permission, such as `view mymodule pages`:

   ```
   view mymodule pages:
   ```

3. Each permission is a YAML array of data. We will need to provide a `title` key that will be displayed on the permissions page:

   ```
   view mymodule pages:
      title: 'View my module pages'
   ```

4. Permissions have a `description` key to provide details of the permission on the permissions page:

   ```
   view mymodule pages:
      title: 'View my module pages'
      description: 'Allows users to view pages provided by My Module'
   ```

5. Save your `permissions.yml` and edit the module's `routing.yml` to use the permission for controlling access to a route.

6. Modify the route's `requirements` key to have a `_permission` key that is equal to the defined permission:

   ```
   mymodule.mypage:
     path: '/mypage'
     defaults:
     _controller:
   '\Drupal\mymodule\Controller\MyPageController::customPage'
     _title: 'My custom page'
   ```

```
requirements:
  _permission: 'view mymodule pages'
```

7. Go to **Configuration** and then to **Performance** in the **DEVELOPMENT** section and click on **Clear all caches** to rebuild Drupal's routes.

8. Go to **People** and then to **Permissions** to add your permission as the authenticated user and anonymous user roles for **My module!**:

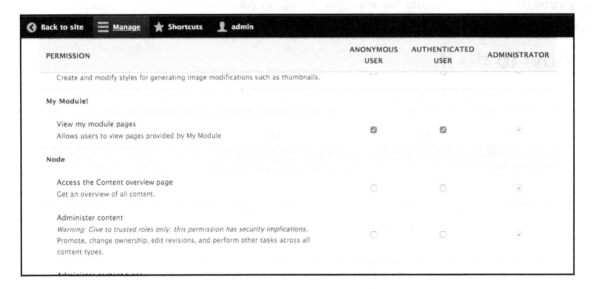

9. Log out of your Drupal site and view the /mypage page. You will see the content, and will not receive an access denied page.

How it works...

Permissions and roles are provided by the User module. The user.permissions service discovers the permissions.yml provided by installed modules. By default, the service is defined through the \Drupal\user\PermissionHandler class.

Drupal does not save a list of all permissions that are available. The permissions for a system are loaded when the permissions page is loaded. Roles contain an array of permissions.

When checking a user's access for a permission, Drupal checks all the user's roles to see whether they support that permission.

You can pass an undefined permission to a user access check and not receive an error. The access check will simply fail unless the user is UID 1, which bypasses access checks.

There's more...

We will cover more ways to work with permissions in your modules in the upcoming sections.

Restrict access flag for permissions

Permissions can be flagged as having a security risk if enabled; this is the `restrict access` flag. When this flag is set to `restrict access: TRUE`, it will add a warning to the permission description.

This allows module developers to provide more context to the amount of control a permission may give a user:

PERMISSION	ANONYMOUS USER	AUTHENTICATED USER	ADMINISTRATOR
Administer content *Warning: Give to trusted roles only; this permission has security implications.* Promote, change ownership, edit revisions, and perform other tasks across all content types.	☐	☐	☑

The permission definition from our recipe would look like the following:

```
view mymodule pages:
  title: 'View my module pages'
  description: 'Allows users to view pages provided by My Module'
  restrict access: TRUE
```

Defining permissions programmatically

Permissions can be defined by a module programmatically or statically in a YAML file. A module needs to provide a `permission_callbacks` key in its `permissions.yml` that contains either an array of classes and their methods or a procedural function name.

For example, the Filter module provides granular permissions based on the different text filters created in Drupal:

```
permission_callbacks:
  - Drupal\filter\FilterPermissions::permissions
```

This tells the `user_permissions` service to execute the permissions method of the `\Drupal\Filter\FilterPermissions` class. The method is expected to return an array that matches the same structure as that of the `permissions.yml` file.

An example of using generated permissions will be covered in *Implementing custom access control for an entity* recipe of `Chapter 10`, *The Entity API*.

Checking whether a user has permissions

The user account interface provides a method for checking whether a user entity has a permission. To check whether the current user has a permission, you will get the current user, and you need to invoke the `hasPermission` method:

```
\Drupal::currentUser()->hasPermission('my permission');
```

The `\Drupal::currentUser()` method returns the current active user object. This allows you to check whether the active user has the necessary permissions to perform certain types of actions.

Providing the configuration on the installation or update

Drupal provides a configuration management system, which is discussed in `Chapter 9`, *Configuration Management - Deploying in Drupal 8*, and modules can provide configuration on an installation or through an update system. Modules provide the configuration through YAML files when they are first installed. Once the module is enabled, the configuration is then placed in the configuration management system; however updates can be made to the configuration in code through the Drupal update system.

In this recipe, we will provide a configuration YAML that creates a new contact form and then manipulates it through a schema version change in the update system.

Getting ready

Create a new module like the one in the first recipe. We will refer to the module as `mymodule` throughout the recipe. Use your module's appropriate name where necessary.

How to do it...

1. Create a `config` folder in your module's base directory. Drupal requires its configuration YAML to be in a subfolder of `config`.

2. Create a folder named `install` in the `config` folder. The configuration YAML in this folder will be imported on module installation.

3. In the `install` folder, create a `contact.form.contactus.yml` to store the YAML definition of the contact form, **Contact Us**:

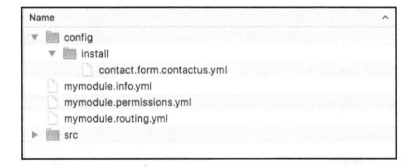

4. We will define the configuration of a contact form based on the `contact.schema.yml` file provided by the Contact module. Add the following YAML content into the file:

```
langcode: en
status: true
dependences: {}
id: contactus
label: 'Contact Us'
recipients:
  - webmaster@example.com
reply: ''
weight: 0
```

The configuration entry is based on a schema definition, which we will cover in *Chapter 9, Configuration Management - Deploying in Drupal 8*. The `langcode`, `status`, and `dependencies` are the required configuration management keys.

The `id` is the contact form's machine name and the label is the human display name. The `recipients` key is a YAML array of valid email addresses. The reply key is a string of text for the **Auto-reply** field. Finally, the `weight` defines the form's weight in the administrative list.

5. Go to **Extend** and enable your module to import the configuration item.
6. The **Contact Us** form will now be located on the **Contact forms** overview page, located under **Structure**:

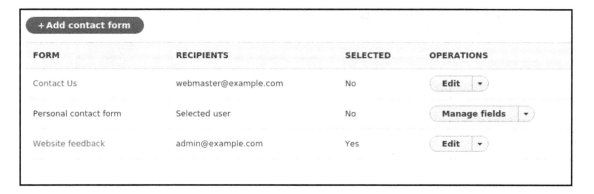

7. Create a `mymodule.install` file in the module's base directory. Drupal checks `.install` files for update hooks.
8. We will create a function called `mymodule_update_8001()` that will be read by the update system and make our configuration changes:

```php
<?php

/**
 * Update "Contact Us" form to have a reply message.
 */
function mymodule_update_8001() {
  $contact_form =
\Drupal\contact\Entity\ContactForm::load('contactus');
  $contact_form->setReply(t('Thank you for contacting us, we will
reply shortly'));
  $contact_form->save();
}
```

This function uses the entity's class to load our configuration entity object. It loads `contactus`, which our module has provided, and sets the reply property to a new value.

9. Go to `/update.php` in your browser to run the Drupal's database update system. Click on **Apply pending updates** to run the update system:

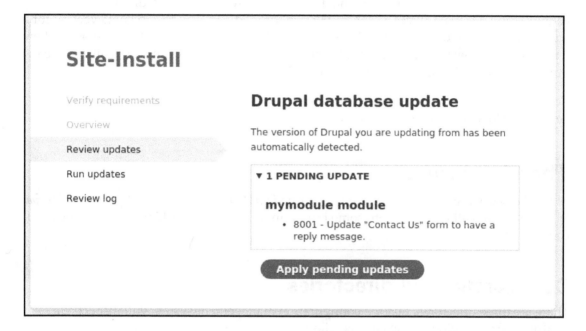

10. Review the **Contact Us** form settings and verify that the reply message has been set.

How it works...

Drupal's `moduler_installer` service, provided through `\Drupal\Core\Extension\ModuleInstaller`, ensures that configuration items defined in the module's `config` folder are processed on installation. When a module is installed, the `config.installer` service, provided through `\Drupal\Core\Config\ConfigInstaller`, is called to process the module's default configuration.

In the event, the `config.installer` service makes an attempt to import the configuration from the `install` folder that already exists, and an exception will be thrown. Modules cannot provide changes made to the existing configuration through static YAML definitions.

Since modules cannot adjust configuration objects through static YAML definitions provided to Drupal, they can utilize the database update system to modify the configuration. Drupal utilizes a schema version for modules. The base schema version for a module is `8000`. Modules can provide update hooks in the form of `hook_update_N`, where `N` represents the next schema version. When Drupal's updates are run, they will execute the proper update hooks and update the module's schema version.

Configuration objects are immutable by default. To edit a configuration, a mutable object needs to be loaded through the configuration factory service.

There's more...

We will discuss configuration in *Chapter 9*, *Configuration Management - Deploying in Drupal 8*; however, we will now dive into some important notes when working with modules and configurations.

Configuration subdirectories

There are three directories that the configuration management system will inspect in a module's `config` folder, which are as follows:

- `install`
- `optional`
- `schema`

The `install` folder specifies the configuration that will be imported. If the configuration object exists, the installation will fail. The `optional` folder contains the configuration that will be installed if the following conditions are met:

- The configuration does not already exist
- It is a configuration entity
- Its dependencies can be met

If any one of the conditions fails, the configuration will not be installed, but it will not halt the module's installation process.

The `schema` folder provides configuration object definitions. This uses YAML definitions to structure configuration objects, and is covered in depth in *Chapter 9, Configuration Management - Deploying in Drupal 8*.

Modifying the existing configuration on installation

The configuration management system does not allow modules to provide configuration on an installation that already exists. For example, if a module tries to provide `system.site` and defines the site's name, it would fail to install. This is because the system module provides this configuration object when you first install Drupal.

Drupal provides `hook_install()` that modules can implement in their `.install` file. This hook is executed during the module's installation process. The following code will update the site's title to *Drupal 8 Cookbook*! on the module's installation:

```
/**
 * Implements hook_install().
 */
function mymodule_install() {
  // Set the site name.
  \Drupal::configFactory()
    ->getEditable('system.site')
    ->set('name', 'Drupal 8 Cookbook!')
    ->save();
}
```

Configurable objects are immutable by default when loaded by the default `config` service. To modify a configuration object, you will need to use the configuration factory to receive a mutable object. The mutable object can have `set` and `save` methods that are executed to update the configuration in a configuration object.

See also

- Refer to *Chapter 9, Configuration Management - Deploying in Drupal 8*

Creating an event subscriber

New to Drupal 8 is the event dispatcher system. One of the many benefits of Drupal is the ability to react to specific processes and alter or react to them. Unlike the hook system that exists in Drupal 8, and has for many versions of Drupal, the event dispatch system uses explicit registration to an event.

The events dispatcher system comes from the Symfony framework and allows components to easily interact with one another. Within Drupal, and integrated Symfony components, events are dispatched, and event subscribers can listen to the events and react to changes or other processes.

In this recipe, we will subscribe to the REQUEST event, which fires when a request is first handled. If the user is not logged in, we will navigate them to the login page.

How to do it...

1. Create `src/EventSubscriber/RequestSubscriber.php` in your module.
2. Define the `RequestSubscriber` class, which implements the `EventSubscriberInterface` interface:

   ```php
   <?php

   namespace Drupal\mymodule\EventSubscriber;

   use Symfony\Component\EventDispatcher\EventSubscriberInterface;

   class RequestSubscriber implements EventSubscriberInterface {

   }
   ```

3. To satisfy the interface requirements, we must add a `getSubscribedEvents` method. This tells the system which events we are subscribing to and the method that needs to be invoked:

   ```php
   <?php

   namespace Drupal\mymodule\EventSubscriber;

   use Symfony\Component\EventDispatcher\EventSubscriberInterface;
   use Symfony\Component\HttpKernel\KernelEvents;

   class RequestSubscriber implements EventSubscriberInterface {
   ```

```
/**
 * {@inheritdoc}
 */
public static function getSubscribedEvents() {
  return [
    KernelEvents::REQUEST => ['doAnonymousRedirect', 28],
  ];
}

}
```

The `KernelEvents` class provides constants for available events. Our returned array specifies the method to invoke and its priority for that event.

 Priorities will be discussed in the *How it works...* section. It is provided in the example to resolve possible conflicts when the `dynamic_page_cache` module is enabled.

4. Create the `doAnonymousRedirect` method we specified, which will receive a `GetResponseEvent` argument:

```
<?php

namespace Drupal\mymodule\EventSubscriber;

use Drupal\Core\Url;
use Symfony\Component\EventDispatcher\EventSubscriberInterface;
use Symfony\Component\HttpFoundation\RedirectResponse;
use Symfony\Component\HttpKernel\Event\GetResponseEvent;
use Symfony\Component\HttpKernel\KernelEvents;

class RequestSubscriber implements EventSubscriberInterface {

  /**
   * Redirects all anonymous users to the login page.
   *
   * @param \Symfony\Component\HttpKernel\Event\GetResponseEvent $event
   *   The event.
   */
  public function doAnonymousRedirect(GetResponseEvent $event) {
    // Make sure we are not on the user login route.
    if (\Drupal::routeMatch()->getRouteName() == 'user.login') {
      return;
    }
```

```
    // Check if the current user is logged in.
    if (\Drupal::currentUser()->isAnonymous()) {
      // If they are not logged in, create a redirect response.
      $url = Url::fromRoute('user.login')->toString();
      $redirect = new RedirectResponse($url);

      // Set the redirect response on the event, cancelling
default response.
      $event->setResponse($redirect);
    }
  }

  /**
   * {@inheritdoc}
   */
  public static function getSubscribedEvents() {
    return [
      KernelEvents::REQUEST => ['doAnonymousRedirect', 28],
    ];
  }

}
```

To prevent a redirect loop, we will use the RouteMatch service to get the current route object and verify that we are not already on the user.login route page.

Then we check whether the user is anonymous and, if the user is anonymous, set the event's response to a redirect response.

5. Now that we have created our class, create a mymodule.services.yml file in your module's directory.
6. We must register our class with the service container so that Drupal understands that it will act as an event subscriber.

```
services:
  mymodule.request_subscriber:
    class: Drupal\mymodule\EventSubscriber\RequestSubscriber
    tags:
      - { name: event_subscriber }
```

The event_subscriber tag tells the container to invoke the getSubscribedEvents method and register its methods.

7. Install the module or rebuild Drupal's caches if it has been already installed.
8. Navigate to any page as an anonymous user--you will be redirected to the login form.

How it works...

Throughout Drupal and Symfony components, and even other third-party PHP libraries, events can be passed to the event dispatcher. The event_dispatcher service in Drupal is an optimized version of the one provided by Symfony, but is completely interoperable.

When the container is built, all services tagged as event_subscribers are gathered. They are then registered into the event_dispatcher service, keyed by the events returned in the getSubscribedEvents method.

When the event_dispatcher service is told to dispatch an event, it invokes the proper methods on all subscribed services. With KernelEvents::REQUEST, KernelEvents::EXCEPTION and KernelEvents::VIEW, you have the opportunity to provide a response before the controller is invoked. Then there are events, such as ConfigEvents::SAVE and ConfigEvents::DELETE, that are dispatched and allow you to react to a configuration being saved or deleted but are not actually able to adjust the configuration entity directly through the event object.

There's more...

Event subscribers require knowledge of creating services, registering them, and even dependency injection. We'll discuss this some more in the next section.

Using dependency injection

With Drupal 8 and the implementation of a service container comes the concept of dependency injection. Dependency injection is a software design concept, and at its base level, it provides a means to use a class without having to directly reference it. In our example, we retrieve services multiple times using the global static class \Drupal. This is bad practice within services, and can make testing more difficult.

To implement dependency injection, first, we will add a constructor to our class that accepts the services used (`current_route_match` and `current_user`) and matches protected properties to store them:

```
/**
 * The route match.
 *
 * @var \Drupal\Core\Routing\RouteMatchInterface
 */
protected $routeMatch;

/**
 * Account proxy.
 *
 * @var \Drupal\Core\Session\AccountProxyInterface
 */
protected $accountProxy;

/**
 * Creates a new RequestSubscriber object.
 *
 * @param \Drupal\Core\Routing\RouteMatchInterface $route_match
 *    The route match.
 * @param \Drupal\Core\Session\AccountProxyInterface $account_proxy
 *    The current user.
 */
public function __construct(RouteMatchInterface $route_match,
AccountProxyInterface $account_proxy) {
  $this->routeMatch = $route_match;
  $this->accountProxy = $account_proxy;
}
```

We can then replace any calls to `\Drupal::` with `$this->`:

```
/**
 * Redirects all anonymous users to the login page.
 *
 * @param \Symfony\Component\HttpKernel\Event\GetResponseEvent $event
 *    The event.
 */
public function doAnonymousRedirect(GetResponseEvent $event) {
  // Make sure we are not on the user login route.
  if ($this->routeMatch->getRouteName() == 'user.login') {
    return;
  }

  // Check if the current user is logged in.
  if ($this->accountProxy->isAnonymous()) {
```

```
    // If they are not logged in, create a redirect response.
    $url = Url::fromRoute('user.login')->toString();
    $redirect = new RedirectResponse($url);

    // Set the redirect response on the event, cancelling default
response.
    $event->setResponse($redirect);
  }
}
```

Finally, we will update `mymodule.services.yml` to specify our constructor arguments so that they will be injected when the container runs our event subscriber:

```
services:
  mymodule.request_subscriber:
    class: Drupal\mymodule\EventSubscriber\RequestSubscriber
    arguments: ['@current_route_match', '@current_user']
    tags:
      - { name: event_subscriber }
```

Dependency injection feels and seems magical at first. However, with use and practice, it will begin to make more sense and become second nature when developing with Drupal 8.

See also

- Refer to the Drupal.org API documentation for events and a list of available events
  at https://api.drupal.org/api/drupal/core%21core.api.php/group/events/8.3.x
- Refer to the Drupal.org API documentation on services and dependency injection
  at https://api.drupal.org/api/drupal/core%21core.api.php/group/container/8.3.x

Using Features 3.0

Many Drupal users create custom modules to provide specific sets of features that they can reuse across multiple sites. In fact, there is a module for the sole purpose of providing a means to export configuration and create modules that provide features. This is how the Features module received its name, in fact.

The Features module has two submodules. The main Features module provides all the functionalities. The Features UI module provides a user interface to create and manage features.

We will use Features to export a module with a configuration that contains the default page and article content types provided by the standard installation so that they can be used on other installation profiles.

How to do it...

1. First, we will install the Features module using Composer, which will also download its dependency, the **Configuration Update Manager** module:

```
$ cd /path/to/drupal8
$ composer require drupal/features
```

2. Go to **Extend** and install the **Features UI** module, confirming the requirements to install **Features and Configuration Update Manager** as well.

3. Go to **Configuration**, and in the **DEVELOPMENT** section, you will find the link to access the Features user interface; click on **Features**:

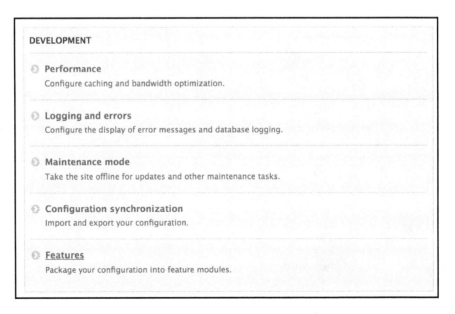

4. Click on **Create new feature** to start making a custom Feature module.

5. Provide a `Name` for the feature, such as **Content Authoring**.

6. Optionally, you can provide a description. This acts as the `description` key in the module's `info.yml`.

7. Toggle the **Content types** grouping and check the **Article** and **Basic Page** checkboxes to mark them for export.

8. The Features module will automatically add detected dependencies or important configuration items to also be exported, such as fields and view modes:

9. Click on **Write** to write the module to export the module and configuration to the `/modules/custom` directory in your Drupal site.

10. Go to **Extend**, search for the **Content Authoring** module, and install your newly created module.

How it works...

Features exports static YAML configuration files into the module's `config/install` folder. Features modifies the standard configuration management workflow by ensuring that a specific kind of configuration exists. Configuration management does not allow modules to overwrite existing configuration objects, but Features manages and allows this to happen.

To accomplish this, Features provides `\Drupal\features\FeaturesConfigInstaller`, which extends the default `config.install` service class. It then alters the services definition to use its `FeaturesConfigInstaller` class instead of the default `\Drupal\Core\Config\ConfigInstaller` class.

Beyond adjusting the `config.install` service, Features harnesses all the functionalities of the configuration management system to provide a simpler way to generate modules.

 Any module can be considered a Feature's module by adding the `features: true` key to its `info.yml`. This will allow it to be managed through the Features UI.

There's more...

Features is a robust tool to easily provide bundled configuration; we will discuss more ways to use the Features module in the next section.

Suggested feature modules

The Features module provides an intelligent bundling method that reviews the current Drupal site's configuration and suggests feature modules that should be created to preserve the configuration. These are provided through package assignment plugins.

These plugins use logic to assign configurations to specific packages:

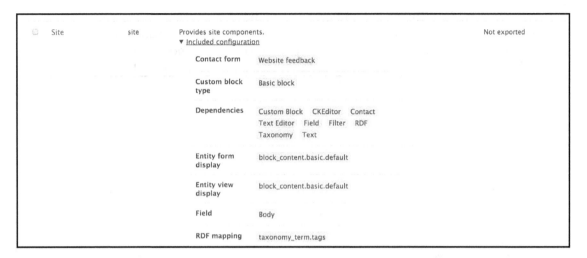

When you visit the Features UI, it will present you with suggested feature modules to be exported. Expanding the items will list the configuration items that will be bundled. Clicking on the suggested feature's link opens the creation form. Alternatively, the checkbox can be used in conjunction with the **Download archive** or **Write** button at the bottom of the form.

> The unpackaged section shows a configuration that has not met any of the packaging rules to group the configuration into a specified module. This will need to be manually added to a created feature module.

Features bundles

In the Features module, there are bundles, and bundles have their own assignment method configurations. The purpose of bundles inside Features is to provide an automatic assignment of configuration that can be grouped into exported modules:

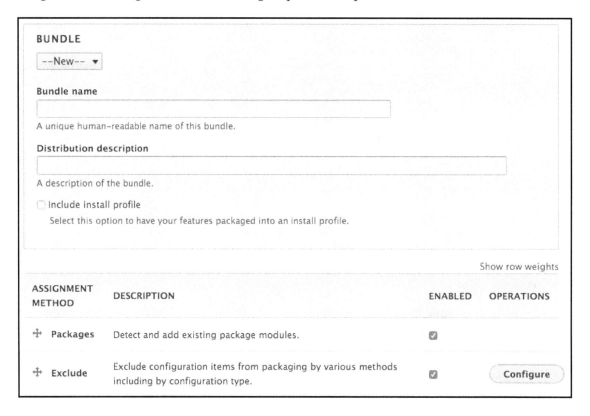

A bundle has a human display name and machine name. The bundle's machine name will be prefixed on all feature modules generated under this bundle. You also can specify the bundle to act as an installation profile. The features UI was heavily used in Drupal 7 to construct distributions and spawn the concept of the bundle functionality.

Assignment methods can be rearranged and configured to your liking.

Managing the configuration state of Features

The Features UI provides a means to review changes to the feature's configuration that may have been made. If a configuration item controlled by a feature module has been modified, it will show up under the differences section of the Features UI. This will allow you to import or update the Feature module with the change.

The **Import** option will force the site to use the configuration defined in the module's configuration YAML files. For example, in the following screenshot we have an exported content type whose description was modified in the user interface after being exported:

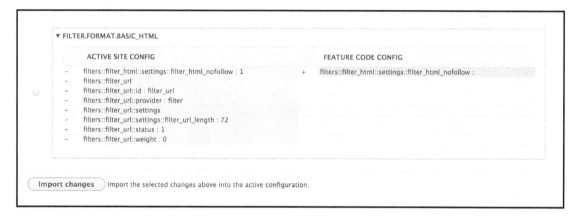

The difference created by the feature module is highlighted. If the difference was checked, and if you click on **Import changes**, the content type's description would be reset to that defined in the configuration.

From the main features overview table, the feature module can be re-exported to include the change and update the exported YAML files.

See also

- Refer to the Drupal.org handbook for the Features module at https://www.drupal.org/docs/8/modules/features

5
Frontend for the Win

In this chapter, we will explore the world of frontend development in Drupal 8. In this chapter, we will cover the following recipes:

- Creating a custom theme based on Classy
- Using the new asset management system
- Twig templating
- Using the Breakpoint module
- Using the Responsive Image module

Introduction

Drupal 8 brought many changes with regard to the frontend. It is now focused on mobile-first responsive design. Frontend performance has been given a high priority, unlike in the previous versions of Drupal. There is a new asset management system based on libraries that will deliver only the minimum required assets for a page that comes with Drupal 8.

In Drupal 8, we have a new feature, the Twig templating engine, that replaces the previously used PHPTemplate engine. Twig is part of the large PHP community and embraces more of Drupal 8's *made elsewhere* initiative. Drupal 7 supported libraries to define JavaScript and CSS resources. However, it was very rudimentary and did not support the concept of library dependencies.

There are two modules provided by the Drupal core that implement the responsive design with server-side components. The Breakpoint module provides a representation of media queries that modules can utilize. The Responsive Image module implements the HTML5 picture tag for image fields.

This chapter dives into harnessing Drupal 8's frontend features to get the most out of them.

Creating a custom theme based on Classy

Drupal 8 ships with a new base theme that is intended to demonstrate best practice and CSS class management. The Classy theme is provided by the Drupal core and is the base theme for the default frontend theme, Bartik, and the administrative theme, Seven.

Unlike the previous versions of Drupal, Drupal 8 provides two base themes--Classy and Stable--to jump start Drupal theming. Stable provides a leaner approach to frontend theming with fewer classes and wrapping elements and is guaranteed to not introduce changes that may disrupt your child theme. In this recipe, we will create a new theme called `mytheme` that uses Classy as its base.

How to do it...

1. In the root directory of your Drupal site, create a folder called `mytheme` in the `themes` folder.
2. Inside the `mytheme` folder, create a `mytheme.info.yml` file so that Drupal can discover the `theme`. We will then edit this file:

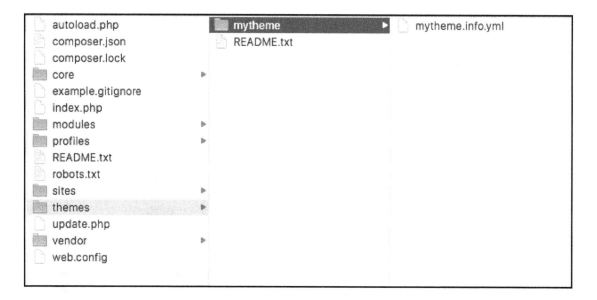

3. First, we will need to define the `themes` name using the `name` key:

```
name: My Theme
```

4. All the themes need to provide a `description` key, that will be displayed on the **Appearance** page:

```
description: My custom theme
```

5. Next, we will need to define the type of extension, that is, a theme and the version of core that is supported:

```
type: theme
core: 8.x
```

6. The `base theme` call allows us to instruct Drupal to use a specific theme as a base:

```
base theme: classy
```

7. The final item is a `regions` key that is used to define the regions of the blocks that can be placed, which is a YAML-based array of key/value pairs:

```
regions:
  header: 'Header'
  primary_menu: 'Primary menu'
  page_top: 'Page top'
  page_bottom: 'Page bottom'
  breadcrumb: 'Breadcrumb'
  content: 'Content'
```

Regions are rendered in the page `template` file, which will be covered in the next recipe, *Twig templates*.

8. Log in to your Drupal site, and go to **Appearance** from the administrative toolbar.

9. Click on **Install and set default** in the **My theme** entry to enable and use the new custom theme:

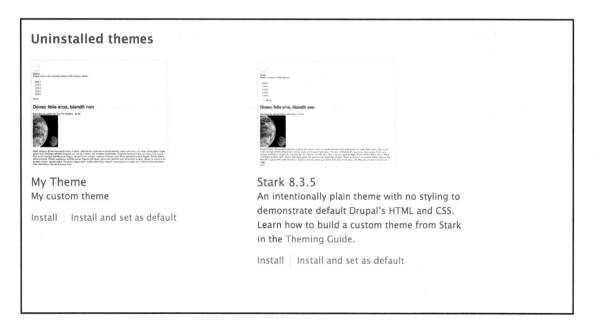

How it works...

In Drupal 8, the `info.yml` files define Drupal themes and modules. The first step to create a theme is to provide the `info.yml` file so that the theme can be discovered. Drupal will parse these values and register the theme.

The following keys are required, as a minimum, when you define a theme:

- `name`
- `description`
- `type`
- `base theme`
- `core`

The `name` key defines the human-readable name of the theme that will be displayed on the **Appearance** page. The **description** will be shown under the **themes** display name on the **Appearance** page. All Drupal projects need to define the `type` key to indicate the kind of extension that is being defined. For themes, the type must always be `theme`. You will also need to define which version of Drupal the project is compatible with using the core value. All Drupal 8 projects will use the `core:  8.x` value. When you define a theme, you will also need to provide the base `theme` key. If your theme does not use a base theme, then you need to set the value to `false`.

The `libraries` and `region` keys are optional, but these are keys that most themes provide. Drupal's asset management system parses a theme's `info.yml` and adds those libraries, if required. Regions are defined in an `info.yml` file and provide the areas into which the Block module may place blocks.

There's more...

Next, we will dive into additional information on themes.

Theme screenshots

Themes can provide a screenshot that shows up on the **Appearance** page. A theme's screenshot can be provided by placing a `screenshot.png` image file in the `theme` folder or a file specified in the `info.yml` file under the `screenshot` key.

If the screenshot is missing, a `default` is used, as seen with the Classy and Stark themes. Generally, a screenshot is a Drupal site with generic content using the theme.

Themes, logos, and favicons

Drupal controls the site's favicon and logo settings as a theme setting. Theme settings are active on a theme-by-theme basis and are not global. Themes can provide a default logo by providing `logo.svg` in the `theme` root folder. A `favicon.ico` placed in a `theme` folder will also be the default value of the `favicon` for the website.

Currently, there is no way to specify a logo of a different file type for a theme. Previous versions of Drupal looked for `logo.png`. A feature has been planned for Drupal 8.5 to allow the `themes` to define the logo's filename and extension. Refer to the core issue for more information at `https://www.drupal.org/node/1507896`.

You can change the site's logo and favicon by navigating to **Appearance** and then clicking on **Settings** for your current theme. Unchecking the **use default** checkboxes for the favicon and logo settings allows you to provide custom files:

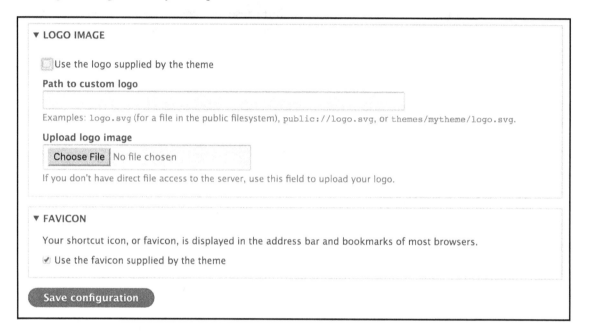

Base themes and shared resources

Many content management systems that have a theme system which supports base (or parent) themes differ mostly in the terminology used. The concept of a base theme is used to provide established resources that are shared, reducing the amount of work required to create a new theme.

All libraries defined in the base theme will be inherited and used by default, allowing subthemes to reuse existing styles and JavaScript. This allows frontend developers to reuse their work and only create specific changes that are required for the subtheme.

The subthemes will also inherit all Twig template overrides provided by the base theme. This was one of the initiatives used for the creation of the Classy theme. Drupal 8 makes many fewer assumptions compared to the previous version as to what class names to provide on elements. Classy overrides all the core's templates and provides sensible default classes, giving themes the ability to use them and accept those class names or be given a blank slate.

CKEditor style sheets

As discussed in `Chapter 2`, *The Content Authoring Experience*, Drupal ships with the WYSIWYG support and CKEditor as the default editor. The CKEditor module will inspect the active theme and its base theme, if provided, and load any style sheets defined in the `ckeditor_stylesheets` key as an array of values.

For example, the following code can be found in `bartik.info.yml`:

```
ckeditor_stylesheets:
  - css/base/elements.css
  - css/components/captions.css
  - css/components/table.css
```

This allows themes to provide style sheets that will style elements within the CKEditor module to enhance the *what you see is what you get* experience of the editor.

See also

- To define a theme with an `info.yml` file, refer to https://www.drupal.org/node/2349827
- To use Classy as a base theme, refer to the community documentation at https://www.drupal.org/theme-guide/8/classy
- Refer to Core themes documentation at https://www.drupal.org/docs/8/core/themes
- To create a Drupal 8 subtheme, refer to the community documentation at https://www.drupal.org/node/2165673

Using the new asset management system

The asset management system is the most recent one to Drupal 8. The asset management system allows modules and themes to register libraries. Libraries define CSS style sheets and JavaScript files that need to be loaded with the page. Drupal 8 takes this approach for the frontend performance. Rather than loading all CSS or JavaScript assets, only those required for the current page in the specified libraries will be loaded.

In this recipe, we will define a `libraries.yml` file that will define a CSS style sheet and JavaScript file provided by a custom theme.

Getting ready

This recipe assumes that you have created a custom theme, such as the one you created in the first recipe. When you see `mytheme` in this recipe, use the machine name of the theme that you created.

How to do it...

1. Create a folder named `css` in your theme's base directory.
2. In your `css` folder, add a `style.css` file that will hold the theme's CSS declarations. For the purpose of demonstration, add the following CSS declaration to `style.css`:

   ```
   body {
      background: cornflowerblue;
   }
   ```

3. Then, create a `js` folder in your theme's directory and add a `scripts.js` file that will hold the theme's JavaScript items.

4. In your theme folder, create a `mytheme.libraries.yml` file, as shown in the following screenshot:

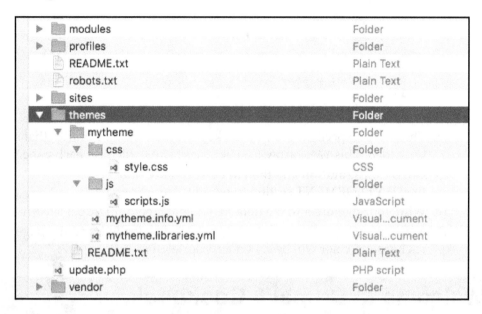

5. Edit the `mytheme.libraries.yml` file. Add the following YAML text to define the `global-styling` library for your theme that will load the CSS and JavaScript files:

```
global-styling:
  version: VERSION
  css:
    theme:
      css/style.css: {}
  js:
    js/scripts.js: {}
```

6. The preceding text tells Drupal that there is a `global-styling` library. You can specify a library version and use the VERSION defaults for your themes. It also defines the `css/styles.css` style sheet as part of the library under the `theme` group.

7. Edit your `mytheme.info.yml`, and add the declaration to your `global-styling` library:

```
name: My Theme
description: My custom theme
type: theme
core: 8.x
base theme: classy
libraries:
  - mytheme/global-styling
```

8. Themes can specify a `libraries` key that defines the libraries that should always be loaded. This `YAML` array lists libraries to be loaded for each page.

9. Go to **Configuration** and then to **Performance** under the **DEVELOPMENT** section to rebuild Drupal's caches.

10. With your theme set to the default, navigate to your Drupal site's home page.

11. Your theme's `global-styling` library will be loaded, and the page's background color will be styled appropriately:

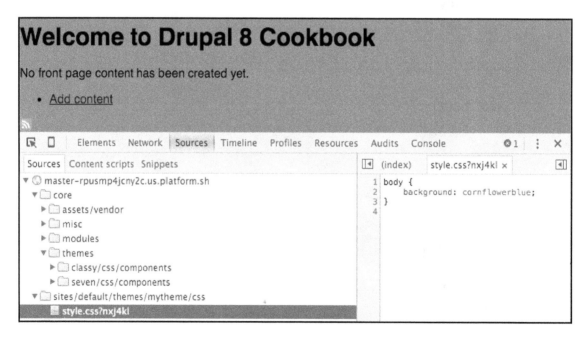

How it works...

Drupal aggregates all the available `library.yml` files and passes them to the `library.discovery.parser` service. The `default` class for this service provider is `\Drupal\Core\Asset\LibraryDiscoveryParser`. This service reads the library definition from each `library.yml` and returns its value to the system. Before parsing the file, the parser allows themes to provide overrides and extensions to the library.

Libraries are enqueuers, as they are attached to rendered elements. Themes can generically add libraries through their `info.yml` files via the `libraries` key. These libraries will always be loaded on the page when the theme is active.

CSS style sheets are added to the data that will build the head tag of the page. JavaScript resources, by default, are rendered in the footer of the page for performance reasons.

There's more...

We will explore the options surrounding libraries in Drupal 8 in more detail in the next section.

CSS groups

With libraries, you can specify CSS by different groups. Drupal's asset management system provides the following CSS groups:

- Base
- Layout
- Component
- State
- Theme

Style sheets are loaded in the order in which the groups are listed. Each one of them relates to a PHP constant defined in `/core/includes/common.inc`. This allows separation of concerns when working with style sheets. Drupal 8's CSS architecture borrows concepts from the **Scalable and Modular Architecture for CSS (SMACSS)** system to organize CSS declarations. You can learn more about this technique for building flexible and scalable CSS style sheets at `https://smacss.com/`.

Library asset options

Library assets can have configuration data attached to them. If there are no configuration items provided, a simple set of empty brackets is added. Therefore, in each example, lines end with { }.

The following example, taken from `core.libraries.yml`, adds `HTML5shiv`:

```
assets/vendor/html5shiv/html5shiv.min.js: { weight: -22, browsers: { IE:
'lte IE 8', '!IE': false }, minified: true }
```

Let's take a look at the attributes of `html5shiv.min.js`:

- The `weight` key ensures that the script is rendered earlier than other libraries
- The `browser` tag allows you to specify conditional rules to load the scripting
- You should always pass `minified` as `true` if the asset has already been minified

For CSS assets, you can pass a media option to specify a media query for the asset. Reviewing classes that implement `\Drupal\Core\Asset\AssetCollectionRendererInterface`.

Library dependencies

Libraries can specify other libraries as dependencies. This allows Drupal to provide a minimum footprint on the frontend performance.

 jQuery is only loaded if a JavaScript library specifies it as a dependency; for more information on library dependencies, refer to `https://www.drupal.org/node/1541860`.

Here's an example from the Quick Edit module's `libraries.yml` file:

```
quickedit:
  version: VERSION
  js:
    ...
  css:
    ...
  dependencies:
    - core/jquery
    - core/jquery.once
    - core/underscore
    - core/backbone
```

```
        - core/jquery.form
        - core/jquery.ui.position
        - core/drupal
        - core/drupal.displace
        - core/drupal.form
        - core/drupal.ajax
        - core/drupal.debounce
        - core/drupalSettings
    - core/drupal.dialog
```

The Quick Edit module defines *jQuery*, the *jQuery Once plugin*, *Underscore*, and *Backbone*, and selects other defined libraries as dependencies. Drupal will ensure that these are present whenever the `quickedit/quickedit` library is attached to a page.

A complete list of the default libraries provided by Drupal core can be found in `core.libraries.yml`, which is in `core/core.libraries.yml`.

Overriding and extending other libraries

Themes have the ability to override libraries using the `libraries-override` and `libraries-extend` keys in their `info.yml`. This allows themes to easily customize the existing libraries without having to add the logic to conditionally remove or add their assets when a particular library is attached to a page.

The `libraries-override` key can be used to replace an entire library, replace selected files in a library, remove an asset from a library, or disable an entire library. The following code will allow a theme to provide a custom jQuery UI theme:

```
libraries-override:
  core/jquery.ui:
    css:
      component:
        assets/vendor/jquery.ui/themes/base/core.css: false
      theme:
        assets/vendor/jquery.ui/themes/base/theme.css: css/jqueryui.css
```

The override declaration mimics the original configuration. Specifying `false` will remove the asset, or else a supplied path will replace that asset.

The `libraries-extend` key can be used to load additional libraries with an existing library. The following code will allow a theme to associate a CSS style sheet with selected jQuery UI declaration overrides, without always having them included in the rest of the theme's assets:

```
libraries-extend:
  core/jquery.ui:
    - mytheme/jqueryui-theme
```

Using a CDN or external resource as a library

Libraries also work with external resources, such as assets loaded over a CDN. This is done by providing a URL for the file location along with selected file parameters.

Here is an example to add the `FontAwesome` font icon library from the `BootstrapCDN` provided by MaxCDN:

```
mytheme.fontawesome:
  remote: http://fontawesome.io/
  version: 4.4.0
  license:
    name: SIL OFL 1.1
    url: http://fontawesome.io/license/
    gpl-compatible: true
  css:
    base:
https://maxcdn.bootstrapcdn.com/font-awesome/4.4.0/css/font-awesome.min.css
: { type: external, minified: true }
```

Remote libraries require additional metainformation to work properly:

```
remote: http://fontawesome.io/
```

The `remote` key describes the library as using external resources. While this key is not validated beyond its existence, it is best to define it with the external resource's primary website:

```
version: 4.4.0
```

Like all libraries, a version is required. This should match the version of the external resource being added:

```
license:
    name: SIL OFL 1.1
    url: http://fontawesome.io/license/
    gpl-compatible: true
```

If a library defines the `remote` key, it also needs to define the `license` key. This defines the license name, the URL for the license, and checks whether it is GPL-compatible. If this key is not provided, a `\Drupal\Core\Asset\Extension\LibraryDefinitionMissingLicenseException` will be thrown:

```
css:
    base:
    https://maxcdn.bootstrapcdn.com/font-awesome/4.4.0/css/font-awesome.min.css
    : { type: external, minified: true }
```

Finally, specific external resources are added as normal. Instead of providing a relative file path, the external URL is provided.

Manipulating libraries from hooks

Modules have the ability to provide dynamic library definitions and alter libraries. A module can use the `hook_library_info()` hook to provide a library definition. This is not the recommended way to define a library, but it is provided for edge use cases.

Modules do not have the ability to use `libraries-override` or `libraries-extend`, and need to rely on the `hook_library_info_alter()` hook. You can check out this hook in `core/lib/Drupal/Core/Render/theme.api.php` or at `https://api.drupal.org/api/drupal/core!lib!Drupal!Core!Render!theme.api.php/function/hook_library_info_alter/8`.

Placing JavaScript in the header

By default, Drupal ensures that JavaScript is placed last on the page. This improves the page's load performance by allowing the critical portions of the page to load first. Placing JavaScript in the header is now an opt-in option.

In order to render a library in the header, you will need to add the `header: true` key/value pair:

```
js-library:
  header: true
  js:
    js/myscripts.js: {}
```

This will load a custom JavaScript library and its dependencies into the header of a page.

See also

- Refer to the CSS architecture for Drupal 8: Separate concerns at `https://www.drupal.org/node/1887918#separate-concerns`
- For more information on SMACSS, refer to `http://smacss.com/book/`

Twig templating

Drupal 8's theming layer is complemented by Twig, a component of the Symfony framework. Twig is a template language that uses a syntax similar to Django and Jinja templates. The preceding version of Drupal used PHPTemplate, which required frontend developers to have a rudimentary understanding of PHP.

In this recipe, we will override the Twig template to provide customizations for the email form element. We will use the basic Twig syntax to add a new class and provide a default placeholder.

Getting ready

This recipe assumes that you have already created a custom theme, such as the one you created in the first recipe. When you see `mythemein` in the following recipe, use the machine name of the theme you created.

 At the time of writing this book, the Classy theme does not provide a template suggestion for the email input nor any customization for the input template that differs from Drupal core.

How to do it...

1. Create a `templates` folder in your theme's base directory to hold your Twig templates.

2. To begin, you will need to copy the `input.html.twig` file from `core/themes/classy/templates/form/input.html.twig` to your theme's `templates` folder.

3. Rename the `input.html.twig` file to `input--email.html.twig` in order to use the proper theme hook suggestion, as shown in the following screenshot:

4. We will use the `addClass` Twig function to add an `input__email` class:

   ```
   <input{{ attributes.addClass('input__email') }}/>{{ children }}
   ```

5. Before the preceding line, we will create a Twig variable using ternary operators to provide a customer placeholder:

   ```
   {% set placeholder = attributes.placeholder ?
   attributes.placeholder : 'email@example.com' %}
   <input{{
   attributes.addClass('input__email').setAttribute('placeholder',
   placeholder) }}/>{{ children }}
   ```

6. This creates a new variable called `placeholder` using the set operator. The question mark (?) operator checks whether the `placeholder` property is empty in the `attributes` object. If it is not empty, it uses the existing value. If the value is empty, it provides a default value.

7. Go to the **Configuration** tab and then to **Performance** under the **DEVELOPMENT** section to rebuild Drupal's cache. We need to do this because Drupal caches the generated Twig output and template overrides.

> New Twig template overrides provided by a theme and any changes made to a Twig template require a cache rebuild.

8. Assuming that you have used the standard Drupal install, go to the Feedback contact form installed at `/contact/feedback`, while logged out, and review the changes to the email field:

```
<!-- END OUTPUT from 'core/themes/classy/templates/form/form-element-label.html.twig' -->
<!-- THEME DEBUG -->
<!-- THEME HOOK: 'input__email' -->
<!-- FILE NAME SUGGESTIONS:
   x input--email.html.twig
   x input--email.html.twig
   * input.html.twig
-->
<!-- BEGIN OUTPUT from 'sites/default/themes/mytheme/templates/input--email.html.twig' -->
<input data-drupal-selector="edit-field-email-0-value" type="email" id="edit-field-email-0-value" name="field_email[0]
[value]" value size="60" maxlength="254" placeholder="email@example.com" class="form-email input__email">
<!-- END OUTPUT from 'sites/default/themes/mytheme/templates/input--email.html.twig' -->
```

> This screenshot contains theme debug output. In the *There's more...* section of this chapter, we will discuss how to enable the output of theming debug comments.

How it works...

Drupal's theme system is built around hooks and hook suggestions. The element definition of the email input element defines the `input__email` theme hook. If there is no `input__email` hook implemented through a Twig template or PHP function, it will step down to just input.

> Drupal theme hooks are defined with underscores (_), but use hyphens (-) when used in Twig template files.

A processor, such as Drupal's theme layer, passes variables to Twig. Variables or properties of objects can be printed by wrapping the variable name with curly brackets. All of Drupal core's default templates provide information in the file's document block that details the available Twig variables.

Twig has a simplistic syntax with basic logic and functions. The `addClass` method will take the `attributes` variable and add the class provided in addition to the existing contents.

When providing a theme hook suggestion or altering an existing template, you will need to rebuild Drupal's cache. The compiled Twig template, as PHP, is cached by Drupal so that Twig does not need to compile each time the template is invoked.

There's more...

We will discuss more on using Twig in the following sections.

Security first

Twig automatically escapes the output by default, making Drupal 8 one of the most secure versions yet. For Drupal 7, most security advisors were for **cross-site scripting** (**XSS**) vulnerabilities in contributed projects. With Drupal core, these security advisories should be severely reduced using Twig.

Theme hook suggestions

Drupal utilizes theme hook suggestions for ways to allow output variations based on different conditions. It allows site themes to provide a more specific template for certain instances.

When a theme hook has double underscores (__), Drupal's theme system understands this, and it can break apart the theme hook to find a more generic template. For instance, the email element definition provides `input__email` as its theme hook. Drupal understands this as follows:

- Look for a Twig template named `input--email.html.twig` or a theme hook that defines `input__email`
- If you are not satisfied, look for a Twig template named `input.html.twig` or a theme hook that defines the input

Theme hook suggestions can be provided by the `hook_theme_suggestions()` hook in a `.module` or `.theme` file.

Debugging template file selection and hook suggestions

Debugging can be enabled to inspect the various template files that make up a page and their theme hook suggestions, and check which are active. This can be accomplished by editing the `sites/default/services.yml` file. If a `services.yml` file does not exist, copy the `default.services.yml` to create one.

You need to change `debug: false` to `debug: true` under the `twig.config` section of the file. This will cause the Drupal theming layer to print out the source code comments containing the template information. When debug is on, Drupal will not cache the compiled versions of Twig templates and render them on the fly.

There is another setting that prevents you from having to rebuild Drupal's cache on each template file change, but do not leave debug enabled. The `twig.config.auto_reload` boolean can be set to `true`. If this is set to `true`, the Twig templates will be recompiled if the source code changes.

The Twig logic and operators

The Twig has ternary operators for logic. Using a question mark (?), we can perform a basic *is true or not empty* operation, whereas a question mark and colon (?:) perform a basic *is false or is empty* operation.

You may also use the `if` and `else` logic to provide different outputs based on variables.

See also

- Refer to the Twig documentation at
  `http://twig.sensiolabs.org/documentation`
- Refer to the API documentation for `hook_theme_suggestions` at
  `https://api.drupal.org/api/drupal/core%21lib%21Drupal%21Core%21Render%21theme.api.php/function/hook_theme_suggestions_HOOK/8`

Using the Breakpoint module

The Breakpoint module provides a method to create media query breakpoint definitions within Drupal. These can be used by other components, such as the responsive image and toolbar modules, to make Drupal responsive.

Breakpoints are a type of plugin that can be defined in a module's or theme's `breakpoints.yml` in its directory. In this recipe, we will define three different breakpoints under a custom group.

> Breakpoints are defined solely in YAML files from installed modules and themes and are not configurable through the user interface.

Getting ready

Ensure that the Breakpoint module is enabled--if you have used the standard Drupal installation, the module is enabled.

This recipe assumes that you have already created a custom module. When you see `mymodule`, use the machine name of the module that you created.

How to do it...

1. Create `mymodule.breakpoints.yml` in your module's base directory. This file will hold the breakpoint configurations.
2. Firstly, we will add a standard mobile breakpoint that does not have a media query, following mobile first practices:

```
mymodule.mobile:
  label: Mobile
  mediaQuery: ''
  weight: 0
```

3. Secondly, we will create a standard breakpoint that will run on a larger viewport:

```
mymodule.standard:
  label: Standard
  mediaQuery: 'only screen and (min-width: 60em)'
  weight: 1
```

4. Thirdly, we will create a wide breakpoint for devices that have a large viewport:

```
mymodule.wide:
  label: Wide
  mediaQuery: 'only screen and (min-width: 70em)'
  weight: 2
```

5. Your `mymodule.breakpoints.yml` should resemble the following:

```
mymodule.mobile:
  label: Mobile
  mediaQuery: ''
  weight: 0
mymodule.standard:
  label: Standard
  mediaQuery: 'only screen and (min-width: 60em)'
  weight: 1
mymodule.wide:
  label: Wide
  mediaQuery: 'only screen and (min-width: 70em)'
  weight: 2
```

6. Go to the **Configuration** tab and then to **Performance** to rebuild Drupal's cache and make the system aware of the new breakpoints.

How it works...

The Breakpoint module defines the breakpoint configuration entity. Breakpoints do not have any specific form of direct functionalities, beyond providing a way to save media queries and grouping them.

The Breakpoint module provides a default manager service. This service is used by other modules to discover breakpoint groups and then all of the breakpoints within a group.

There's more...

Additional information on using the Breakpoint module will be covered in the upcoming sections.

Caveat for providing breakpoints from themes

Themes have the ability to provide breakpoints; however, they cannot be automatically discovered if new ones are added once they have been installed. Drupal only reads breakpoints provided by themes when a theme is either installed or uninstalled.

Inside `breakpoint.manager`, there are two hooks: one for the `theme install`, and one for the `theme uninstall`. Each hook retrieves the breakpoint manager service and rebuilds the breakpoint definitions. Without any extra deployment steps, new breakpoints added to a theme will not be discovered unless these hooks are fired.

Accessing breakpoints programmatically

Breakpoints are utility configurations for other modules. Breakpoints can be loaded using the breakpoint manager service and by specifying a group. For example, the following code returns all breakpoints used by the Toolbar module:

```
\Drupal::service('breakpoint.manager')->getBreakpointsByGroup('toolbar');
```

This code invokes the Drupal container to return the service to manage breakpoints, which, by default, is `\Drupal\breakpoint\BreakpointManager`. The `getBreakpointsByGroup` method returns all breakpoints within a group, which are initiated as the `\Drupal\breakpoint\BreakpointInterface` objects.

The Toolbar element class utilizes this workflow to push the breakpoint media query values as JavaScript settings for the JavaScript model to interact with.

Multipliers

The multipliers value is used to support pixel resolution multipliers. This multiplier is used in coordination with *retina* displays. It is a measure of the viewport's device resolution as a ratio of the device's physical size and independent pixel size. The following is an example of standard multipliers:

- 1x is normal
- 5x supports Android
- 2x supports Mac retina devices

See also

- To work with breakpoints in Drupal 8, refer to the community documentation at `https://www.drupal.org/documentation/modules/breakpoint`

Using the Responsive Image module

The Responsive Image module provides a field formatter for image fields that use the HTML5 picture tag and source sets. Utilizing the Breakpoint module, mappings to breakpoints are made to denote an image style to be used at each breakpoint.

The responsive image field formatter works with using a defined responsive image style. Responsive image styles are configurations that map image formats to specific breakpoints and modifiers. First, you will need to define a responsive image style, and then you can apply it to an image field.

In this recipe, we will create a responsive image style set called `Article image` and apply it to the `Article` content type's image field.

Getting ready

You will need to enable the `Responsive Image` module, as it is not automatically enabled with the standard installation.

How to do it...

1. Go to **Configuration** and then to **Responsive image styles** under the **MEDIA** section. Click on **Add responsive image style** to create a new style set.
2. Provide a label that will be used to administratively identify the **Responsive image style** set.
3. Select a breakpoint group that will be used as a source of breakpoints to define the image style map.
4. Each breakpoint will have a `fieldset`. Expand the `fieldset` and choose **Select a single image style**, and then, pick an appropriate image style:

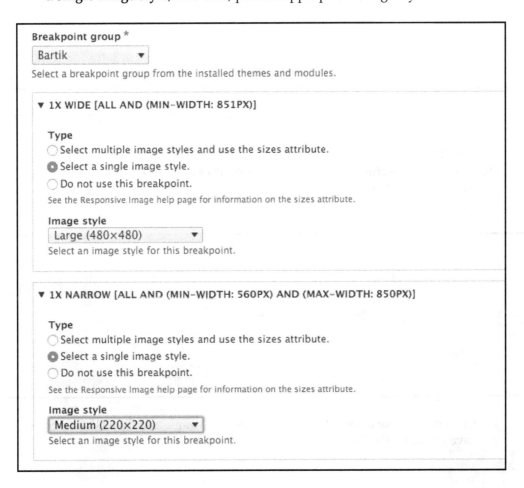

5. Additionally, choose a fallback image style in the event of a browser that doesn't support source sets, such as Internet Explorer 8.

6. Click on **Save** to save the configuration, and add the new style set:

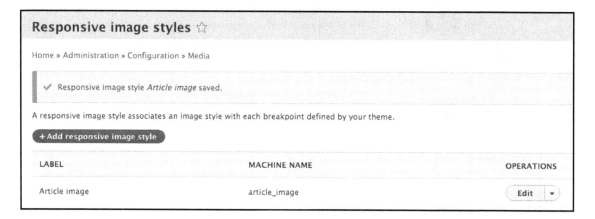

7. Go to **Structure** and **Content types** and select **Manage Display** from the **Article** content type's drop-down menu.

8. Change the **Image** field's formatter to **Responsive image**.

9. Click on the **Settings** tab of the field formatter to choose your new **Responsive image style** set. Select **Article image** from the **Responsive image style** dropdown:

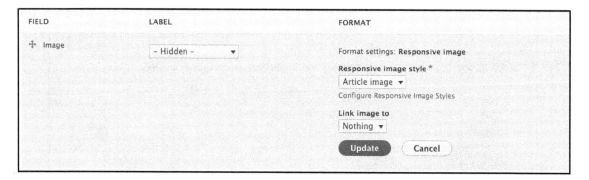

10. Click on **Update** to save the field formatter settings, and then click on **Save** to save the field display settings.

How it works...

The **Responsive image style** provides three components: a responsive image element, the responsive image style configuration entity, and the responsive image field formatter. The configuration entity is consumed by the field formatter and displayed through the responsive image element.

The responsive image style entity contains an array of breakpoints to image style mappings. The available breakpoints are defined by the selected breakpoint groups. Breakpoint groups can be changed anytime; however, the previous mappings will be lost.

The responsive image element prints a `picture` element with each breakpoint, defining a new `source` element. The breakpoint's media query value is provided as the `media` attribute for the element.

 For Internet Explorer 9, Drupal 8 ships with the `picturefill` polyfill. Internet Explorer 9 does not recognize source elements wrapped by a `picture` element. The polyfill wraps the sources around a video element within the `picture` element.

There's more...

In the following sections, we will discuss the responsive image field in more detail.

Performance first delivery

A benefit of using the responsive image formatter is performance. Browsers will only download the resources defined in the `srcset` of the appropriate `source` tag. This not only allows you to deliver a more appropriate image size, but also carries a smaller payload on smaller devices.

Removing picturefill polyfill

The Responsive Image module attaches the `picturefill` library to the responsive image element definition. The element's template also provides HTML to implement the polyfill. The polyfill can be removed by overriding the element's template and overriding the `picturefill` library to be disabled.

The following snippet, when added to a theme's `info.yml`, will disable the `picturefill` library:

```
libraries-override:
  core/picturefill: false
```

Then, the `responsive-image.html.twig` must be overridden by the theme to remove the extra HTML generated in the template for the polyfill:

1. Copy `responsive-image.html.twig` from `core/modules/responsive_image/templates` to the `theme` templates folder.
2. Edit `responsive-image.html.twig` and delete the Twig comment and IE conditional to output the initial video tag.
3. Remove the last conditional, that provides the closing video tag.

See also

- Refer to the picture element on the **Mozilla Developer Network (MDN)** at `https://developer.mozilla.org/en-US/docs/Web/HTML/Element/picture`
- Refer to `picturefill` for IE9 at `http://scottjehl.github.io/picturefill/#ie9`

6

Creating Forms with the Form API

In this chapter, we will explore the various recipes to work with forms in Drupal:

- Creating a form
- Using new HTML5 elements
- Validating form data
- Processing submitted form data
- Altering other forms

Introduction

Drupal provides a robust API for creating and managing forms without writing any HTML. Drupal handles form building, validation, and submission. Drupal handles the request to either build the form or process the HTTP POST request. This allows developers to simply define the elements in a form, provide any additional validation if needed, and then handle a successful submission through specific methods.

This chapter contains various recipes to work with forms in Drupal through the Form API. In Drupal 8, forms and form states are objects.

Creating a form

In this recipe, we will create a form, which will be accessible from a menu path. This will involve creating a route that tells Drupal to invoke our form and display it to the end user.

Forms are defined as classes, which implement `\Drupal\Core\Form\FormInterface`. The `\Drupal\Core\Form\FormBase` serves as a utility class that is intended to be extended. We will extend this class to create a new form.

Getting ready

Since we will write the code, you will want to have a custom module. Creating a custom module in Drupal is simple: create a folder and an `info.yml` file. For this recipe, we will create a folder under `/modules` in your Drupal folder called `drupalform`.

In the `drupalform` folder, create `drupalform.info.yml`. Drupal will parse the `info.yml` file to discover modules. An example of a module's `info.yml` file is as follows:

```
name: Drupal form example
description: Create a basic Drupal form, accessible from a route
type: module
version: 1.0
core: 8.x
```

The name will be your module's name, and the description will be listed on the **Extend** page. Specifying the core tells Drupal what version of Drupal it is built for. *Chapter 4, Extending Drupal*, covers how to create a module in depth.

How to do it...

1. Create an `src` folder in your module directory. In this directory, create a `Form` directory, which will hold the class that defines your form.
2. Next, create a file called `ExampleForm.php` in your module's `src/Form` directory.

Drupal utilizes PSR4 to discover and autoload classes. For brevity, this defines that there should be one class per file, with each filename matching the class name. The folder structure will also mimic the namespace expected.

3. We will edit the `ExampleForm.php` file and add the proper PHP namespace, classes used, and the class itself:

```php
<?php

namespace Drupal\drupalform\Form;

use Drupal\Core\Form\FormBase;
use Drupal\Core\Form\FormStateInterface;

class ExampleForm extends FormBase {

}
```

The `namespace` defines the class in your module's `Form` directory. The `autoloader` will now look at the `drupalform` module path and load the `ExampleForm` class from the `src/Form` directory.

The use statement allows us to use just the class name when referencing `FormBase`, and, in the next steps, `FormStateInterface`. Otherwise, we would be forced to use the fully qualified namespace path for each class whenever it is used.

4. The `\Drupal\Core\Form\FormBase` is an abstract class and requires us to implement four remaining interface methods: `getFormId`, `buildForm`, `validateForm`, and `submitForm`. The latter two will be covered in the following recipes; however, we will need to define the method stubs:

```php
class ExampleForm extends FormBase {

  /**
   * {@inheritdoc}
   */
  public function getFormId() {
    return 'drupalform_example_form';
  }

  /**
   * {@inheritdoc}
```

```
    */
    public function buildForm(array $form, FormStateInterface
$form_state) {
        // Return array of Form API elements.
    }

    /**
     * {@inheritdoc}
     */
    public function validateForm(array &$form,  FormStateInterface
$form_state) {
        // Validation covered in later recipe, required to satisfy
interface.
    }

    /**
     * {@inheritdoc}
     */
    public function submitForm(array &$form,  FormStateInterface
$form_state) {
        // Validation covered in later recipe, required to satisfy
interface.
    }
}
```

This code flushes out the initial class definition from the preceding step.
`FormBase` provides `utility` methods and does not satisfy the interface
requirements for `FormStateInterface`. We define those here, as they are unique
across each form definition.

The `getFormId` method returns a unique string to identify the form, for example,
`site_information`. You may encounter some forms that append _form to the
end of their form ID. This is not required, and it is just a naming convention often
found in previous versions of Drupal.

 The `buildForm` method is covered in the following steps. The
`validateForm` and `submitForm` methods are both called during the
Form API processes and are covered in later recipes.

5. The `buildForm` method will be invoked to return Form API elements that are
rendered to the end user. We will add a simple text field to ask for a company
name and a **submit** button:

```
    /**
     * {@inheritdoc}
```

```
*/
public function buildForm(array $form, FormStateInterface
$form_state) {
  $form['company_name'] = [
    '#type' => 'textfield',
    '#title' => $this->t('Company name'),
  ];
  $form['submit'] = [
    '#type' => 'submit',
    '#value' => $this->t('Save'),
  ];
  return $form;
}
```

We added a form element definition to the `form` array. Form elements are defined with a minimum of a type to specify what the element is and a title to act as the label. The title uses the `t` method to ensure that it is translatable.

Adding a **submit** button is done by providing an element with the type submit.

6. To access the form, we will create `drupalform.routing.yml` in the module's folder. A route entry will be created to instruct Drupal to use `\Drupal\Core\Form\FormBuilder` to create and display our form:

```
drupalform.form:
  path: '/drupal-example-form'
  defaults:
    _title: 'Example form'
    _form: '\Drupal\drupalform\Form\ExampleForm'
  requirements:
    _access: 'TRUE'
```

In Drupal, all routes have a name, and this example defines it as `drupalform.form`. Routes then define a path attribute and override default variables. This route definition has altered the route's title, specified it as a form, and given the fully qualified namespace path to this form's class.

Routes need to be passed a `requirements` property with specifications, or else the route will be denied access.

7. Go to the **Extend** page and install the Drupal form example module that we created.

8. Go to /drupal-example-form, and the form should be now visible, as shown in the following screenshot:

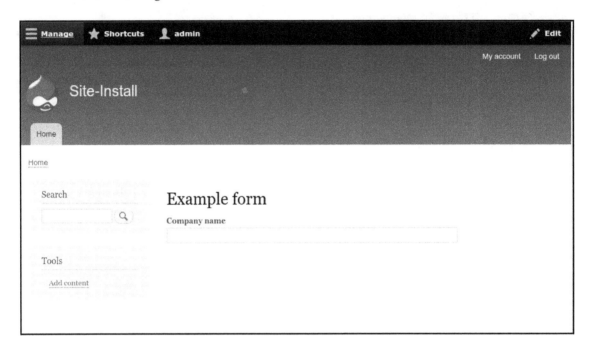

How it works...

This recipe creates a route to display the form. By passing the _form variable in the defaults section of our route entry, we are telling the route controller how to render our route's content. The fully qualified class name, which includes the namespace, is passed to a method located in the form builder. The route controller will invoke \Drupal::formBuilder()->getForm(\Drupal\drupalform\Form\ExampleForm) based on the recipe. At the same time, this can be manually called to embed the form elsewhere.

A form builder instance that implements \Drupal\Core\Form\FormBuilderInterface will then process the form by calling buildForm and initiate the rendering process. The buildForm method is expected to return an array of form elements and other API options. This will be sent to the render system to output the form as HTML.

There's more...

Many components make up a form created through Drupal's Form API. We will explore a few of them in depth.

Form element definitions

A form is a collection of form elements, which are types of plugin in Drupal 8. Plugins are small pieces of swappable functionalities in Drupal 8. Plugins and plugin development are covered in *Chapter 7*, *Plug and Play with Plugins*.

Here are some of the most common element properties that can be used:

- `weight`: This is used to alter the position of a form element in a form. By default, elements will be displayed in the order in which they were added to the form array. Defining a weight allows a developer to control element positions.
- `default_value`: This gives a developer the ability to prefill the element with a value, for example, when building configuration forms that have existing data or when editing an entity.
- `placeholder`: This is new to Drupal 8. Drupal 8 provides a new HTML5 support, and this attribute will set the placeholder attribute on the HTML input.

 For a complete reference of available form elements and their properties, check out the Drupal.org API documentation page at `https://api.drupal.org/api/drupal/elements/`.

The form state

The `\Drupal\Core\Form\FormStateInterface` object represents the current state of the form and its data. The form state contains user-submitted data for the form along with build state information. Redirection after the form submission is handled through the form state, as well. You will interact more with the form state during the validation and submission recipes.

The form cache

Drupal utilizes a cache table for forms. This holds the build table, as identified by form build identifiers. This allows Drupal to validate forms during AJAX requests and easily build them when required. It is important to keep the form cache in persistent storage; otherwise, there may be repercussions, such as loss of form data or invalidating forms.

See also

- Form API in Drupal 8 at `https://www.drupal.org/node/2117411`
- The Drupal 8 Form API reference at `https://api.drupal.org/api/drupal/elements/`
- Refer to *Chapter 4*, *Extending Drupal*
- Refer to *Chapter 7*, *Plug and Play with Plugins*, to learn more about derivatives

Using new HTML5 elements

With the release of Drupal 8, Drupal has finally entered into the realm of HTML5. The Form API now allows utilization of HTML5 input elements out of the box. These include the following element types:

- `tel`
- `email`
- `number`
- `date`
- `url`
- `search`
- `range`

This allows your forms in Drupal to leverage native device input methods along with native validation support.

Getting ready

This recipe will walk you through adding elements to a Drupal form. You will need to have a custom form implemented through a module, such as the one created in the *Creating a form* recipe of this chapter.

How to do it...

1. To use the telephone input, you will need to add a new form element definition of the tel type to your buildForm method:

```
$form['phone'] = [
  '#type' => 'tel',
  '#title' => $this->t('Phone'),
];
```

2. To use the email input, you will need to add a new form element definition of the email type to your buildForm method. It will validate the format of email addresses in the Form API:

```
$form['email'] = [
  '#type' => 'email',
  '#title' => $this->t('Email'),
];
```

3. To use the number input, you will need to add a new form element definition of the number type to your buildForm method. It will validate the range and format of the number:

```
$form['integer'] = [
  '#type' => 'number',
  '#title' => $this->t('Some integer'),
  // The increment or decrement amount
  '#step' => 1,
  // Miminum allowed value
  '#min' => 0,
  // Maxmimum allowed value
  '#max' => 100,
];
```

4. To use the date input, you will need to add a new `form` element definition of the `date` type to your `buildForm` method. You can also pass the `#date_date_format` option to alter the format used by the input:

```
$form['date'] = [
  '#type' => 'date',
  '#title' => $this->t('Date'),
  '#date_date_format' => 'Y-m-d',
];
```

5. To use the URL input, you will need to add a new `form` element definition of the `url` type to your `buildForm` method. The element has a validator to check the format of the URL:

```
$form['website'] = [
  '#type' => 'url',
  '#title' => $this->t('Website'),
];
```

6. To use the search input, you will need to add a new `form` element definition of the `search` type to your `buildForm` method. You can specify a route name that the search field will query for autocomplete options:

```
$form['search'] = [
  '#type' => 'search',
  '#title' => $this->t('Search'),
  '#autocomplete_route_name' => FALSE,
];
```

7. To use the `range` input, you will need to add a new `form` element definition of the `range` type to your `buildForm` method. It is an extension of the number element and accepts `min`, `max`, and `step` properties to control the values of the range input:

```
$form['range'] = [
  '#type' => 'range',
  '#title' => $this->t('Range'),
  '#min' => 0,
  '#max' => 100,
  '#step' => 1,
];
```

How it works...

Each type references an extended class of
\Drupal\Core\Render\Element\FormElement. It provides the element's definition and
additional functions. Each element defines a prerender method in the class that defines
the input type attribute along with other additional attributes.

Each input defines its theme as input__TYPE, allowing you to copy the input.html.twig
base to input.TYPE.html.twig for templating. The template then parses the attributes
and renders the HTML.

Some elements, such as emails, provide validators for the element. The email element
defines the validateEmail method. Here is an example of the code from
\Drupal\Core\Render\Element\Email::valdateEmail:

```
/**
 * Form element validation handler for #type 'email'.
 *
 * Note that #maxlength and #required is validated by _form_validate()
already.
 */
public static function validateEmail(&$element, FormStateInterface
$form_state, &$complete_form) {
    $value = trim($element['#value']);
    $form_state->setValueForElement($element, $value);

    if ($value !== '' &&
!\Drupal::service('email.validator')->isValid($value)) {
        $form_state->setError($element, t('The email address %mail is not
valid.', array('%mail' => $value)));
    }
}
```

This code will be executed on form submission and validate the provider's email. It does
this by taking the current value and trimming any whitespaces and using the form state
object to update the value. The email.validator service is invoked to validate the email.
If this method returns false, the form state is invoked to mark the element as the one that
has an error. If the element has an error, the form builder will prevent form submission,
returning the user to the form to fix the value.

There's more...

Elements are provided through Drupal's plugin system and are explored in detail in the upcoming sections.

Specific element properties

Elements can have their own unique properties along with individual validation methods. You can refer to the available elements through the Drupal.org API documentation page at `https://api.drupal.org/api/drupal/elements/`. However, the classes can also be examined, and the definition method can be read to learn about the properties of each element. These classes are under the `\Drupal\Core\Render\Element` namespace located in `/core/lib/Drupal/Core/Render/Element`:

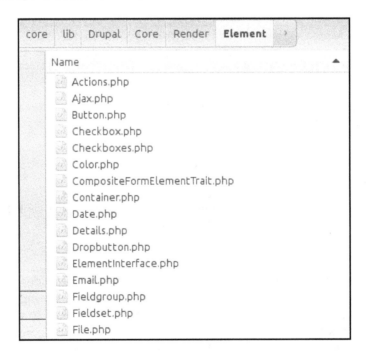

Creating new elements

Each element used in the Form API extends the `\Drupal\Core\Render\Element\FormElement` class, which is a plugin. Modules can provide new element types by adding classes to their `Plugins/Element` namespace. Refer to Chapter 7, *Plug and Play with Plugins*, for more information on how to implement a plugin.

See also

- Form API in Drupal 8 at `https://www.drupal.org/node/2117411`
- Refer to Chapter 7, Plug and Play with Plugins

Validating form data

All forms must implement the `\Drupal\Core\Form\FormInterface`. The interface defines a `validation` method. The `validateForm` method is invoked once a form has been submitted and provides a way to validate the data and halt the processing of the data if required. The form state object provides methods for marking specific fields as having the error, providing a user experience tool to alert your users to specify the problem input.

In this recipe, we will be validating the length of the submitted field.

Getting ready

This recipe will use the module and custom form created in the first *Creating a form* recipe.

How to do it...

1. Open and edit the `\Drupal\drupalform\Form\ExampleForm` class in the `src/Form` directory of the module.

2. Before validating the `company_name` value, we will need to check whether the value is empty using the `isValueEmpty()` method from the `\Drupal\Core\Form\FormStateInterface` object:

```
/**
 * {@inheritdoc}
 */
public function validateForm(array &$form,  FormStateInterface
$form_state) {
  if (!$form_state->isValueEmpty('company_name')) {
    // Value is set, perform validation.
  }
}
```

3. The `\Drupal\Form\FormStateInterface::isValueEmpty` method takes the key name of the form element; for example, `$form['company_name']` from the `buildForm` method is referenced through `company_name` in the `isValueEmpty` method.

4. Next, we will check whether the value's length is greater than five:

```
/**
 * {@inheritdoc}
 */
public function validateForm(array &$form,  FormStateInterface
$form_state) {
  if (!$form_state->isValueEmpty('company_name')) {
    if (strlen($form_state->getValue('company_name')) <= 5) {
      // Set validation error.
    }
  }
}
```

5. The `getValue` takes a form element's key and returns the value. Since we have already verified that the value is not empty, we can retrieve the value.

If you had any experience with previous versions of Drupal, note that the form state is now an object and not an array.

6. If the logic check finds a value with a length of five or fewer characters, it will throw a form error to prevent submission:

```
/**
 * {@inheritdoc}
 */
public function validateForm(array &$form,  FormStateInterface
$form_state) {
  if (!$form_state->isValueEmpty('company_name')) {
    if (strlen($form_state->getValue('company_name')) <= 5) {
      $form_state->setErrorByName('company_name', t('Company name
is less than 5 characters'));
    }
  }
}
```

We can place the setErrorByName method in our strlen logic check. If the string is fewer than five characters, an error is set on the element. The first parameter is the element's key, and the second parameter is the message to be presented to the user.

7. When the form is submitted, the **Company name** text field will have more than five characters or be empty to be submitted.

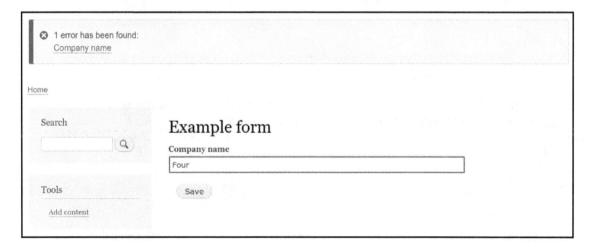

How it works...

Before the form builder service invokes the form object's `submitForm` method, it invokes the object's `validateForm` method. In the validation method, the form state can be used to check values and perform logic checks. In the event that an item is deemed *invalid* and an error is set on an element, the form cannot be submitted and will show errors to the user.

When an error is added to an element, an overall counter for the number of errors on the form is incremented. If the form has any errors, the form builder service will not execute the submit method.

This process is executed through the `\Drupal\Core\Form\FormValidator` class, which is run through the form builder service.

There's more...

Form validation can be done through multiple handlers and at the element level. The following sections will cover those.

Multiple validation handlers

A form can have multiple validation handlers. By default, all forms come with at least one validator, which is its own `validateForm` method. There is more that can be added. However, by default, the form will merely execute `::validateForm` and all element validators. This allows you to invoke methods on other classes or other forms.

If a class provides `method1` and `method2`, which it would like to execute as well, the following code can be added to the `buildForm` method:

```
$form_state->setValidateHandlers([
  ['::validateForm'],
  ['::method1'],
  [$this, 'method2'],
]);
```

This sets the validator array to execute the default `validateForm` method and the two additional methods. You can reference a method in the current class using two colons (`::`) and the method name. Alternatively, you can use an array that consists of a class instance and the method to be invoked.

Accessing multidimensional array values

Forms support nested form elements in the form array. The default
\Drupal\Core\Form\FormStateInterface implementation,
\Drupal\Core\Form\FormState, supports accessing multidimensional array values.
Instead of passing a string, you can pass an array that represents the parent array structure
in the form array.

If the element is defined as in $form['company']['company_name'], then we will pass
['company', 'company_name'] to the form state's methods.

Element validation methods

Form elements can have their own validators. The form state will aggregate all of the
element validation methods and pass them to the form validation service. This will run with
the form's validation.

There is a limit_validation_errors option, which can be set to allow selected invalid
errors to be passed. This option allows you to bypass validation on specific elements in your
form. This is useful if a form has two submit buttons and each intends to validate and
submit specific data. This attribute is defined in the submit button, also known as the
triggering element in the form state. It is an array value consisting of form element keys.

Processing submitted form data

A form's purpose is to collect data and do something with the data that was submitted. All
forms need to implement the \Drupal\Core\Form\FormInterface interface. The
interface defines a submit method. Once the Form API has invoked the class's validation
method, the submit method can be run.

This recipe will be based on the custom module and form created in the *Creating a form*
recipe of this chapter. We will convert the form to \Drupal\Core\FormConfigBaseForm,
allowing us to save our configuration and reuse code provided by Drupal core.

Getting ready

In this recipe, we will use the module and custom form created in the first *Creating a form* recipe.

How to do it...

1. In your module's directory, create a `config` directory, and then create a directory inside it named `install`.

2. Create a file named `drupalform.schema.yml`. This file will tell Drupal about the configuration item that we want to save.

3. Add the following configuration schema definition to `drupalform.schema.yml`:

```
drupalform.company:
  type: config_object
  label: 'Drupal form settings'
  mapping:
    company_name:
      type: string
      label: 'A company name'
```

This tells Drupal that we have the configuration with the name `drupalform.company`, and it has a valid option of `company_name`. We will cover this in more detail in Chapter 9, *Configuration Management - Deploying in Drupal 8*.

4. Next, edit the module's `src/Form/ExampleForm.php` file. Replace the `FormBase` use statement to use the `ConfigFormBase` class:

```php
<?php

namespace Drupal\drupalform\Form;

use Drupal\Core\Form\ConfigFormBase;
use Drupal\Core\Form\FormStateInterface;
```

5. Update the `ExampleForm` class to extend `ConfigFormBase` instead, to harness its existing methods and provided code:

```php
<?php

namespace Drupal\drupalform\Form;
```

```
use Drupal\Core\Form\ConfigFormBase;
use Drupal\Core\Form\FormStateInterface;

class ExampleForm extends ConfigFormBase {
  ...
}
```

This allows us to reuse methods from the `ConfigFormBase` class and write less about our own implementation.

6. For `ExampleForm` to implement `ConfigFormBase`, the `getEditableConfigNames` method needs to be implemented to satisfy the `\Drupal\Core\Form\ConfigBaseTrait` trait. This method can be added anywhere in the class:

```php
<?php

namespace Drupal\drupalform\Form;

use Drupal\Core\Form\ConfigFormBase;
use Drupal\Core\Form\FormStateInterface;

class ExampleForm extends ConfigFormBase {
  ...
  /**
   * {@inheritdoc}
   */
  protected function getEditableConfigNames() {
    return ['drupalform.company'];
  }
  ...
}
```

This function defines the configuration names, which will be editable by the form. This brings all the attributes under the `drupalform.company` object to be editable when accessed through the form with the `config` method provided by `ConfigFormBaseTrait`.

7. We will remove the submit form element (`$form['submit']`) and update the `buildForm` method to return data from the parent's method rather than from `$form` itself. We will also need to add a `#default_value` option to `company_name` so that it uses an existing value the next time our form is loaded:

```
/**
 * {@inheritdoc}
 */
```

```
public function buildForm(array $form, FormStateInterface
$form_state) {
  $form['company_name'] = [
    '#type' => 'textfield',
    '#title' => $this->t('Company name'),
    '#default_value' =>
$this->config('drupalform.company')->get('company_name'),
  ];
  return parent::buildForm($form, $form_state);
}
```

The `ConfigFormBase` class implements the `buildForm` method to provide a reusable submit button. It also unifies the presentation across Drupal configuration forms:

Example form

Company name

Save configuration

8. The `ConfigFormBase` provides a configuration factory method. We will add a `default_value` property to our element with the currently saved item:

```
/**
 * {@inheritdoc}
 */
public function buildForm(array $form, FormStateInterface
$form_state) {
  $form['company_name'] = [
    '#type' => 'textfield',
    '#title' => $this->t('Company name'),
    '#default_value' =>
$this->config('drupalform.company')->get('name'),
  ];
  return parent::buildForm($form, $form_state);
}
```

The `#default_value` key is added to the element's definition. It invokes the `config` method provided by `ConfigFormBaseTrait` to load our configuration group and access a specific configuration value.

9. The final step is to save the configuration in the `submitForm` method. Add the following method to your class:

```
/**
 * {@inheritdoc}
 */
public function submitForm(array &$form, FormStateInterface
$form_state) {
  parent::submitForm($form, $form_state);
  $this->config('drupalform.company')->set('name',
$form_state->getValue('company_name'));
}
```

The `config` method is invoked by specifying our configuration group. We will then use the set method to define the name as the value of the `company name` text field.

10. Your form class should resemble the following when complete:

```
<?php

namespace Drupal\drupalform\Form;

use Drupal\Core\Form\ConfigFormBase;
use Drupal\Core\Form\FormStateInterface;

class ExampleForm extends ConfigFormBase {

  /**
   * {@inheritdoc}
   */
  protected function getEditableConfigNames() {
      return ['drupalform.company'];
  }

  /**
   * {@inheritdoc}
   */
  public function getFormId() {
    return 'drupalform_example_form';
  }

  /**
```

```
 * {@inheritdoc}
 */
public function buildForm(array $form, FormStateInterface
$form_state) {
    $form['company_name'] = array(
      '#type' => 'textfield',
      '#title' => t('Company name'),
      '#default_value' =>
$this->config('drupalform.company')->get('name'),
    );
    return parent::buildForm($form, $form_state);
  }

/**
 * {@inheritdoc}
 */
public function validateForm(array &$form, FormStateInterface
$form_state) {
    if (!$form_state->isValueEmpty('company_name')) {
      if (strlen($form_state->getValue('company_name')) <= 5) {
        $form_state->setErrorByName('company_name', t('Company name
is less than 5 characters'));
      }
    }
  }
/**
 * {@inheritdoc}
 */
public function submitForm(array &$form, FormStateInterface
$form_state) {
    parent::submitForm($form, $form_state);
    $this->config('drupalform.company')->set('name',
$form_state->getValue('company_name'));
  }
}
```

11. When you edit your form and click on the **Submit** button, the value that you entered in the **Company name** field will now be saved in the configuration.

How it works...

The `ConfigFormBase` utilizes the `ConfigFormBaseTrait` to provide easy access to a configuration factory. The class's implementation of `buildForm` also adds a `submit` button and theme styling to forms. The submit handler displays a configuration saved message, but relies on implementing a module to save the configuration.

The form saves its data under the drupalform.company namespace. The company name value is stored as name and can be accessed as drupalform.company.name. Note that the configuration name does not have to match the form element's key.

There's more...

In the next section, we will cover how to handle multiple submit callbacks.

Multiple submit handlers

A form can have multiple submit handlers. By default, all forms implement a submit handler, which is its own submitForm method. The form will execute ::submitForm automatically and any other methods defined on the triggering element. There is more that can be added. However, this allows you to invoke static methods on other classes or other forms.

If a class provides method1 and method2, which it would like to execute as well, the following code can be added to the buildForm method:

```
$form_state->setSubmitHandlers([
  ['::submitForm'],
  ['::method1'],
  [$this, 'method2']
]);
```

This sets the submit handler array to execute the default submitForm method and two additional methods. You can reference a method in the current class using two colons (::) and the method name. Alternatively, you can use an array consisting of a class instance and the method to be invoked.

See also

- Refer to *Chapter 9, Configuration Management- Deploying in Drupal 8*

Altering other forms

Drupal's Form API does not just provide a way to create forms. There are ways to alter forms through a custom module that allows you to manipulate the core and contributed forms. Using this technique, new elements can be added, default values can be changed, or elements can even be hidden from view to simplify the user experience.

The altering of a form does not happen in a custom class; this is a hook defined in the module file. In this recipe, we will use the `hook_form_FORM_ID_alter()` hook to add a telephone field to the site's configuration form.

Getting ready

This recipe assumes that you have a custom module to add the code to.

How to do it...

1. In the `modules` folder of your Drupal site, create a folder named `mymodule`.

2. In the `mymodule` folder, create a `mymodule.info.yml`, containing the following code:

   ```
   name: My module
   description: Custom module that uses a form alter
   type: module
   core: 8.x
   ```

3. Next, create a `mymodule.module` file in your module's directory:

   ```php
   <?php

   /**
    * @file
    * Custom module that alters forms.
    */
   ```

4. Add the `mymodule_form_system_site_information_settings_alter()` hook. The form ID can be found by viewing the form's class and reviewing the `getFormId` method:

```
/**
 * Implements hook_form_FORM_ID_alter().
 */
function
mymodule_form_system_site_information_settings_alter(&$form,
\Drupal\Core\Form\FormStateInterface $form_state) {
    // Code to alter form or form state here
}
```

Drupal will call this hook and pass the current form array and its form state object. The form array is passed by reference, allowing our hook to modify the array without returning any values. This is why the `$form` parameter has the ampersand (`&`) before it. In PHP, all objects are passed by reference, which is why we have no ampersand (`&`) before `$form_state`.

When calling a class in a normal file, such as the module file, you will need to either use the fully qualified class name or add a use statement at the beginning of the file. In this example, we can add `\Drupal\Core\Form\FormStateInterface`.

5. Next, we add our `telephone` field to the form so that it can be displayed and saved:

```
/**
 * Implements hook_form_FORM_ID_alter().
 */
function
mymodule_form_system_site_information_settings_alter(&$form,
\Drupal\Core\Form\FormStateInterface $form_state) {
    $form['site_phone'] = [
        '#type' => 'tel',
        '#title' => t('Site phone'),
        '#default_value' =>
Drupal::config('system.site')->get('phone'),
    ];
}
```

We retrieve the current phone value from `system.site` so that it can be modified if already set.

6. Go to the **Extend** page and install the module **My module** that we created.

7. Note the **Basic site settings** form under **Configuration,** and test setting the site telephone number:

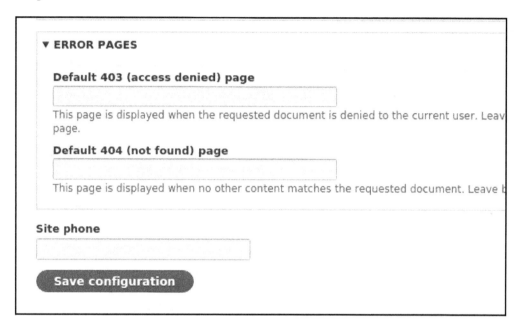

```
▼ ERROR PAGES

Default 403 (access denied) page
┌─────────────────────────────────────┐
│                                     │
└─────────────────────────────────────┘
This page is displayed when the requested document is denied to the current user. Leav
page.

Default 404 (not found) page
┌─────────────────────────────────────┐
│                                     │
└─────────────────────────────────────┘
This page is displayed when no other content matches the requested document. Leave

Site phone
┌─────────────────────────────────────┐
│                                     │
└─────────────────────────────────────┘

  Save configuration
```

8. We then need to add a submit handler in order to save the configuration for our new field. We will need to add a submit handler to the form and a submit handler callback:

```
/**
 * Implements hook_form_FORM_ID_alter().
 */
function
mymodule_form_system_site_information_settings_alter(&$form,
\Drupal\Core\Form\FormStateInterface $form_state) {
  $form['site_phone'] = [
    '#type' => 'tel',
    '#title' => t('Site phone'),
    '#default_value' => Drupal::config('system.site')->get('phone'),
  ];
  $form['#submit'][] =
'mymodule_system_site_information_phone_submit';
}

/**
```

```
 * Form callback to save site_phone
 * @param array $form
 * @param \Drupal\Core\Form\FormStateInterface $form_state
 */
function mymodule_system_site_information_phone_submit(array
&$form,  \Drupal\Core\Form\FormStateInterface $form_state) {
  $config = Drupal::configFactory()->getEditable('system.site');
  $config
  ->set('phone', $form_state->getValue('site_phone'))
  ->save();
}
```

The $form['#submit'] modification adds our callback to the form's
submit handlers. This allows our module to interact with the form
once it has been submitted.

The mymodule_system_site_information_phone_submit callback is
passed the form array and form state. We load the current
configuration factory to receive the configuration that can be
edited. We then load system.site and save phone based on the value
from the form state.

9. Submit the form, and verify that the data has been saved.

How it works...

The \Drupal\system\Form\SiteInformationForm class extends
\Drupal\Core\Form\ConfigFormBase to handle the writing of form elements as
individual configuration values. However, it does not write the values automatically to the
form state. In this recipe, we needed to add a submit handler to manually save our added
field via a procedural function in our mymodule.module file.

The form array is passed by reference, allowing modifications to be made in the hook to
alter the original data. This allows us to add an element or even modify existing items, such
as titles or descriptions.

There's more...

We will discuss how to add additional handlers to other forms using form alters.

Adding additional validate handlers

Using a form alter hook, we can add additional validators to a form. The proper way to do this is to load the current validators and add the new one to the array and reset the validators in the form state:

```
$validators = $form_state->getValidateHandlers();
$validators[] = 'mymodule_form_validate';
$form_state->setValidateHandlers($validators);
```

First, we will receive all of the currently set validators from the form state as the $validators variable. We then append a new callback to the end of the array. Once the $validators variable has been modified, we will override the form state's validator array by executing the setValidateHandlers method.

 You can also use PHP array manipulation functions to add your validators in different execution orders. For example, array_unshift will place your validator at the beginning of the array so that it can run first.

Adding additional submit handlers

Using a form alter hook, we can add additional submit handlers to a form. The proper way to do this is to load the current submit handlers, add the new one to the array, and reset the validators in the form state:

```
$submit_handlers = $form_state->getSubmitHandlers();
$submit_handlers[] = 'mymodule_form_submit';
$form_state->setSubmitHandlers($submit_handlers );
```

First, we will receive all of the currently set submit handlers from the form state as the $submit_handlers variable. We then append a new callback to the end of the array. Once the $submit_handlers variable has been modified, we will override the form state's submit handler array by executing the setSubmitHandlers method.

 You can also use PHP array manipulation functions to add your callback in different execution orders. For example, array_unshift will place your callback at the beginning of the array so that it can run first.

7
Plug and Play with Plugins

In this chapter, we will dive into the new Plugin API provided in Drupal 8:

- Creating blocks using plugins
- Creating a custom field type
- Creating a custom field widget
- Creating a custom field formatter
- Creating a custom plugin type

Introduction

Drupal 8 introduces plugins. Plugins power many items in Drupal, such as blocks, field types, and field formatters. Plugins and plugin types are provided by modules. They provide a swappable and specific functionality. Breakpoints, as discussed in Chapter 5, *Front End for the Win*, are plugins. In this chapter, we will discuss how plugins work in Drupal 8 and show you how to create blocks, fields, and custom plugin types.

Each version of Drupal has subsystems, which provided pluggable components and contributed modules. However, the implementation and management of these subsystems presented a problem. Blocks, fields, and image styles each had an entirely different system to be learned and understood. The Plugin API exists in Drupal 8 to mitigate this problem and provide a base API to implement pluggable components. This has greatly improved the developer experience when working with Drupal core's subsystems. In this chapter, we will implement a block plugin. We will use the Plugin API to provide a custom field type along with a widget and formatter for the field. The last recipe will show you how to create and use a custom plugin type.

Creating blocks using plugins

In Drupal, a block is a piece of content that can be placed in a region provided by a theme. Blocks are used to present specific kinds of content, such as a user login form, a snippet of text, and many more.

Blocks are annotated plugins. Annotated plugins use documentation blocks to provide details of the plugin. They are discovered in the module's `Plugin` class namespace. Each class in the `Plugin/Block` namespace will be discovered by the Block module's plugin manager.

In this recipe, we will define a block that will display a copyright snippet and the current year and place it in the footer region.

Getting ready

Create a new module like the one shown in this recipe, with a defined `info.yml` so that it can be discovered by Drupal. We will refer to the module as `mymodule` throughout the recipe. Use your module's appropriate name.

How to do it...

1. Create a `src/Plugin/Block` directory in your module. This will translate the `\Drupal\mymodule\Plugin\Block` namespace and allow a block plugin discovery.
2. Create a `Copyright.php` file in the newly created folder so that we can define the `Copyright` class for our block:

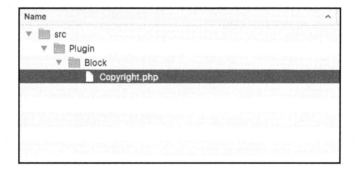

3. The `Copyright` class will extend the `\Drupal\Core\Block\BlockBase` class:

```php
<?php

namespace Drupal\mymodule\Plugin\Block;

use Drupal\Core\Block\BlockBase;

class Copyright extends BlockBase {

}
```

We will extend the `BlockBase` class, which implements `\Drupal\Core\Block\BlockPluginInterface` and provides us with an implementation of nearly all of the interface's methods.

4. We will provide the block's identifier, administrative label, and category:

```php
<?php

namespace Drupal\mymodule\Plugin\Block;

use Drupal\Core\Block\BlockBase;

/**
 * @Block(
 *   id = "copyright_block",
 *   admin_label = @Translation("Copyright"),
 *   category = @Translation("Custom")
 * )
 */
class Copyright extends BlockBase {

}
```

The annotation document block of the class identifies the type of plugin through `@Block`. Drupal will parse this and initiate the plugin with the properties defined inside it. The `id` is the internal machine name, the `admin_label` is displayed on the block listing page, and `category` shows up in the block select list.

5. We will need to provide a `build` method to satisfy the `\Drupal\Core\Block\BlockPluginInterface` interface. This returns the output to be displayed:

```php
<?php

namespace Drupal\mymodule\Plugin\Block;

use Drupal\Core\Block\BlockBase;

/**
 * @Block(
 *   id = "copyright_block",
 *   admin_label = @Translation("Copyright"),
 *   category = @Translation("Custom")
 * )
 */
class Copyright extends BlockBase {

  /**
   * {@inheritdoc}
   */
  public function build() {
    $date = new \DateTime();
    return [
      '#markup' => t('Copyright @year&copy; My Company', [
          '@year' => $date->format('Y'),
      ]),
    ];
  }
}
```

The `build` method returns a render array that uses Drupal's `t` function to substitute `@year` for the `\DateTime` object's output that is formatted as a full year.

Since PHP 5.4, a warning will be displayed if you have not set a timezone explicitly in your PHP's configuration.

6. Install your module if it has not yet been installed by going to the **Extend** page. If you have already installed your module, go to the **Performance** page and rebuild Drupal's caches.

7. Go to the **Black layout** page from **Structure** in the administrative menu. In the **Footer fourth** region, click on **Place block**.

8. Review the block list and add the custom block to your regions, for instance, the footer region. Find the **Copyright** block, and click on **Place block**:

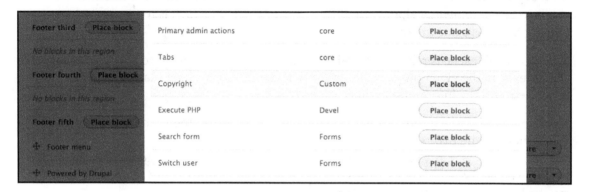

9. Uncheck the **Display title** checkbox so that only our block's content can be rendered. Click on **Save block** and accept all of the other defaults.

10. View your Drupal site, and verify that the copyright statement will always keep the year dynamic:

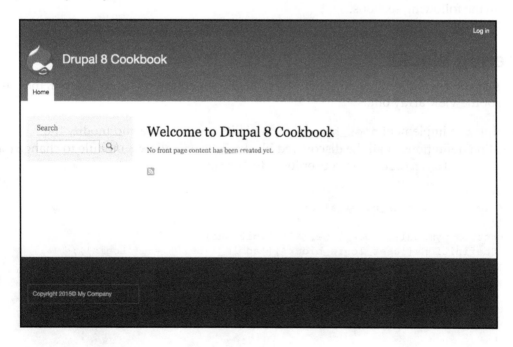

How it works...

The plugin system works through plugin definitions and plugin managers for those definitions. The `\Drupal\Core\Block\BlockManager` class defines the block plugins that need be located in the `Plugin/Block` namespace. It also defines the base interface that needs to be implemented along with the `Annotation` class, which is to be used when parsing the class's document block.

When Drupal's cache is rebuilt, all available namespaces are scanned to check whether classes exist in the given plugin namespace. The definitions, via annotation, will be processed, and the information will be cached.

Blocks are then retrieved from the manager, manipulated, and their methods are invoked. When viewing the `Block layout` page to manage blocks, the `\Drupal\Core\Block\BlockBase` class's `label` method is invoked to display the human-readable name. When a block is displayed on a rendered page, the `build` method is invoked and passed to the theming layer to be output.

There's more...

There are more in-depth items that can be used when creating a block plugin. We will cover those in the following sections.

Altering blocks

Blocks can be altered in three different ways: the plugin definition can be altered, the build array, or the view array out.

A module can implement `hook_block_alter` in its `.module` file and modify the annotation definitions of all the discovered blocks. This will allow a module to change the default `user_login_block` from user login to `Login`:

```
/**
 * Implements hook_block_alter().
 */
function mymodule_block_alter(&$definitions) {
  $definitions['user_login_block']['admin_label'] = t('Login');
}
```

A module can implement `hook_block_build_alter` and modify the build information of a block. The hook is passed through the build array and the `\Drupal\Core\Block\BlockPluginInterface` instance for the current block. Module developers can use this to add cache contexts or alter the cache ability of the metadata:

```
/**
 * Implements hook_block_build_alter().
 */
function hook_block_build_alter(array &$build,
\Drupal\Core\Block\BlockPluginInterface $block) {
  // Add the 'url' cache the block per URL.
  if ($block->getBaseId() == 'myblock') {
    $build['#contexts'][] = 'url';
  }
}
```

 You can test the modification of the cache metadata by altering the recipe's block to output a timestamp. With caching enabled, you will see that the value persists on the same URL, but it will be different across each page.

Finally, a module can implement `hook_block_view_alter` in order to modify the output to be rendered. A module can add content to be rendered or removed. This can be used to remove the `contextual_links` item, which allows inline editing on the front page of a site:

```
/**
 * Implements hook_block_view_alter().
 */
function hook_block_view_alter(array &$build,
\Drupal\Core\Block\BlockPluginInterface $block) {
  // Remove the contextual links on all blocks that provide them.
  if (isset($build['#contextual_links'])) {
    unset($build['#contextual_links']);
  }
}
```

Block settings forms

Blocks can provide a `setting` form. This recipe provides the text *My Company* for the copyright text. Instead, this can be defined through a text field in the block's setting form.

Let's readdress the `Copyright.php` file that holds our block's class. We will override methods provided by our base class. The following methods will be added to the class written in this recipe.

A block can override the default `defaultConfiguration` method, which returns an array of setting keys and their default values. The `blockForm` method can then override the `\Drupal\Core\Block\BlockBase` empty array implementation to return a Form API array to represent the settings form:

```php
/**
 * {@inheritdoc}
 */
public function defaultConfiguration() {
  return [
    'company_name' => '',
  ];
}

/**
 * {@inheritdoc}
 */
public function blockForm($form, \Drupal\Core\Form\FormStateInterface
$form_state) {
  $form['company_name'] = [
    '#type' => 'textfield',
    '#title' => t('Company name'),
    '#default_value' => $this->configuration['company_name'],
  ];
  return $form;
}
```

The `blockSubmit` method must then be implemented, which updates the block's configuration:

```php
/**
 * {@inheritdoc}
 */
public function blockSubmit($form, \Drupal\Core\Form\FormStateInterface
$form_state) {
  $this->configuration['company_name'] =
$form_state->getValue('company_name');
}
```

Finally, the `build` method can be updated to use the new configuration item:

```
/**
 * {@inheritdoc}
 */
public function build() {
  $date = new \DateTime();
  return [
    '#markup' => t('Copyright @year&copy; @company', [
      '@year' => $date->format('Y'),
      '@company' => $this->configuration['company_name'],
    ]),
  ];
}
```

You can now return to the `Block layout` form, and click on **Configure** in the **Copyright** block. The new setting will be available in the block instance's configuration form.

Defining access to a block

Blocks, by default, are rendered for all users. The default access method can be overridden. This allows a block to only be displayed to authenticated users or based on a specific permission:

```
/**
 * {@inheritdoc}
 */
protected function blockAccess(AccountInterface $account) {
  $route_name = $this->routeMatch->getRouteName();
  if ($account->isAnonymous() && !in_array($route_name,
      array('user.login', 'user.logout'))) {
    return AccessResult::allowed()
      ->addCacheContexts(['route.name',
          'user.roles:anonymous']);
  }
  return AccessResult::forbidden();
}
```

The preceding code is taken from the `user_login_block`. It allows access to the block if the user is logged out and is not in the login or logout page. The access is cached based on the current route name and the user's current role being anonymous. If these are not passed, the access returned is forbidden and the block is not built.

Other modules can implement `hook_block_access` to override the access of a block:

```
/**
 * Implements hook_block_access().
 */
function mymodule_block_access(\Drupal\block\Entity\Block $block,
$operation, \Drupal\Core\Session\AccountInterface $account) {
  // Example code that would prevent displaying the Copyright' block in
  // a region different than the footer.
  if ($operation == 'view' && $block->getPluginId() == 'copyright') {
    return
\Drupal\Core\Access\AccessResult::forbiddenIf($block->getRegion() !=
'footer');
  }

  // No opinion.
  return \Drupal\Core\Access\AccessResult::neutral();
}
```

A module implementing the preceding hook will deny access to our **Copyright** block if it is not placed in the footer region.

See also

- Refer to the *Creating a custom plugin type* recipe of this chapter
- Refer to annotations-based plugins at
  https://www.drupal.org/docs/8/api/plugin-api/annotations-based-plugins
- Information on `block.api.php` is available
  at https://api.drupal.org/api/drupal/core%21modules%21block%21block.api
  .php/8

Creating a custom field type

Field types are defined using the plugin system. Each field type has its own class and definition. A new field type can be defined through a custom class that will provide schema and property information.

In this example, we will create a simple field type called *real name* to store the first and last names.

 Field types define ways in which data can be stored and handled through the Field API. Field widgets provides means for editing a field type in the user interface. Field formatters provide means for displaying the field data to users. Both are plugins and will be covered in later recipes.

Getting ready

Create a new module like the one shown in this recipe, with a defined `info.yml` so that it can be discovered by Drupal. We will refer to the module as `mymodule` throughout the recipe. Use your module's appropriate name.

How to do it...

1. We will need to create the `src/Plugin/Field/FieldType` directory in the module's base location. The `Field` module discovers field types in the `Plugin\Field\FieldType` namespace.

2. We will create a `RealName.php` file in the newly created directory so that we can define the `RealName` class. This will provide our `realname` field for the first and last names:

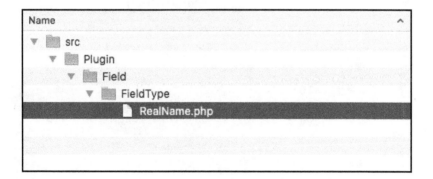

3. The `RealName` class will extend the `\Drupal\Core\Field\FieldItemBase` class:

```php
<?php

namespace Drupal\mymodule\Plugin\Field\FieldType;

use Drupal\Core\Field\FieldItemBase;
use Drupal\Core\Field\FieldStorageDefinitionInterface;
use Drupal\Core\TypedData\DataDefinition;

class RealName extends FieldItemBase {

}
```

The `\Drupal\Core\Field\FieldItemBase` satisfies methods defined by inherited interfaces, except for `schema` and `propertyDefinitions`.

4. Field types are annotated plugins. Annotated plugins use documentation blocks to provide details of the plugin. We will provide the field type's identifier, label, description, category, and default widget and formatter:

```php
<?php

namespace Drupal\mymodule\Plugin\Field\FieldType;

use Drupal\Core\Field\FieldItemBase;
use Drupal\Core\Field\FieldStorageDefinitionInterface;
use Drupal\Core\TypedData\DataDefinition;

/**
 * Plugin implementation of the 'realname' field type.
 *
 * @FieldType(
 *   id = "realname",
 *   label = @Translation("Real name"),
 *   description = @Translation("This field stores a first and last name."),
 *   category = @Translation("General"),
 *   default_widget = "string_textfield",
 *   default_formatter = "string"
 * )
 */

class RealName extends FieldItemBase {

}
```

The @FieldType tells Drupal that this is a FieldType plugin. The following properties are defined:

- Id: This is the plugin's machine name
- Label: This is the human-readable name for the field
- description: This is the human-readable description of the field
- category: This is the category where the field shows up in the user interface
- default_widget: This is the default form widget to be used for editing
- default_formatter: This is the default formatter with which you can display the field

5. The RealName class needs to implement the schema method defined in the \Drupal\Core\Field\FieldItemInterface. This returns an array of the database API schema information. Add the following method to your class:

```php
/**
 * {@inheritdoc}
 */
public static function
schema(\Drupal\Core\Field\FieldStorageDefinitionInterface
$field_definition) {
  return [
    'columns' => [
      'first_name' => [
        'description' => 'First name.',
        'type' => 'varchar',
        'length' => '255',
        'not null' => TRUE,
        'default' => '',
      ],
      'last_name' => [
        'description' => 'Last name.',
        'type' => 'varchar',
        'length' => '255',
        'not null' => TRUE,
        'default' => '',
      ],
    ],
    'indexes' => [
      'first_name' => ['first_name'],
      'last_name' => ['last_name'],
    ],
  ];
}
```

The `schema` method defines the columns in the field's data table. We will define a column to hold the `first_name` and `last_name` values.

6. We will also need to implement the `propertySchema` method to satisfy `\Drupal\Core\TypedData\ComplexDataDefinitionInterface`. This returns a typed definition of the values defined in the `schema` method. Add the following method to your class:

```
/**
 * {@inheritdoc}
 */
public static function
propertyDefinitions(\Drupal\Core\Field\FieldStorageDefinitionInterf
ace $field_definition) {
  $properties['first_name'] =
\Drupal\Core\TypedData\DataDefinition::create('string')
->setLabel(t('First name'));
  $properties['last_name'] =
\Drupal\Core\TypedData\DataDefinition::create('string')
->setLabel(t('Last name'));
  return $properties;
}
```

This method returns an array that is keyed with the same column names provided in `schema`. It returns a typed data definition to handle the field type's values.

7. Install your module, if it has not yet been installed, by going to the **Extend** page. If you have already installed your module, go to the **Performance** page and rebuild Drupal's caches.

8. The field will now appear on the field type management screen. To use it, go to **Structure** and then to **Comment Types**. You can now go to **Manage Fields** and click on **Add field** to add a real name entry for your comments:

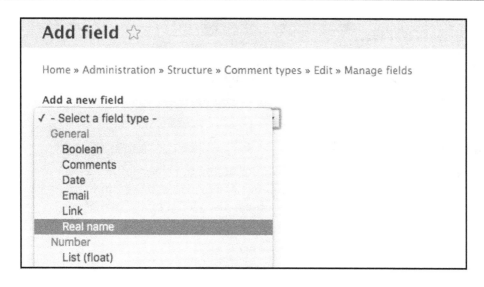

How it works...

Drupal core defines a `plugin.manager.field.field_type` service. By default, this is handled through the `\Drupal\Core\Field\FieldTypePluginManager` class. This plugin manager defines the field type plugins that should be in the `Plugin/Field/FieldType` namespace, and all the classes in this namespace will be loaded and assumed to be field type plugins.

The manager's definition also sets `\Drupal\Core\Field\FieldItemInterface` as the expected interface that all the field type plugins will implement. This is why most field types extend `\Drupal\Core\Field\FieldItemBase` to meet these method requirements.

As field types are annotated plugins, the manager provides `\Drupal\Core\Field\Annotation\FieldType` as the class that fulfills the annotation definition.

When the user interface defines the available fields, the `plugin.manager.field.field_type` service is invoked to retrieve a list of available field types.

There's more...

Existing field types can be altered to modify their definitions, and custom field types can implement a method to define whether the value is empty or not. We will cover these in the next sections.

Altering field types

The \Drupal\Core\Field\FieldTypePluginManager class defines the alter method as field_info. Modules that implement hook_field_info_alter in their .module files have the ability to modify field type definitions discovered by the manager:

```
/**
 * Implements hook_field_info_alter().
 */
function mymodule_field_info_alter(&$info) {
  $info['email']['label'] = t('E-mail address');
}
```

The preceding alter method will change the human-readable label for the email field to **E-mail address** when selecting the field in the user interface.

Defining whether a field is empty

The \Drupal\Core\TypedDate\ComplexDataInterface interface provides an isEmpty method. This method is used to check whether the field's value is empty, for example, when verifying that the required field has data. The \Drupal\Core\TypedData\Plugin\DataType\Map class implements the method. By default, the method ensures that the values are not empty.

Field types can provide their own implementations to provide a more robust verification. For instance, the field can validate that the first name can be entered but not the last name, or the field can require both the first and the last name.

See also

- Refer to the *Creating blocks using plugins* recipe of this chapter

Creating a custom field widget

Field widgets provide the form interface to edit a field. These integrate with the Form API to define how a field can be edited and the way in which the data can be formatted before it is saved. Field widgets are chosen and customized through the form display interface.

In this recipe, we will create a widget for the field created in the *Creating a custom field type* recipe in this chapter. The field widget will provide two text fields for entering the first and last name items.

Getting ready

Create a new module, such as the one from the *Creating a custom field type* recipe. We will refer to the module as `mymodule` throughout the recipe. Use your module's appropriate name.

How to do it...

1. We will need to create the `src/Plugin/Field/FieldWidget` directory in the module's base location. The `Field` module discovers field widgets in the `Plugin\Field\FieldWidget` namespace.

2. Create a `RealNameDefaultWidget.php` file in the newly created directory so that we can define the `RealNameDefaultWidget` class. This will provide a custom form element to edit the first and last name values of our field:

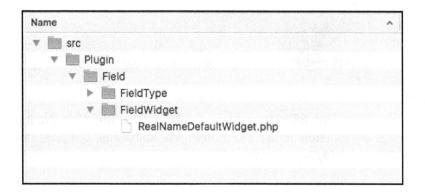

3. The `RealNameDefaultWidget` class will extend the `\Drupal\Core\Field\WidgetBase` class:

```php
<?php

namespace Drupal\mymodule\Plugin\Field\FieldWidget;

use Drupal\Core\Field\WidgetBase;

class RealNameDefaultWidget extends WidgetBase {

}
```

4. We will provide the field widget's identifier, label, and supported field types in the plugin's annotation:

```php
<?php

namespace Drupal\mymodule\Plugin\Field\FieldWidget;

use Drupal\Core\Field\WidgetBase;
use Drupal\Core\Field\FieldItemListInterface;
use Drupal\Core\Form\FormStateInterface;

/**
 * Plugin implementation of the 'realname_default' widget.
 *
 * @FieldWidget(
 *   id = "realname_default",
 *   label = @Translation("Real name"),
 *   field_types = {
 *     "realname"
 *   }
 * )
 */
class RealNameDefaultWidget extends WidgetBase {

}
```

The `@FieldWidget` tells Drupal that this is a field widget plugin. It defines `id` to represent the machine name, the human-readable name as `label`, and the field types that the widget interacts with.

5. We will need to implement the `formElement` method to satisfy the remaining `interface` methods after extending `\Drupal\Core\Field\WidgetBase`. Add the following method to your class:

```
/**
 * {@inheritdoc}
 */
public function formElement(FieldItemListInterface $items, $delta,
array $element, array &$form, FormStateInterface $form_state) {
  $element['first_name'] = [
    '#type' => 'textfield',
    '#title' => t('First name'),
    '#default_value' => '',
    '#size' => 25,
    '#required' => $element['#required'],
  ];
  $element['last_name'] = [
    '#type' => 'textfield',
    '#title' => t('Last name'),
    '#default_value' => '',
    '#size' => 25,
    '#required' => $element['#required'],
  ];
  return $element;
}
```

The `formElement` method returns a Form API array that represents the widget to be set and edits the field data.

6. Next, we will need to modify our original `RealName` field type plugin class to use the default widget that we created. Modify the `src/Plugin/FieldType/RealName.php` file, and update the `default_widget` annotation property as `realname_default`:

```
/**
 * Plugin implementation of the 'realname' field type.
 *
 * @FieldType(
 *   id = "realname",
 *   label = @Translation("Real name"),
 *   description = @Translation("This field stores a first and last
name."),
 *   category = @Translation("General"),
 *   default_widget = "realname_default",
 *   default_formatter = "string"
 * )
```

```
 */
class RealName extends FieldItemBase {
```

7. Rebuild Drupal's cache so that the plugin system can discover the new field widget.

8. Add a `Real name` field and use the new `Real name` widget. For example, add it to a comment type:

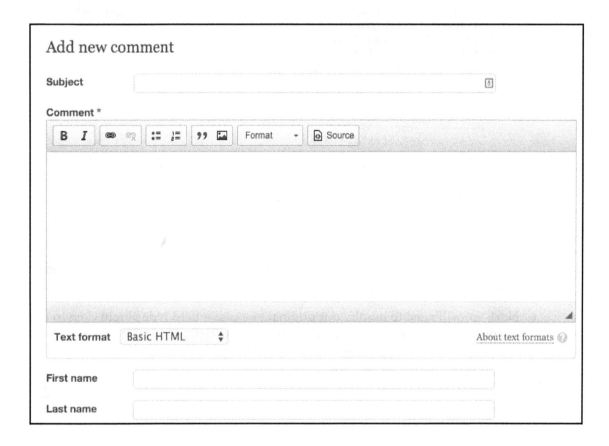

How it works...

Drupal core defines a `plugin.manager.field.widget` service. By default, this is handled through the `\Drupal\Core\Field\FieldWidgetPluginManager` class. This plugin manager defines the field widget plugins that should be in the `Plugin/Field/FieldWidget` namespace, and all the classes in this namespace will be loaded and assumed to be field widget plugins.

The manager's definition also sets `\Drupal\Core\Field\FieldWidgetInterface` as the expected interface that all the field widget plugins will implement. This is why most field types extend `\Drupal\Core\Field\WidgetBase` to meet these method requirements.

As field widgets are annotated plugins, the manager provides `\Drupal\Core\Field\Annotation\FieldWidget` as the class that fulfills the annotation definition.

The entity form display system uses the `plugin.manager.field.widget` service to load field definitions and add the field's element returned from the `formElement` method to the entity form.

There's more...

Field widgets have additional methods to provide more information; they are covered in the next section.

Field widget settings and summary

The `\Drupal\Core\Field\WidgetInterface` interface defines three methods that can be overridden to provide a settings form and a summary of the current settings:

- `defaultSettings`: This returns an array of the setting keys and default values
- `settingsForm`: This returns a Form API array that is used for the settings form
- `settingsSummary`: This allows an array of strings to be returned and displayed on the manage display form for the field

Widget settings can be used to alter the form presented to the user. A setting can be created that allows the field element to be limited to only enter the first or last name with one text field.

See also

- The *Creating a custom plugin type* recipe of this chapter

Creating a custom field formatter

Field formatters define the way in which a field type will be presented. These formatters return the render array information to be processed by the theming layer. Field formatters are configured on the display mode interfaces.

In this recipe, we will create a formatter for the field created in the *Creating a custom field type* recipe in this chapter. The field formatter will display the first and last names with some settings.

Getting ready

Create a new module like the one existing in the first recipe. We will refer to the module as `mymodule` throughout the recipe. Use your module's appropriate name.

How to do it...

1. We will need to create the `src/Plugin/Field/FieldFormatter` directory in the module's base location. The `Field` module discovers field formatters in the `Plugin\Field\FieldFormatter` namespace.
2. Create a `RealNameFormatter.php` file in the newly created directory so that we can define the `RealNameFormatter` class. This will provide a custom form element to display the field's values:

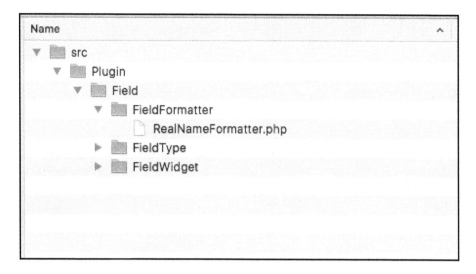

3. The `RealNameFormatter` class will extend the `\Drupal\Core\Field\FormatterBase` class:

```php
<?php

namespace Drupal\mymodule\Plugin\Field\FieldFormatter;

use Drupal\Core\Field\FormatterBase;
use Drupal\Core\Field\FieldItemListInterface;

class RealNameFormatter extends FormatterBase {

}
```

4. We will provide the field widget's identifier, label, and supported field types:

```php
<?php

namespace Drupal\mymodule\Plugin\Field\FieldFormatter;

use Drupal\Core\Field\FormatterBase;
use Drupal\Core\Field\FieldItemListInterface;

/**
 * Plugin implementation of the 'realname_one_line' formatter.
 *
 * @FieldFormatter(
 *   id = "realname_one_line",
 *   label = @Translation("Real name (one line)"),
```

```
 *     field_types = {
 *        "realname"
 *     }
 * )
 */
class RealNameFormatter extends FormatterBase {

}
```

5. We will need to implement the `viewElements` method to satisfy the `\Drupal\Core\Field\FormatterInferface` interface. This is used to render the field data. Add the following method to your class:

```
/**
{@inheritdoc}
*/
public function viewElements(FieldItemListInterface $items,
$langcode) {
  $element = [];

  foreach ($items as $delta => $item) {
    $element[$delta] = [
      '#markup' => $this->t('@first @last', [
        '@first' => $item->first_name,
        '@last' => $item->last_name,
      ]),
    ];
  }
  return $element;
}
```

6. Next, we will need to modify our original `RealName` field type's `plugin` class to use the default formatter that we created. Open the `src/Plugin/FieldType/RealName.php` file, and update the `default_formatter` annotation property as `realname_one_line`:

```
/**
 * Plugin implementation of the 'realname' field type.
 *
 * @FieldType(
 *    id = "realname",
 *    label = @Translation("Real name"),
 *    description = @Translation("This field stores a first and last
name."),
 *    category = @Translation("General"),
 *    default_widget = " string_textfield ",
 *    default_formatter = "realname_one_line"
```

```
 *  )
 */
```

7. Rebuild Drupal's cache so that the plugin system can discover the new field widget.

8. Update an entity view mode with a `Real name` field to use the **Real name (one line)** formatter:

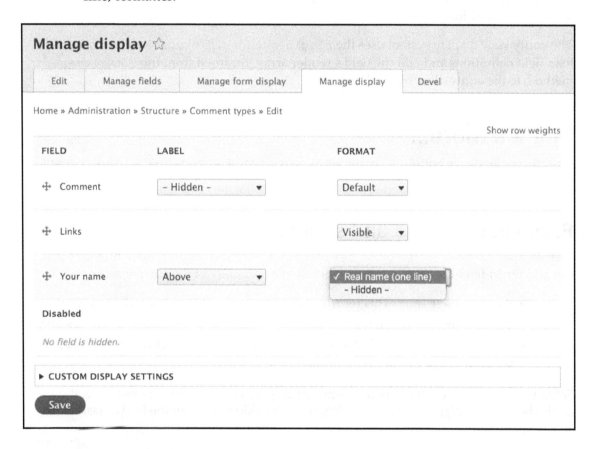

How it works...

Drupal core defines a `plugin.manager.field.formatter` service. By default, this is handled through the `\Drupal\Core\Field\FormatterPluginManager` class. This plugin manager defines the field formatter plugins that should be in the `Plugin/Field/FieldFormatter` namespace, and all the classes in this namespace will be loaded and assumed to be field formatter plugins.

The manager's definition also sets `\Drupal\Core\Field\FormatterInterface` as the expected interface that all field formatter plugins will implement. This is why most field formatters extend `\Drupal\Core\Field\FormatterBase` to meet these method requirements.

As field formatters are annotated plugins, the manager provides `\Drupal\Core\Field\Annotation\FieldFormatter` as the class that fulfills the annotation definition.

The entity view display system uses the `plugin.manager.field.formatter` service to load field definitions and add the field's render array, returned from the `viewElements` method, to the entity view render array.

There's more...

Field formatters have additional methods to provide more information; they are covered in the next section.

Formatter settings and summary

The `\Drupal\Core\Field\FormatterInterface` interface defines three methods that can be overridden to provide a settings form and a summary of the current settings:

- `defaultSettings`: This returns an array of the setting keys and default values
- `settingsForm`: This returns a Form API array that is used for the settings form
- `settingsSummary`: This allows an array of strings to be returned and displayed on the manage display form for the field

Settings can be used to alter how the formatter displays information. For example, these methods can be implemented to provide settings to hide or display the first or last name.

See also

- Refer to the *Creating a custom plugin type* recipe of this chapter.

Creating a custom plugin type

The plugin system provides a means to create specialized objects in Drupal that do not require the data storage features of the entity system.

This recipe is based on the **GeoIP API** module port to Drupal 8 that was started by the author. The **GeoIP API** module provides a way to get the country from a website visitor's IP address.

In this recipe, we will create a new plugin type called `GeoLocator` that will return the country code for a given IP address. We will create a plugin manager, a default plugin interface, a plugin annotation definition, and provide a default plugin to find the country via the website's CDN.

Getting ready

We will use the `geoip` namespace and module name in this recipe.

How to do it...

1. All plugins need to have a service that acts as a plugin manager. Create a new file in your module's `src` directory called `GeoLocatorManager.php`. This will hold the `GeoLocatorManager` class.

2. Create the `GeoLocatorManager` class by extending the `\Drupal\Core\Plugin\DefaultPluginManager` class:

```php
<?php

namespace Drupal\geoip;

use Drupal\Core\Plugin\DefaultPluginManager;
use Drupal\Core\Cache\CacheBackendInterface;
use Drupal\Core\Extension\ModuleHandlerInterface;

class GeoLocatorManager extends DefaultPluginManager {

}
```

3. When creating a new plugin type, it is recommended that the plugin manager provides a set of defaults for new plugins, in case an item is missing from the definition:

```php
<?php

namespace Drupal\geoip;

use Drupal\Core\Plugin\DefaultPluginManager;
use Drupal\Core\Cache\CacheBackendInterface;
use Drupal\Core\Extension\ModuleHandlerInterface;

class GeoLocatorManager extends DefaultPluginManager {

  /**
   * Default values for each plugin.
   *
   * @var array
   */
  protected $defaults = [
    'label' => '',
    'description' => '',
    'weight' => 0,
  ];

}
```

4. Next, we will need to override the `\Drupal\Core\Plugin|DefaultPluginManager` class constructor to define the module handler and cache backend:

```php
<?php

namespace Drupal\geoip;

use Drupal\Core\Plugin\DefaultPluginManager;
use Drupal\Core\Cache\CacheBackendInterface;
use Drupal\Core\Extension\ModuleHandlerInterface;

class GeoLocatorManager extends DefaultPluginManager {

  /**
   * Default values for each plugin.
   *
   * @var array
   * /
  protected $defaults = [
```

```
      'label' => '',
      'description' => '',
      'weight' => 0,
    ];

    /**
     * Constructs a new GeoLocatorManager object.
     *
     * @param \Traversable $namespaces
     *   An object that implements \Traversable which contains the
root paths
     *   keyed by the corresponding namespace to look for plugin
implementations.
     * @param \Drupal\Core\Cache\CacheBackendInterface $cache_backend
     *   Cache backend instance to use.
     * @param \Drupal\Core\Extension\ModuleHandlerInterface
$module_handler
     *   The module handler.
     */
    public function __construct(\Traversable $namespaces,
CacheBackendInterface $cache_backend, ModuleHandlerInterface
$module_handler) {
      parent::__construct(
        'Plugin/GeoLocator',
        $namespaces,
        $module_handler,
        'Drupal\geoip\Plugin\GeoLocator\GeoLocatorInterface',
        'Drupal\geoip\Annotation\GeoLocator'
      );
      $this->setCacheBackend($cache_backend, 'geolocator_plugins');
    }

}
```

We override the constructor so that we can specify a specific cache key. This allows plugin definitions to be cached and cleared properly; otherwise, our plugin manager will continuously read the disk to find plugins.

5. The next step will be to create a `geoip.services.yml` file in our module's root directory. This will describe our plugin manager to Drupal, allowing a plugin discovery:

```
services:
  plugin.manager.geolocator:
    class: Drupal\geoip\GeoLocatorManager
    parent: default_plugin_manager
```

Drupal utilizes services and dependency injection. By defining our class as a service, we are telling the application container how to initiate our class. We can use the `parent` definition to tell the container to use the same arguments as the `default_plugin_manager` definition.

6. All annotation-based plugins must provide a class, which serves as the annotation definition. Create `GeoLocator.php` in `src/Annotation` to provide the `GeoLocator` annotation class:

```php
<?php

namespace Drupal\geoip\Annotation;

use Drupal\Component\Annotation\Plugin;

/**
 * Defines a GeoLocator annotation object.
 *
 * @Annotation
 */
class GeoLocator extends Plugin {

  /**
   * The human-readable name.
   *
   * @var \Drupal\Core\Annotation\Translation
   *
   * @ingroup plugin_translatable
   */
  public $label;

  /**
   * A description of the plugin.
   *
   * @var \Drupal\Core\Annotation\Translation
   *
   * @ingroup plugin_translatable
   */
  public $description;

}
```

Each property is an item that can be defined in the plugin's annotation. The annotated definition will start with `@GeoLocator` for our plugins.

7. Next, we will define the plugin interface that we defined in the plugin manager. The plugin manager will validate the `GeoLocator` plugins that implement this interface. Create a `GeoLocatorInterface.php` file in our module's `src/Plugin/GeoLocator` directory to hold the interface:

```php
<?php

namespace Drupal\geoip\Plugin\GeoLocator;

/**
 * Interface GeoLocatorInterface.
 */
interface GeoLocatorInterface {

  /**
   * Get the plugin's label.
   *
   * @return string
   *    The geolocator label
   */
  public function label();

  /**
   * Get the plugin's description.
   *
   * @return string
   *    The geolocator description
   */
  public function description();

  /**
   * Performs geolocation on an address.
   *
   * @param string $ip_address
   *    The IP address to geolocate.
   *
   * @return string|NULL
   *    The geolocated country code, or NULL if not found.
   */
  public function geolocate($ip_address);

}
```

We provide an interface so that we can guarantee that we have these expected methods when working with a `GeoLocator` plugin, and that we have an output, regardless of the logic behind each method.

8. Next, we will create a default plugin, which returns the country code from CDN headers, if available. In `src/Plugin/GeoLocator`, create a `Cdn.php` file for our `Cdn` plugin class:

```php
<?php

namespace Drupal\geoip\Plugin\GeoLocator;

use Drupal\Core\Plugin\PluginBase;

/**
 * CDN geolocation provider.
 *
 * @GeoLocator(
 *   id = "cdn",
 *   label = "CDN",
 *   description = "Checks for geolocation headers sent by CDN
services",
 *   weight = -10
 * )
 */
class Cdn extends PluginBase implements GeoLocatorInterface {

  /**
   * {@inheritdoc}
   */
  public function label() {
    return $this->pluginDefinition['label'];
  }

  /**
   * {@inheritdoc}
   */
  public function description() {
    return $this->pluginDefinition['description'];
  }

  /**
   * {@inheritdoc}
   */
  public function geolocate($ip_address) {
    // Check if CloudFlare headers present.
    if (!empty($_SERVER['HTTP_CF_IPCOUNTRY'])) {
      $country_code = $_SERVER['HTTP_CF_IPCOUNTRY'];
    }
    // Check if CloudFront headers present.
    elseif (!empty($_SERVER['HTTP_CLOUDFRONT_VIEWER_COUNTRY'])) {
```

```
        $country_code = $_SERVER['HTTP_CLOUDFRONT_VIEWER_COUNTRY'];
      }
      else {
        $country_code = NULL;
      }

      return $country_code;
    }
  }
```

9. The `GeoLocator` plugin type is now set, with a default CDN-based plugin.

How it works...

Drupal 8 implements a service container, a concept adopted from the Symfony framework. In order to implement a plugin, there needs to be a manager who can discover and process plugin definitions. This manager is defined as a service in a module's `services.yml` with its required constructor parameters. This allows the service container to initiate the class when it is required.

In our example, the `GeoLocatorManager` plugin manager discovers the `GeoLocator` plugin definitions through annotated plugin discovery. After the first discovery, all the known plugin definitions are then cached under the `geolocator_plugins` cache key.

Plugin managers also provide a method to return these definitions or create an object instance based on an available definition. For the CDN plugin, this would be a full instantiated `Cdn` class object.

Let's consider the following example:

```
// Load the manager service.
$geolocator_manager = \Drupal::service('plugin.manager.geolocator');

// Create a class instance through the manager.
$cdn_instance = $unit_manager->createInstance('cdn');

// Get country code.
$country_code = $cdn_instance->geolocate('127.0.0.1');
```


There's more...

There are many additional items for creating a custom plugin type; we will discuss some of them in the following sections.

Specifying an alter hook

Plugin managers have the ability to define an alter hook. The following line of code will be added to the `GeoLocatorManager` class's constructor to provide `hook_geolocator_plugins_alter`. This is passed to the module handler service for invocations:

```
/**
 * Constructs a new GeoLocatorManager object.
 *
 * @param \Traversable $namespaces
 * An object that implements \Traversable which contains the root paths
 * keyed by the corresponding namespace to look for plugin implementations.
 * @param \Drupal\Core\Cache\CacheBackendInterface $cache_backend
 * Cache backend instance to use.
 * @param \Drupal\Core\Extension\ModuleHandlerInterface $module_handler
 * The module handler.
 */
public function __construct(\Traversable $namespaces, CacheBackendInterface
$cache_backend, ModuleHandlerInterface $module_handler) {
  parent::__construct(
    'Plugin/GeoLocator',
    $namespaces,
    $module_handler,
    'Drupal\geoip\Plugin\GeoLocator\GeoLocatorInterface',
    'Drupal\geoip\Annotation\GeoLocator'
  );
  $this->alterInfo('geolocator_info');
  $this->setCacheBackend($cache_backend, 'geolocator_plugins');
}
```

Modules implementing `hook_geolocator_plugins_alter` in the `.module` file have the ability to modify all the discovered plugin definitions. They also have the ability to remove defined plugin entries or alter any information provided for the annotation definition.

Using a cache backend

Plugins can use a cache backend to improve performance. This can be done by specifying a cache backend with the `setCacheBackend` method in the manager's constructor. The following line of code will allow the `Unit` plugins to be cached and only discovered on a cache rebuild.

The $cache_backend variable is passed to the constructor. The second parameter provides the cache key. The cache key will have the current language code added as a suffix.

There is an optional third parameter that takes an array of strings to represent cache tags that will cause the plugin definitions to be cleared. This is an advanced feature, and plugin definitions should normally be cleared through the manager's clearCachedDefinitions method. The cache tags allow the plugin definitions to be cleared when a relevant cache is cleared as well.

Accessing plugins through the manager

Plugins are loaded through the manager service, which should always be accessed through the service container. The following line of code will be used in your module's hooks or classes to access the plugin manager:

```
$geolocator_manager = \Drupal::service('plugin.manager.geolocator');
```

Plugin managers have various methods for retrieving plugin definitions, which are as follows:

- getDefinitions: This method will return an array of plugin definitions. It first makes an attempt to retrieve cached definitions, if any, and sets the cache of discovered definitions before returning them.
- getDefinition: This takes an expected plugin ID and returns its definition.
- createInstance: This takes an expected plugin ID and returns an initiated class for the plugin.
- getInstance: This takes an array that acts as a plugin definition and returns an initiated class from the definition.

See also

- Refer to services and dependency injection at
  https://www.drupal.org/node/2133171

8
Multilingual and Internationalization

In this chapter, we will cover the following recipes to make sure that your site is multilingual and internationalized:

- Translating administrative interfaces
- Translating configurations
- Translating content
- Creating multilingual views

Introduction

This chapter will cover the multilingual and internationalization features of Drupal 8, which have been greatly enhanced since Drupal 7. The preceding version of Drupal required many extra modules to provide internationalization efforts, but now the majority is provided by Drupal core.

Drupal core provides the following multilingual modules:

- **Language**: This provides you with the ability to detect and support multiple languages
- **Interface translation**: This takes installed languages and translates strings that are presented through the user interface

- **Configuration translation**: This allows you to translate configuration entities, such as date formats and views
- **Content translation**: This brings the power of providing content in different languages and displaying it according to the current language of the user

Each module serves a specific purpose in creating the multilingual experience for your Drupal site. Behind the scenes, Drupal supports the language code for all entities and cache contexts. These modules expose the interfaces to implement and deliver internationalized experiences.

Translating administrative interfaces

The interface translation module provides a method to translate strings found in the Drupal user interface. Harnessing the Language module, interface translations are automatically downloaded from the Drupal translation server. By default, the interface language is loaded through the language code as a path prefix. With the default **Language** configuration, paths will be prefixed with the default language.

Interface translations are based on strings provided in the code that are passed through the internal translation functions.

In this recipe, we will enable Spanish, import the language files, and review the translated interface strings to provide missing or custom translations.

Getting ready

Drupal 8 provides an automated installation process of translation files. For this to work, your web server must be able to communicate with `https://localize.drupal.org/`. If your web server cannot automatically download the files from the translation server, you can refer to the manual installation instructions, which will be covered in the *There's more...* section of this recipe.

How to do it...

1. Go to **Extend** and install the **Interface Translation** module. It will prompt you to enable the **Language**, **File**, and **Field** modules to be installed, if they are not.
2. After the module is installed, click on **Configuration**. Go to the **Languages** page under the **Regional and Language** section.
3. Click on **Add language** in the languages overview table:

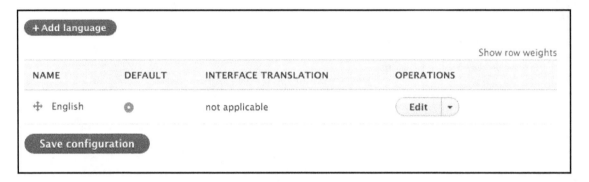

4. The **Add language** page provides a select list of all available languages that the interface can be translated to. Select **Spanish**, and then click on **Add language**.
5. A batch process will run, install the translation language files, and import them.
6. The **INTERFACE TRANSLATION** column specifies the percentage of active translatable interface strings that have a matching translation. Clicking on the link allows you to view the **User interface translation** form:

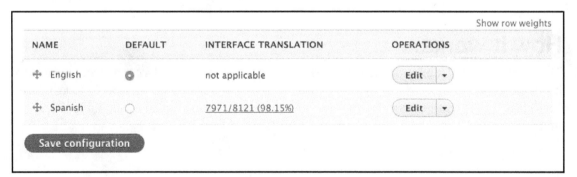

7. The **Filter Translatable Strings** form allows you to search for translated strings or untranslated strings. Select **Only untranslated strings** from the **Search in** list and click on **Filter**.

8. Using the textbox on the right-hand side of the screen, a custom translation can be added to **Only untranslated strings**. Type in a translation for the item:

9. Click on **Save translations** to save the modification.

10. Go to /es/node/add, and you will note that the **Basic page** content type description will now match your translation.

How it works...

The interface translation module provides \Drupal\locale\LocaleTranslation, which implements \Drupal\Core\StringTranslation\Translator\TranslatorInterface. This class is registered under the string_translation service as an available lookup method.

When the t function or the
\Drupal\Core\StringTranslation\StringTranslationTrait::t method is
invoked, the string_translation service is called to provide a translated string. The
string_translation service will iterate through the available translators and return a
translated string, if possible.

> Developers need to note that this is a key reason to ensure that module
> strings are passed through translation functions. It allows you to identify
> strings that need to be translated.

The translator provided in the interface translation will then attempt to resolve the
provided string against known translations for the current language. If a translation has
been saved, it will be returned.

There's more...

We will explore ways to install other languages, check translation statuses, and do much
more in the following sections.

Manually installing language files

Translation files can be manually installed by downloading them from the Drupal.org
translation server and uploading them through the language interface. You can also use the
import interface to upload custom **gettext portable object (.po)** files.

Drupal core and most contributed projects have .po files available at the Drupal translations site, https://localize.drupal.org. On the site, click on **Download** to download a .po file for Drupal core in all available languages. Additionally, clicking on a language will provide more translations for a specific language across projects, as follows:

Spanish overview

Overview Board Translate

Spanish translation team – Grupo de traducción al Español

Nuevo!: Ayuda a probar la nueva versión de localize.drupal.org en Drupal 7!

- Diccionario – Libro de estilo Wiki para crear un glosario de términos, manuales para traductores y libro de estilo en Español.
- Traducción de Drupal core Paquete de archivos .po que componen la traducción de Drupal, y los módulos del Core, al español neutro.
- Interfaz de traducción: Aportar sugerencias de traducción para cadenas de texto pendientes de traducir. Los moderadores validarán las sugerencias y seleccionarán la que será finalmente utilizada por la comunidad. Permite importar nuevas cadenas de texto (actualizaciones de módulos) y exportarlas para ser utilizadas en producción.
- Foro de traducciones: Iniciar y seguir debates sobre palabras o cadenas de texto concretas. Las discusiones sobre palabras establecen una base sólida sobre la que luego construir las sugerencias que serán posteadas en localize.drupal.org
- Glosario de términos: Establece una relación de traducción "automática" para los términos más comunes.
- Directrices para la traducción: Ofrece ideas sobre cómo realizar la traducción al español, de modo que los traductores tengamos un criterio homogéneo. Son ideas abiertas a discusión y por tanto no son realmente un "Libro de Estilo".
- Moderadores de la traducción: Cómo convertirse en moderador y líneas guía para moderar las traducciones.

Top downloads

Drupal core

Project	Version	Downloads	Date created	Up to date as of
Drupal core	5.23	Download (414.14 KB)	2011–Jun–23	2011–Jul–14
Drupal core	6.37	Download (529.03 KB)	2015–Oct–01	2015–Dec–06
Drupal core	7.41	Download (679.04 KB)	2015–Nov–03	2015–Dec–06
Drupal core	8.0.1	Download (1.04 MB)	2015–Dec–04	2015–Dec–06

You can import a .po file by going to the User interface translation form and selecting the Import tab. You will need to select the .po file and then the appropriate language. You can treat the uploaded files as custom-created translations. This is recommended if you are providing a custom translation file that was not provided by Drupal.org. If you are updating Drupal.org translations manually, make sure that you check the box that overwrites existing noncustom translations. The final option allows you to replace customized translations if the .po file provides them. This can be useful if you have translated missing strings that might now be provided by the official translation file.

Checking translation status

As you add new modules, the available translations will grow. The Interface translation module provides a translation status report that is accessible from the Reports page. This will check the default translation server for the project and check whether there is a .po available or if it has changed. In the event of a custom module, you can provide a custom translation server, which is covered in *Providing translations for a custom module*.

If an update is available, you will be alerted. You can then import the translation file updates automatically or download and manually import them.

Exporting translations

In the User interface translation form, there is an Export tab. This form will provide a Gettext Portable Object (.po) file. You can export all the available source text that is discovered in your current Drupal site without translations. This will provide a base .po for translators to work on.

Additionally, you can download a specific language. Specific language downloads can include uncustomized translations, customized translations, and missing translations. Downloading customized translations can be used to help make contributions to the multilingual and internationalization efforts of the Drupal community.

Interface translation permissions

The interface translation module provides a single permission called **Translate interface text**. This permission grants users the permission to interact with all the module's capabilities. It is flagged with a security warning, as it allows users with this permission to customize all the output text presented to them.

However, it does allow you to provide a role for translators and limits their access to just translation interfaces.

Using interface translation to customize default English strings

The interface translation module is useful beyond its typical multilingual purposes. You can use it to customize strings in the interface that are not available to be modified through typical hook methods, or if you are not a developer.

Firstly, you will need to edit the English language from the **Languages** screen. Check the checkbox for **Enable interface translation for English** and click on **Save language**. You will now have the ability to customize existing interface strings.

 This is only recommended for areas of the interface that cannot already be customized through the normal user interface or provided API mechanisms.

Interface text language detection

The Language module provides detection and selection rules. By default, the module will detect the current language based on the URL, with the language code acting as a prefix to the current path. For example, /es/node will display the node listing page in Spanish, as seen in the following screenshot:

Interface text language detection

Order of language detection methods for interface text. If a translation of interface text is available in the detected language, it will be displayed.

Show row weights

DETECTION METHOD	DESCRIPTION	ENABLED	OPERATIONS
⊹ Account administration pages	Account administration pages language setting.	☐	
⊹ URL	Language from the URL (Path prefix or domain).	☑	Configure
⊹ Session	Language from a request/session parameter.	☐	Configure
⊹ User	Follow the user's language preference.	☐	
⊹ Browser	Language from the browser's language settings.	☐	Configure
⊹ Selected language	Language based on a selected language.	☑	Configure

You can have multiple detection options enabled at once and use the ordering to decide which takes precedence. This can allow you to use the language code in the URL first, but, if they are missing, a fallback to the language is specified by the user's browser.

Some detection methods have settings. For instance, the URL detection method can be based on the default path prefix or subdomains.

Providing translations for a custom module

Modules can provide custom translations in their directories or point to a remote file. These definitions are added to the module's `info.yml` file. First, you will need to specify the `interface translation project` key if it differs from the project's machine name.

You will then need to specify a server pattern through the `interface translation server pattern` key. This can be a relative path to Drupal's root, such as `modules/custom/mymodule/translation.po`, or a remote file URL at `http://example.com/files/translations/mymodule/translation.po`.

Distributions (or other modules) can implement `hook_locale_translation_projects_alter` to provide this information on behalf of modules or to alter defaults.

The server pattern accepts the following different tokens:

- `%core`: Indicates the version of a course (for example, 8.x)
- `%project`: Indicates the project's name
- `%version`: Indicates the current version string
- `%language`: Indicates the language code

More information on the interface translation keys and variables can be found in the `local.api.php` document file located in the interface translation module's base folder.

See also

- Refer to the Drupal translation server at `https://localize.drupal.org/translate/drupal8`
- You can contribute using the localization server at `https://www.drupal.org/node/302194`

- Refer to the `locale.api.php` documentation at `https://api.drupal.org/api/drupal/core%21modules%21locale%21locale.api.php/8`
- Refer to PO and POT files at `https://www.drupal.org/node/1814954`

Translating configuration

The **Configuration translation** module provides an interface to translate configurations with interface translation and language as dependencies. This module allows us to translate configuration entities. The ability to translate configuration entities adds an extra level of internationalization.

Interface translation allows us to translate strings provided in our Drupal site's code base. Configuration translation allows us to translate importable and exportable configuration items that we created, such as site title or date formats.

In this recipe, we will translate date format configuration entities. We will provide localized date formats for Danish to provide a more internationalized experience.

Getting ready

Your Drupal site needs to have two languages enabled in order to use **Configuration Translation**. Install **Danish** from the **Languages interface**.

How to do it...

1. Go to **Extend** and install the **Configuration Translation** module. It will prompt you to enable the **Interface Translation**, **Language**, **File**, and **Field** modules to be installed, if they are not.
2. After the module is installed, go to **Configuration**. Then, go to the **Configuration translation** page under the **Regional and Language** section.

3. Click on the list for the **Date format** option in the configuration entity option table:

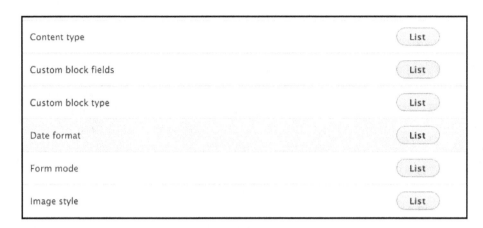

Content type	List
Custom block fields	List
Custom block type	List
Date format	List
Form mode	List
Image style	List

4. We will translate the **Default long date format** to represent the **Danish** format. Click on the **Translate for the Default long date format** row.
5. Click on **Add** to create a **Danish** translation:

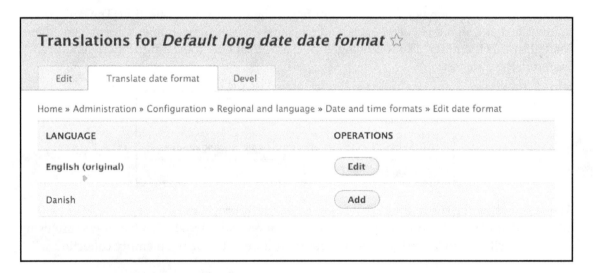

Translations for *Default long date date format* ☆

Edit	Translate date format	Devel

Home » Administration » Configuration » Regional and language » Date and time formats » Edit date format

LANGUAGE	OPERATIONS
English (original)	Edit
Danish	Add

6. For **Danish**, we will provide the following PHP date format: l j. F, Y - H.i. This will display the day of the week, the day of the month, the month, the full year, and the 24-hour notation for the time.

7. Click on **Save translation**.

8. Whenever a user is browsing your Drupal site with **Danish** as their language, the date format will now be localized for their experience.

How it works...

The Configuration Translation module requires Interface Translation; however, it does not work in the same fashion. The module modifies all entity types that extend the `\Drupal\Core\Config\Entity\ConfigEntityInterface` interface. It adds a new handler under the `config_translation_list` key. This is used to build a list of available configuration entities and their bundles.

The module alters the configuration schema in Drupal, and updates the default configuration element definitions to use a specified class under `\Drupal\config_translation\Form`. This allows `\Drupal\config_translation\Form\ConfigTranslationFormBase` and its child classes to properly save translated configuration data, which can then be modified through the configuration translation screens.

When the configuration is saved, it is identified as being part of a collection. The collection is identified as `language.LANGCODE`, and all translated configuration entities are saved and loaded by this identifier. The following is an example of how the configuration items are stored in the database:

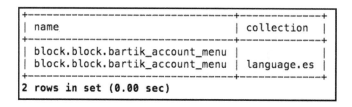

```
+----------------------------------------+---------------+
| name                                   | collection    |
+----------------------------------------+---------------+
| block.block.bartik_account_menu        |               |
| block.block.bartik_account_menu        | language.es   |
+----------------------------------------+---------------+
2 rows in set (0.00 sec)
```

When browsing the site in the `es` language code, the appropriate `block.block.bartik_account_menu` configuration entity will be loaded. If you are using the default site, or no language code, the configuration entity with an empty collection will be used.

There's more...

Configuration entities and the ability to translate them are a big part of Drupal 8's multilingual capabilities. We'll explore them in detail in the next recipe.

Altering configuration translation info definitions

Modules can invoke the `hook_config_translation_info_alter` hook to alter discovered configuration mappers. For instance, the **Node** module does this to modify the `node_type` configuration entity:

```
/**
 * Implements hook_config_translation_info_alter().
 */
function node_config_translation_info_alter(&$info) {
  $info['node_type']['class'] =
'Drupal\node\ConfigTranslation\NodeTypeMapper';
}
```

This updates the `node_type` definition to use the `\Drupal\node\ConfigTranslation\NodeTypeMapper` custom mapper class. This class adds the node type's title as a configurable translation item.

Translating views

Views are configuration entities. When the Configuration translation module is enabled, it is possible to translate Views. This will allow you to translate display titles, exposed form labels, and other items. Refer to the `Creating a multilingual view` recipe in this chapter for more information.

See also

- Refer to the *Creating a Multilingual View* recipe of `Chapter 8`, *Multilingual and Internationalization*.

Translating content

The content translation module provides a method to translate content entities, such as nodes and blocks. Each content entity needs to have translation enabled, which allows you to granularly decide what properties and fields are translated.

Content translations are duplications of the existing entity, but are flagged with a proper language code. When a visitor uses a language code, Drupal attempts to load content entities using that language code. If a translation is not present, Drupal will render the default untranslated entity.

Getting ready

Your Drupal site needs to have two languages enabled to use Content translation. Install **Spanish** from the **Languages** interface.

How to do it...

1. Go to **Extend** and install the **Content translation** module. It will prompt you to enable the **Language** modules to be installed, if they are not.
2. After the module is installed, go to **Configuration** and then to the **Content language and translation** page under the **Regional and Language** section.
3. Check the checkbox next to **Content** to expose settings for the current content types.
4. Enable the content translation for the **Basic page** and keep the provided default settings that enable translation for each field. Click on **Save configuration**:

5. Create a new **Basic page** node. We will create this in the site's default language.

6. When viewing the new node, click on the **Translate** tab. From the **Spanish** language row, click on **Add** to create a translated version of the node:

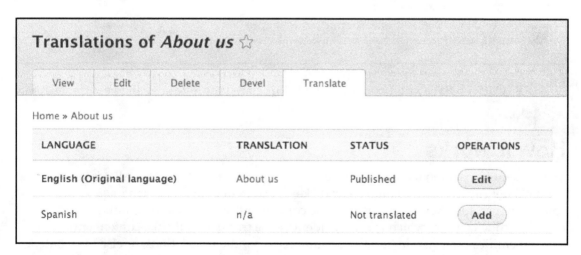

7. The content will be prepopulated with the default language's content. Replace the title and body with the translated text:

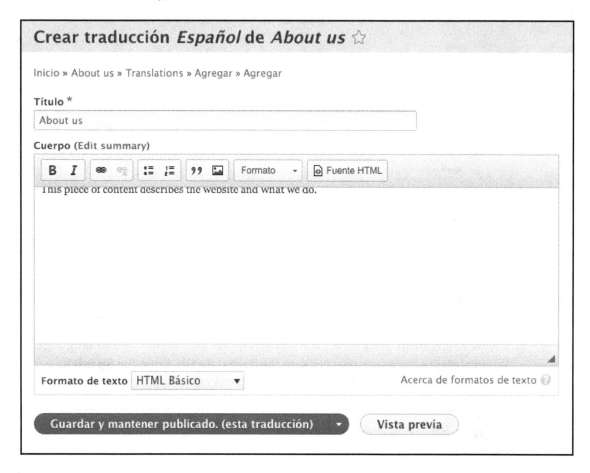

8. Click on **Save and keep published (this translation)** to save the new translation.

How it works

The Content translation module works by utilizing language code flags. All content entities and field definitions have a language code key. A content entity has a language code column, which specifies what language the content entity is for. Field definitions also have a language code column, which is used to identify the translation for the content entity. Content entities can provide handler definitions to handle translations, or else the Content translation module will provide its own.

Each entity and field record is saved with the proper language code to use. When an entity is loaded, the current language code is taken into consideration to ensure that the proper entity is loaded.

There's more...

There are additional operations to translate content; we will cover them in the next sections.

Flagging translations as outdated

The Content translation module provides a mechanism to flag translated entities as possibly being outdated. The **Flag other translations as outdated** flag provides a way to make a note of entities that will need updated translations:

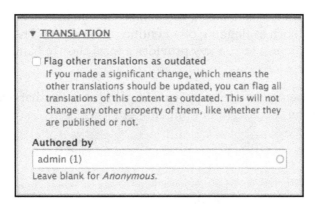

This flag does not change any data, but rather provides a moderation tool. This makes it easy for translators to identify content, which has been changed and requires updating. The translation tab for the content entity will highlight all translations, which are still marked as outdated. As they are changed, the editor can uncheck the flag.

Translating content links

Mostly, Drupal menus contain links to nodes. Menu links are not translated by default, and the **Custom menu links** option must be enabled under **Content translation**. You will need to translate node links manually from the menu administration interface.

Enabling a menu link from the node create and edit form will not work with translations. If you edit the menu settings from a translation, it will edit the untranslated menu link.

Defining translation handlers for entities

The Content translation module requires entity definitions to provide information about translation handlers. If this information is missing, it will provide its own defaults. The *Entity API* is covered in *Chapter 10, The Entity API*, but we will quickly discuss how the content translation module interacts with the Entity API.

Content entity definitions can provide a `translation` handler. If not provided, it will default to `\Drupal\content_translation\ContentTranslationHandler`. A node provides this definition and uses it to place the content translation information into the vertical tabs.

The `content_translation_metadata` key defines how to interact with translation metadata information, such as flagging other entities as outdated. The `content_translation_deletion` key provides a form class to handle entity translation deletion.

Currently, as of 8.0.1, no core modules provide implementations that override the default `content_translation_metadata` or `content_translation_deletion`.

See also

- Refer to *Chapter 10, The Entity API*.

Creating multilingual views

Views, being configuration entities, are available for translation. However, the power of multilingual views does not lie just in configuration translation. Views allow you to build filters that react to the current language code. This ensures that the content, which has been translated into the user's language, is displayed.

In this recipe, we will create a multilingual view that provides a block showing recent articles. If there is no content, we will display a translated `no results` message.

Getting ready

Your Drupal site needs to have two languages enabled in order to use **Content Translation**. Install **Spanish** from the **Languages** interface. Enable content translation for **Articles**. You will also need to have some translated content.

How to do it...

1. Go to **Views** from **Structure**, and click on **Add view**.
2. Provide a view name, such as Recent articles, and change the type of content to **Article**. Mark that you would like to **Create a block** and then click on **Save** and **edit**.
3. Add a new **Filter criteria**. Search for **Translation language** and add the filter for the **Content** category. Click on **Add and configure filter criteria**. Set the filter to check the **Interface text language selected for page**. This will only display that the content that has been translated or the base language is the current language:

4. Click on **Add** next to **No Results** and search for **Text area**. Check the checkbox and click on **Add and configure no results behavior**. Provide some sample text, such as `Currently no recent articles`.

5. Save the view.

6. Click on the **Translate view** tab. Click on **Add** for the **Spanish** row to translate the view for the language.

7. Expand the **Master display settings** and then the **Recent articles** display options fieldsets. Modify the **Display title** option to provide a translated title:

8. Expand **No results behavior** to modify the text on the right-hand side of the screen using the textbox on the left-hand side of the screen as the source for the original text:

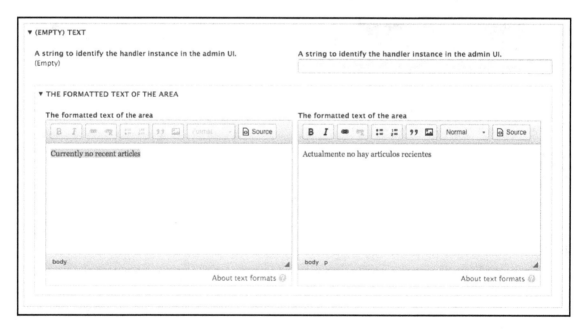

9. Click on **Save translation**.

10. Place the block on your Drupal site by going to **Structure** and then to **Block Layout**.

11. Go to the site through /es and note the translated Views block:

How it works...

Views provide the Translation language filter that builds off this element. The Views plugin systems provide a mechanism to gather and display all available languages. These will be saved as a token internally and then substituted with the actual language code when the query is executed. If a language code is no longer available, the Content language for selected page and views will fall back to the current language when viewed.

 You will come across this option when editing views provided by Drupal core or contributed modules. Although this is not an option in the user interface, it is a default practice to add a language filter defined as ***LANGUAGE_language_content***, which will force the view to be multilingual.

The filter tells **Views** to query based on the language code of the entity and its fields.

Views are configuration entities. The Configuration translation module allows you to translate views. Views can be translated from the main Configuration translation screens from the `Configuration` area or by editing individual views.

Most translation items will be under the **Master display settings** tab unless overridden in specific displays. Each display type will also have its own specific settings.

There's more...

Even more can be done to translate your views; we will discuss in the following section.

Translating exposed form items and filters

Each view can translate the exposed form from the `Exposed Form` section. This does not translate the labels on the form but the form elements. You can translate the `submit` button text, `reset` button label, `sort` label, and `ascending` or `descending`.

You can translate the labels for exposed filters from the `Filters` section. Each exposed filter will show up as a collapsible fieldset, allowing you to configure the administrative label and front-facing label.

By default, available translations need to be imported through the global interface translation context.

Translating display and row format items

Some display formats have translatable items. These can be translated in each display mode's section. For example, the following items can be translated with their display format:

- The `Table` format allows you to translate the table summary
- The `RSS feed` format allows you to translate the feed description
- The `Page` format allows you to translate the page's title
- The `Block` format allows you to translate the block's title

Translating page display menu items

Custom menu links can be translated through the Content translation module. Views which use a page display do not create custom menu link entities. So it must be translated through the View itself. The `Views` module takes all views with a page display and registers their paths into the routing system directly as if defined in a module's `routing.yml` file:

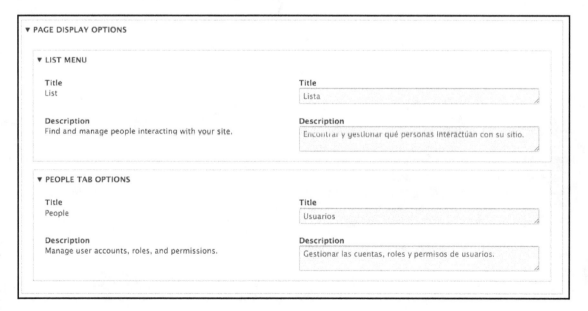

For example, the **People** view that lists all users can be translated to have an updated tab name and link description.

See also

- Refer to *Chapter 3*, *Displaying Content through Views*.

9
Configuration Management - Deploying in Drupal 8

In this chapter, we will explore the configuration management system and deployment of the configuration changes. The following is a list of the recipes covered in this chapter:

- Importing and exporting configurations
- Synchronizing site configurations
- Using command-line workflow processes
- Updating and installing new module configurations

Introduction

Drupal 8 provides a new, unified system to manage configurations. In Drupal 8, all configurations are saved in configuration entities that match a defined configuration schema. This system provides a standard way of deploying the configuration between Drupal site environments and updating the site configuration.

Once the configuration is created, or imported, it goes into an immutable state. If a module tries to install the configuration that exists, it will throw an exception and be prevented. Outside the typical user interface, the configuration can only be modified through the configuration management system.

The configuration management system can be manipulated through a user interface provided by the Configuration management module or through the command-line interface tools. These tools allow you to follow the development paradigm of utilizing a production site and a development site, where changes are made to the development site and then pushed to production.

Instead of creating two different Drupal sites for the recipes in this chapter, you can utilize the Drupal multisite functionality. For more information on this functionality, refer to the *Installing Drupal* recipe of `Chapter 1`, *Up and Running with Drupal 8*. Note that if you use a multisite, you will need to clone your development site's database into the site acting as your production site to replicate a realistic development and production site workflow.

Importing and exporting configurations

Configuration management in Drupal 8 provides a solution to common problems when working with a website across multiple environments. No matter what the workflow pattern is, at some point, the configuration needs to move from one place to another, such as from production to a local environment. When pushing the development work to production, you will need to have some way to put the configuration in place.

Drupal 8's user interface provides a way to import and export configuration entities via the YAML format. In this recipe, we will create a content type, export its configuration, and then import it into another Drupal site. The configuration YAML export will be imported into the production site to update its configuration.

Getting ready

You will need a base Drupal site to act as the development site. Another Drupal site, which is a clone of the development site, must be available to act as a production Drupal site.

How to do it...

1. To get started, create a new content type on the development site. Name the content type **Staff Page** and click on **Save and manage fields** to save the content type. We will not add any additional fields.
2. Once the content type has been saved, go to **Extend** and install the **Configuration Manager** module if it is not installed:

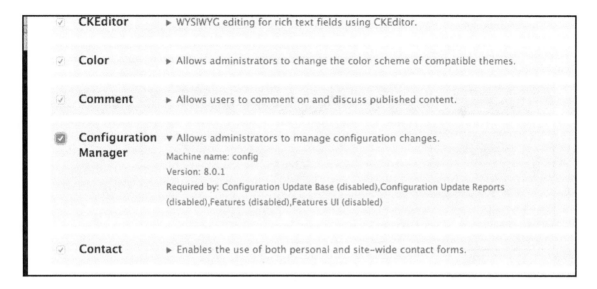

3. From your Drupal site's **Configuration** page, go to **Configuration synchronization** under the **Development** group. This section allows you to import and export configuration:

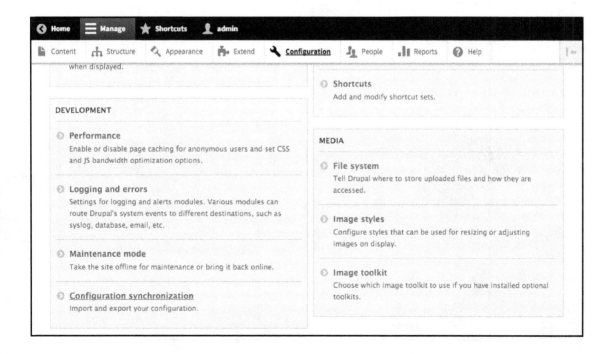

4. Click on the **Export** tab at the top of the page. The default page will be for a **Full archive** export, that contains the configuration of your entire Drupal site. Click on the **Single item** subtab to export a single configuration entity instead:

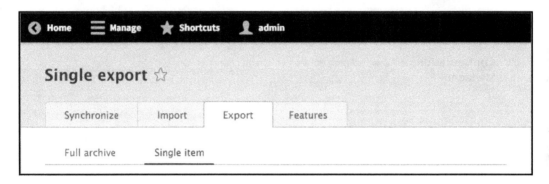

5. Select **Content type** from the **Configuration type** drop-down menu. Then, choose your content type from the **Configuration name** drop-down menu. Its configuration will populate the configuration textbox:

6. Copy the YAML content from the textbox so that you can import it into your other Drupal site.
7. On your production Drupal site, install the Configuration management module just as you did for the development site, if it is not yet installed.
8. Go to the **Configuration synchronization** page and click on the **Import** tab.
9. Click on **Single item** and select **Content type** from the **Configuration type**:

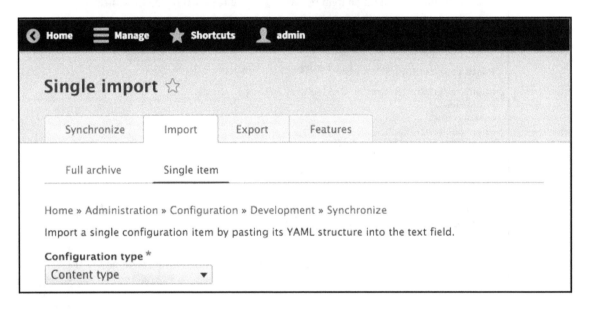

10. Paste your exported configuration YAML into the textbox and click on **Import**:

Full archive   Single item

Home » Administration » Configuration » Development » Synchronize

Import a single configuration item by pasting its YAML structure en el text field.

Configuration type *

Content type ▼

Paste your configuration here *

```
uuid: f33fa230-28ee-4f56-8751-81c30742e04d
langcode: en
status: true
dependencies:
  module:
    - menu_ui
third_party_settings:
  menu_ui:
    available_menus:
      - main
    parent: 'main:'
name: 'Staff pages'
type: staff_pages
description: 'Add a new <em>staff page</em> to add staff profile page on the site.'
help: ''
new_revision: false
preview_mode: 1
display_submitted: true
```

▶ ADVANCED

Import

11. Click on **Confirm** on the confirmation form to finalize your import to the production Drupal site for your custom content type.

12. Go to the **Structure** page and then to the **Content Types** page to verify that your content type has been imported.

How it works...

At the most basic level, configurations are just a mapping of keys and values, which can be represented as a PHP array and translated into the YAML format.

Configuration management uses schema definitions for configuration entities. The schema definition provides a configuration namespace and the available keys and data types. The schema definition provides a typed data definition for each option that allows validation of the individual values and configuration.

The export process reads the configuration data and translates it into the YAML format. The configuration manager then receives the configuration in the form of YAML and converts it back to a PHP array. The data is then updated in the database.

When importing the configuration, Drupal checks the value of the configuration YAML's `uuid` key, if present, against any current configuration with the same **Universally Unique Identifier** (**UUID**). A UUID is a pattern used in software to provide a method of identifying an object across different environments. This allows Drupal to correlate a piece of data from its UUID since the database identifier can differ across environments. If the configuration item has a matching machine name, but a mismatching UUID, an error will be thrown.

There's more...

We will discuss importing and exporting configuration within your Drupal site more in depth in a later section.

Configuration dependencies

Configuration entities define dependencies when they are exported. The dependency definitions ensure that the configuration entity's schema and other module functionalities are available.

When you review the configuration export for `field.storage.node.body.yml`, it defines `node` and `text` as dependencies:

```
dependencies:
  module:
    - node
    - text
```

If the `node` or `text` module is not enabled, the import will fail and throw an error.

Saving to a YAML file for a module's configuration installation

The *Providing configuration on install or update* recipe of `Chapter 6`, *Creating Forms with the Form API*, discusses how to use a module to provide configurations on the module's installation. Instead of manually writing configuration `YAML` files for installation, the `Configuration management` module can be used to export configurations and save them in your module's `config/install` directory.

Any item exported through the user interface can be used. The only requirement is that you will need to remove the `uuid` key, as it denotes the site's UUID value and invalidates the configuration when it tries to install it.

Configuration schemas

The configuration management system in Drupal 8 utilizes the configuration schema to describe configurations that can exist. Why is this important? It allows Drupal to properly implement typed data on stored configuration values and validate them, providing a standardized way of handling configurations for translation and configuration items.

When a module uses the configuration system to store data, it needs to provide a schema for each configuration definition it wishes to store. The schema definition is used to validate and provide typed data definitions for its values.

The following code defines the configuration schema for the `navbar_awesome` module, which holds two different Boolean configuration values:

```
navbar_awesome.toolbar:
  type: config_object
  label: 'Navbar Awesome toolbar settings'
  mapping:
    cdn:
      type: boolean
      label: 'Use the FontAwesome CDN library'
    roboto:
      type: boolean
      label: 'Include Roboto from Google Fonts CDN'
```

This defines the `navbar_awesome.toolbar` configuration namespace; it belongs to the `navbar_awesome` module and has the `toolbar` configuration. We will then need two `cdn` and `roboto` subvalues that represent typed data values. A configuration YAML for this schema will be named `navbar_awesome.toolbar.yml` after the namespace, and it contains the following code:

```
cdn: true
roboto: true
```

In turn, this is what the values will look like when represented as a PHP array:

```
[
  'navbar_awesome' => [
    'cdn' => TRUE,
    'roboto' => TRUE,
  ]
]
```

The configuration factory classes then provide an object-based wrapper around these configuration definitions and provide validation of their values against the schema. For instance, if you try to save the `cdn` value as a string, a validation exception will be thrown.

See also

- Refer to `Chapter 4`, *Extending Drupal*
- Configuration schema/metadata in the Drupal.org community handbook at `https://www.drupal.org/node/1905070`

Synchronizing site configurations

A key component for managing a Drupal website is configuration integrity. A key part of maintaining this integrity is ensuring that your configuration changes made in development are pushed upstream to your production environments. Maintaining configuration changes by manually exporting and importing through the user interface can be tedious and does not provide a way to track what has or has not been exported or imported. At the same time, manually writing module hooks to manipulate the configuration can be time-consuming. Luckily, the configuration management solution provides you with the ability to export and import the entire site's configuration.

A site export can only be imported into another copy of itself. Each site must have the same UUID, which is set during its installation. This allows you to export your local development environment's configuration and bring it to staging or production, without modifying the content or the database directly.

In this recipe, we will export the development site's complete configuration entities' definitions. We will then take the exported configuration and import it into the production site. This will simulate a typical deployment of a Drupal site with changes created in development that is ready to be released in production.

Getting ready

You will need a base Drupal site to act as the development site. Another Drupal site, which is a duplicate of the development site's database, must be available to act as the production Drupal site.

You will need to have the **Configuration management** module installed if it is not already.

How to do it...

1. Go to the development site. Modify the site to simulate creating changes that need to be deployed to our other Drupal site.
2. For example, let's modify the site's name; go to the **Configuration** page and the **Basic site settings** form.
3. From the **Configuration** page, go to **Configuration synchronization**.
4. Navigate to the **Export** tab; we will land on the **Full archive** page. Click on the **Export** button to begin the export and download process:

5. Save the `gzipped` archive; this contains an archive of all the site's configuration as YAML.

6. Navigate to your other Drupal site and then to its **Configuration synchronization** page.

7. Click on the **Import** tab and then on the **Full archive** tab. Use the **Configuration archive** file input, and click on **Choose File** to select the tarball you just downloaded. Click on **Upload** to begin the import process.

8. You will be taken to the **Synchronize** tab to review changes that need to be imported:

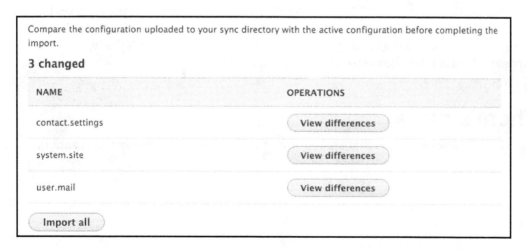

9. Click on **Import all** to update the current site's configuration to the items in the archive.

10. A batch operation will begin with the import process:

How it works...

The **Configuration synchronization** form provides a way to interface with the config database table for your Drupal site. When you go to the **Export** page and create the tarball, Drupal effectively dumps the contents of the config table. Each row represents a configuration entity and will become its own YAML file. The contents of the YAML file represent its database value.

When you import the tarball, Drupal extracts its content. The files are placed in the available CONFIG_SYNC_DIRECTORY directory. The synchronization page parses the configuration entity YAML and provides a difference check against the current site's configuration. Each configuration item can be reviewed, and then all the items can be imported. You cannot choose to selectively import individual items.

There's more...

We will now discuss things that are required for site configuration synchronization.

Universally Unique Identifier

When a Drupal site is installed, the UUID is set. This UUID is added to the exported configuration entities and is represented by the `uuid` key. Drupal uses this key to identify the source of the configuration. Drupal will not synchronize configurations that do not have a matching UUID in their YAML definition.

You can review the site's current UUID value by reviewing the `system.site` configuration object. This can also be done using the Drush or Drupal Console command-line tool.

Using Drush, type the following command:

```
$ drush config-get system.site
```

Using Drupal Console, type the following command:

```
$ drupal debug:config system.site
```

A synchronization folder

Drupal uses a synchronization folder to hold the configuration YAML files that are to be imported into the current site. This folder is represented by the `CONFIG_SYNC_DIRECTORY` constant. If you have not defined this in the global `$config_directories` variable in your site's `settings.php`, then it will be a randomly named directory in your site's file directory.

When Drupal 8 entered its beta release cycle, this folder was referenced as a staging folder and referenced by the `CONFIG_STAGING_DIRECTORY`. This is now deprecated; however, the internals of the configuration management system support reading `CONFIG_STAGING_DIRECTORY` as `CONFIG_SYNC_DIRECTORY`. This will be removed in Drupal 9.

The synchronization form will use the configuration management discovery service to look for configuration changes that need to be imported from this folder.

Installing a configuration from a new site

Drupal's configuration management system will not allow the import of configuration entities that originated at a different Drupal site. When a Drupal site is installed, the `system.site` configuration entity saves a UUID for the current site instance. Only cloned versions of this site's database can accept configuration imports from it.

The configuration installer profile is a custom distribution, that will allow you to import the configuration despite the configuration's site UUID. The profile doesn't install itself. When you use the profile, it will provide an interface to upload a configuration export that will then be imported, as shown in the following screenshot:

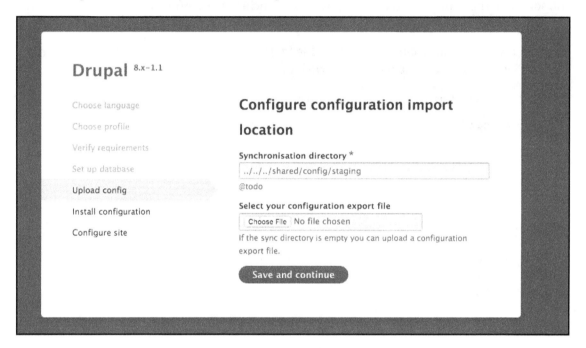

The distribution can be found at `https://www.drupal.org/project/config_installer`.

Using command-line workflow processes

Drupal 8's configuration systems solve many problems encountered when exporting and deploying configurations in Drupal 7. However, the task of synchronizing the configuration is still a user interface task and requires the manipulation of archive files that contain the configuration exports for a Drupal 8 site.

Configuration management can be done on the command line through Drush, without requiring it to be installed. This mitigates any requirement to log in to the production website to import changes. It also opens the ability for more advanced workflows that place the configuration in version control.

In this recipe, we will use Drush to export the development site's configuration to the filesystem. The exported configuration files will then be copied to the production site's configuration directory. Using Drush, the configuration will be imported into production to complete the deployment.

Getting ready...

You will need a base Drupal site to act as the development site. Another Drupal site, which is a clone of the development site, must be available to act as the production Drupal site.

This recipe uses Drush. If you have not installed Drush, instructions can be found at `http://docs.drush.org/en/master/install/`. Drush needs to be installed at the locations of both your Drupal sites.

How to do it...

1. For the purpose of demonstration, change your development site's name to `Drush Config Sync Demo!`. This way, there is at least one configuration change to be imported to the production Drupal site.
2. Open a command-line terminal and change your directory to the working directory of your development Drupal site.
3. Use the `drush config-export` command to export the configuration to a directory. The command will default to the `sync` configuration directory defined in your Drupal 8 site.

 If you have not explicitly defined a sync directory, Drupal automatically creates a protected folder in the current site's uploaded files' directory, with a unique hash suffix on the directory name.

4. You will receive a message that the configuration has been exported to the directory.
5. Using a method of your choice, copy the contents of the configuration `sync` folder to your other Drupal sites that match the `configuration sync` folder. For example, a default folder generated by Drupal can be `sites/default/files/config_XYZ/sync`.

6. Open a command-line terminal and change your directory to your production Drupal site's working directory.
7. Use the `drush config-import` command to begin the process of importing your configuration.
8. Review the changes made to the configuration entity keys and enter `y` to confirm the changes:

```
●  ●  ●                    www — -bash — 85×19
Matts-MacBook-Air:www mglaman$ drush config-get system.site
uuid: d847568b-4c6d-4826-9f41-65d40ede72a7
name: Site-Install
mail: admin@example.com
slogan: ''
page:
  403: ''
  404: ''
  front: /node
admin_compact_mode: false
weight_select_max: 100
langcode: en
default_langcode: en

Matts-MacBook-Air:www mglaman$ ▊
```

9. Check whether your configuration changes have been imported.

How it works...

The **Drush** command-line tool can utilize the code found in Drupal to interact with it. The `config-export` command replicates the functionality provided by the `Configuration management` module's full site export. However, you do not need the Configuration management module enabled for the command to work. The command will extract the available site configuration and write it to a directory, which is unarchived.

The `config-import` command parses the files in a directory. It will make an attempt to run a difference check against the YAML files like the Configuration management module's synchronize overview form does. It will then import all the changes.

There's more...

There are additional ways to work with the configuration management system in Drupal. We will explore those options in the next section.

Drush config-pull

Drush provides a way to simplify the transportation of configuration between sites. The `config-pull` command allows you to specify two Drupal sites and move the export configuration between them. You can either specify a name of a subdirectory under the `/sites` directory or a Drush alias.

The following command will copy a development site's configuration and import it into the staging server's site:

```
drush config-pull @mysite.local @mysite.staging
```

Additionally, you can specify the `--label` option. This represents a folder key in the `$config_directories` setting. The option defaults to `sync` automatically. Alternatively, you can use the `--destination` parameter to specify an arbitrary folder that is not specified in the setting of `$config_directories`.

Using the Drupal Console

Drush has been part of the Drupal community since Drupal 4.7 and is a custom-built command-line tool. The Drupal Console is a Symfony Console-based application used to interact with Drupal. The Drupal Console project provides a means for configuration management over the command line.

> You can learn more about the Drupal Console in *Chapter 13*, *Drupal CLI* or at http://www.drupalconsole.com/.

The workflow is the same, except the naming of the command. The configuration export command is `config:export`, and it is automatically exported to your system's temporary folder until a directory is passed. You can then import the configuration using the `config:import` command.

Editing the configuration from the command line

Both Drush and Drupal Console support the ability to edit the configuration through the command line in YAML format. Both the tools operate in the same fashion and have similar command names:

- **Drush**: `config-edit [name]`
- **Console**: `config:edit [name]`

The difference is that Drush will list all the available options to be edited if you do not pass a name, while Console allows you to search.

When you edit a configuration item, your default terminal-based text editor will open. You will be presented with a YAML file that can be edited. Once you save your changes, the configuration is then saved on your Drupal site:

```
www — web@rpusmp4jcny2c-master--php: ~/public — ssh · php ~/.composer/vendor/b...
uuid: c05bca85-1c2b-438c-a305-5ef617835d77
langcode: en
status: true
dependencies: {  }
name: 'Basic page'
type: page
description: 'Use <em>basic pages</em> for your static content, such as an ''About us''
page.'
help: ''
new_revision: false
preview_mode: 1
display_submitted: false
~
~
~
~
~
~
~
~
~
~
~
~
~
~
~
~
~
"/tmp/drush_tmp_1450234230_5670d1764a157/node.type.page.yml" 11 lines, 283 characters
```

Exporting a single configuration item

Both Drush and Console provide their own mechanisms for exporting a single configuration entity:

- **Drush**: `config-get [name]`
- **Console**: `config:debug [name]`

Drush will print the configuration's output to the terminal, whereas Console's default behavior is to write the output to the file disk. For example, the following commands will output the values from `system.site` in the YAML format:

```
$ drush config-get system.site
$ drupal debug:config system.site
```

```
● ● ●                    ▧ www — -bash — 85×19
Matts-MacBook-Air:www mglaman$ drush config-get system.site
uuid: d847568b-4c6d-4826-9f41-65d40ede72a7
name: Site-Install
mail: admin@example.com
slogan: ''
page:
  403: ''
  404: ''
  front: /node
admin_compact_mode: false
weight_select_max: 100
langcode: en
default_langcode: en

Matts-MacBook-Air:www mglaman$ ▊
```

Using version control and command-line workflow

A benefit of having the configuration exportable to YAML files is the fact that the configuration can be kept in version control. The Drupal site's `CONFIG_SYNC_DIRECTORY` directory can be committed to version control to ensure that it is transported across environments and properly updated. Deployment tools can then use Drush or Console to automatically import changes.

The `config-export` command provided by Drush provides the Git integration:

```
drush config-export --add
```

Appending the `--add` option will run `git add -p` for an interactive staging of the changed configuration files:

```
drush config-export --commit --message="Updating configuration "
```

The `--commit` and optional `--message` options will stage all configuration file changes and commit them with your message:

```
drush config-export --push --message="Updating configuration "
```

Finally, you can also specify `--push` to make a commit and push it to the remote repository.

See also

- Refer to `Chapter 13`, *The Drupal CLI*
- Refer to Drush at `http://docs.drush.org/en/master/`
- Refer to Drupal Console at `http://www.drupalconsole.com/`

Updating and installing new module configurations

Modules in Drupal 8 provide configuration YAML files inside their `config/install` directory. A consequence of the site controlling configuration is that a new configuration in a module's `config/install` directory is not automatically installed. Module developers must write update functions, which will import the new configuration as it is added. While this is a practice contributed modules should follow, this process can be cumbersome for private projects.

Luckily, the Drupal community has come up with a solution that provides a configuration management flow that allows updating of a module's provided default configuration. The module **Configuration Update Manager** allows you to import a new configuration from a module or revert it to the original configuration if modified. In fact, the module is a dependency for the Features module discussed in `Chapter 4`, *Extending Drupal*.

In this recipe, we will use Configuration Update Manager to review configuration differences to a module and revert the modified configuration.

How to do it...

1. Add the Configuration Update Manager project to your Drupal installation using the following Composer command:

```
$ cd /path/to/drupal8
$ composer require drupal/config_update
```

2. Go to the **Extend** page and install the **Configuration Update Reports** module, the user interface for Configuration Update Manager:

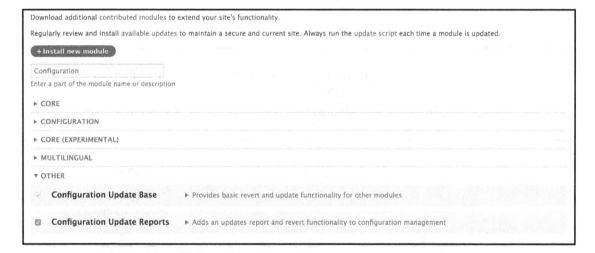

3. To visit the configuration reports, go to **Configuration** in the toolbar under the **Development** section and click on **Configuration synchronization**.
4. Go to the **Updates Report** tab. This provides an overview of configuration reports to generate: by configuration type, module, theme, and profile.
5. Review the System module's configuration. Select the **System** module from the module's drop-down button.

6. For the `system.site` row, click on the **Show differences** button link. This will review a difference report between the default configuration and the current site configuration:

SOURCE CONFIG		SITE CONFIG
	default_langcode : en	default_langcode : en
	langcode : en	langcode : en
−	mail :	+ mail : admin@example.com
−	name : Drupal	+ name : Site-Install
	page	page
−	page::front : /user/login	+ page::front : /node
	page::403 :	page::403 :
	page::404 :	page::404 :
	slogan :	slogan :
	weight_select_max : 100	weight_select_max : 100

Back to 'Updates report' page.

7. Click on the **Back to 'Updates report' page** to go back to the main report so that the configuration can be reverted.
8. Expand the drop-down button so that you can click on **Revert to source**:

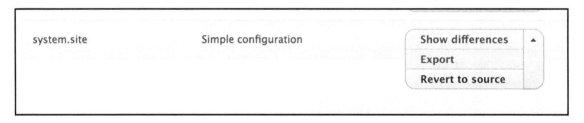

9. Click on **Revert** on the confirmation form to finish the operation.
10. The configuration is now reverted to its original installation.

How it works...

The Configuration Update Manager provides two modules: **Configuration Update Base** and **Configuration Update Reports**. The base module provides an underlying API for listing a configuration, reverting a configuration, and running difference checks with results. It extends Drupal core's configuration operations. The reports module provides a user interface on top of the base module. The Features module uses the base module to provide difference review and automatic reverting of a configuration.

When reverting a configuration, the raw values are collected and then used to overwrite what currently exists in the system. The reports also allow importing a new configuration added to a module.

There's more...

There are other contributed projects and methods for handling a configuration within modules.

The Configuration Development module

For module developers, there is the Configuration Development module. The Configuration Development module provides a command-line method for importing and exporting a configuration. This is useful for contributed module developers. It eases the exporting and update of a configuration intended for the `config/install` directory.

The module looks for a `config_devel` entry in the module's `info.yml` file. An example is taken from the Commerce Store submodule from Drupal Commerce module:

```
config_devel:
  install:
    - commerce_store.commerce_store_type.online
    - commerce_store.settings
    - core.entity_view_display.commerce_store.online.default
    - views.view.commerce_stores
    - system.action.commerce_delete_store_action
```

Using Drush, commands provided by the Configuration Development can then be used to export and import the data. The following command will export the listed configuration to the `config/install` directory:

```
$ drush config-devel-export commerce_store
```

See also

- Refer to Configuration Update Manager project page
  at `https://www.drupal.org/project/config_update`
- Refer to Configuration development, a command-line based alternative
  at `https://www.drupal.org/project/config_devel`

10
The Entity API

In this chapter, we will explore the Entity API to create custom entities and see how they are handled and cover the following recipes:

- Creating a configuration entity type
- Creating a content entity type
- Creating a bundle for a content entity type
- Implementing custom access control for an entity
- Providing a custom storage handler
- Creating a route provider

Introduction

In Drupal, entities are a representation of data that has a specific structure. There are specific entity types, which have different bundles and fields attached to those bundles. Bundles are implementations of entities that can have fields attached to themselves. In terms of programming, you can consider an entity that supports bundles as an abstract class and each bundle as a class that extends that abstract class. The fields are added to bundles. This is part of the reasoning for the terminology: an entity type can contain a *bundle* of fields.

An entity is an instance of an entity type defined in Drupal. Drupal 8 provides two entity types: `configuration` and `content`. Configuration entities are not fieldable and represent a configuration within a site. Content entities are fieldable and can have bundles. Bundles are, most commonly, controlled through configuration entities.

In Drupal 8, there is an **Entity API** module. It was created in Drupal 7 to expand the entity subsystem; most of its functionalities from Drupal 7 are now in its core. The goal of the module is to develop improvements for the developer experience around entities by merging more functionalities into the Drupal core during each minor release cycle (8.1.x, 8.2.x, and so on). There will be a *There's more...* section in each recipe that relates to how the Entity API module can simplify the recipe.

Creating a configuration entity type

Drupal 8 harnesses the entity API for configuration to provide configuration validation and extended functionality. Using the underlying entity structure, the configuration has a proper **Create**, **Read**, **Update**, and **Delete** (**CRUD**) process that can be managed. Configuration entities are not fieldable. All the attributes of a configuration entity are defined in its configuration schema definition.

Most common configuration entities interact with Drupal core's `config_object` type, as discussed in *Chapter 4*, *Extending Drupal*, and *Chapter 9*, *Configuration Management - Deploying in Drupal 8*, to store and manage a site's configuration. There are other uses of configuration entities, such as menus, view displays, form displays, and contact forms, which are all configuration entities.

In this recipe, we will create a new configuration entity type called `SiteAnnouncement`. This will provide a simple configuration entity that allows you to create, edit, and delete simple messages that can be displayed on the site for important announcements.

Getting ready

You will need a custom module to place code into to implement a configuration entity type. Let's create an `src` directory for your classes. Refer to the *Creating a module* recipe of *Chapter 4*, *Extending Drupal*, for information on creating a custom module.

Do not use a module that is currently installed, otherwise Drupal will not install your new entity type.

How to do it...

1. In our module's base directory, let's create a `config` directory with a `schema` subdirectory. In the subdirectory, create a file named `mymodule.schema.yml` that will hold your configuration entity's schema:

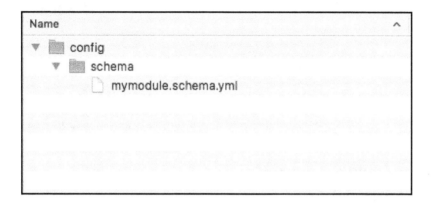

2. In our `mymodule.schema.yml`, add a definition to `mymodule.announcement.*:` to provide our label and message storage:

```
# Schema for the configuration files of the Site Announcement.

mymodule.announcement.*:
  type: config_entity
  label: 'Site announcement'
  mapping:
    id:
      type: string
      label: 'ID'
    label:
      type: label
      label: 'Label'
    message:
      type: text
      label: 'Text'
```

We will define the configuration entity's namespace as an announcement, which we will provide to Drupal in the entity's annotation block. We will then tell Drupal that this is a `config_entity` and provide a label for the schema.

Using the mapping array, we will provide the attributes that make up our entity and the data that will be stored.

3. Create an `Entity` directory in our module's `src` folder. First, we will create an interface for our entity by creating a `SiteAnnouncementInterface.php` file. The `SiteAnnouncementInterface` interface will extend the `\Drupal\Core\Config\Entity\ConfigEntityInterface`:

    ```php
    <?php

    namespace Drupal\mymodule\Entity;

    use Drupal\Core\Config\Entity\ConfigEntityInterface;

    interface SiteAnnouncementInterface extends ConfigEntityInterface {

      /**
       * Gets the message value.
       *
       * @return string
       */
      public function getMessage();

    }
    ```

    This will be implemented by our entity, and will provide the method requirements. It is best practice to provide an interface for entities. This allows you to provide the required methods if another developer extends your entity or if you are doing advanced testing and need to mock an object. We also provide a method to return our custom attribute.

4. Let's create `SiteAnnouncement.php` in our `src/Entity` directory. This file will contain the `SiteAnnouncement` class, which extends `\Drupal\Core\Config\Entity\ConfigEntityBase` and implements our entity's interface:

    ```php
    <?php

    namespace Drupal\mymodule\Entity;

    use Drupal\Core\Config\Entity\ConfigEntityBase;

    class SiteAnnouncement extends ConfigEntityBase implements
    SiteAnnouncementInterface {

      /**
    ```

```
 * The announcement's message.
 *
 * @var string
 */
protected $message;

/**
 * {@inheritdoc}
 */
public function getMessage() {
  return $this->message;
}


}
```

In the preceding code, we added the `message` property defined in our schema as a class property. Our method defined in the entity's interface is used to return that value and interact with our configuration entity.

5. Entities use annotation documentation blocks. We will start our annotation block by providing the entity's ID, label, configuration prefix, and configuration export key names:

```
<?php

namespace Drupal\mymodule\Entity;

use Drupal\Core\Config\Entity\ConfigEntityBase;

/**
 * @ConfigEntityType(
 *    id ="announcement",
 *    label = @Translation("Site Announcement"),
 *    config_prefix = "announcement",
 *    entity_keys = {
 *      "id" = "id",
 *      "label" = "label"
 *    },
 *    config_export = {
 *       "id",
 *       "label",
 *       "message",
 *    }
 * )
 */
class SiteAnnouncement extends ConfigEntityBase implements
SiteAnnouncementInterface {
```

```
/**
 * The announcement's message.
 *
 * @var string
 */
protected $message;

/**
 * {@inheritdoc}
 */
public function getMessage() {
  return $this->message;
}


}
```

The annotation document block tells Drupal that this is an instance of the `ConfigEntityType` plugin. The `id` is the internal machine name identifier for the entity type, and the `label` is its human-readable version. The `config_prefix` matches how we defined our schema with `mymodule.announcement`. The entity keys definition tells Drupal the attributes that represent our identifiers and labels.

When specifying `config_export`, we are telling the configuration management system what properties are exportable when exporting our entity.

6. Next, we will add `handlers` to our entity's annotation. We will define the class that will display the available entity entries and forms to work with our entity:

```
/**
 * @ConfigEntityType(
 *   id ="announcement",
 *   label = @Translation("Site Announcement"),
 *   handlers = {
 *     "list_builder" =
"Drupal\mymodule\SiteAnnouncementListBuilder",
 *     "form" = {
 *       "default" = "Drupal\mymodule\SiteAnnouncementForm",
 *       "add" = "Drupal\mymodule\SiteAnnouncementForm",
 *       "edit" = "Drupal\mymodule\SiteAnnouncementForm",
 *       "delete" = "Drupal\Core\Entity\EntityDeleteForm"
 *     }
 *   },
 *   config_prefix = "announcement",
 *   entity_keys = {
 *     "id" = "id",
 *     "label" = "label"
 *   },
```

```
 *      config_export = {
 *          "id",
 *          "label",
 *          "message",
 *      }
 *   )
 */
```

The `handlers` array specifies classes that provide the interaction functionality with our entity. The `list_builder` class will be created to show you a table of our entities. The `form` array provides classes for forms to be used when creating, editing, or deleting our configuration entity.

7. Lastly, for our entity's annotation, we will need to define routes for our `delete`, `edit`, and `collection` (list) pages. Drupal will automatically build the routes based on our annotation:

```
/**
 * @ConfigEntityType(
 *   id ="announcement",
 *   label = @Translation("Site Announcement"),
 *   handlers = {
 *     "list_builder" =
"Drupal\mymodule\SiteAnnouncementListBuilder",
 *     "form" = {
 *       "default" = "Drupal\mymodule\SiteAnnouncementForm",
 *       "add" = "Drupal\mymodule\SiteAnnouncementForm",
 *       "edit" = "Drupal\mymodule\SiteAnnouncementForm",
 *       "delete" = "Drupal\Core\Entity\EntityDeleteForm"
 *     }
 *   },
 *   config_prefix = "announcement",
 *   entity_keys = {
 *     "id" = "id",
 *     "label" = "label"
 *   },
 *   links = {
 *     "delete-form" = "/admin/config/system/site-
announcements/manage/{announcement}/delete",
 *     "edit-form" = "/admin/config/system/site-
announcements/manage/{announcement}",
 *     "collection" = "/admin/config/system/site-announcements",
 *   },
 *   config_export = {
 *     "id",
 *     "label",
 *     "message",
```

```
 *    }
 * )
 */
```

There is a routing service for entities that will automatically provide Drupal a route with the proper controllers based on this annotation.

8. Create the `SiteAnnouncementListBuilder` class defined in our `list_builder` handler by creating a `SiteAnnouncementListBuilder.php` file in the module's `src` directory and extending the `\Drupal\Core\Config\Entity\ConfigEntityListBuilder`:

```php
<?php

namespace Drupal\mymodule;

use Drupal\Core\Config\Entity\ConfigEntityListBuilder;
use Drupal\mymodule\Entity\SiteAnnouncementInterface;

class SiteAnnouncementListBuilder extends ConfigEntityListBuilder {

  /**
   * {@inheritdoc}
   */
  public function buildHeader() {
    $header['label'] = t('Label');
    return $header + parent::buildHeader();
  }

  /**
   * {@inheritdoc}
   */
  public function buildRow(SiteAnnouncementInterface $entity) {
    $row['label'] = $entity->label();
    return $row + parent::buildRow($entity);
  }
}
```

In our list builder handler, we override the `buildHeader` and `builderRow` methods so that we can add our configuration entity's properties to the table.

9. Now, we will need to create an entity form, as defined in our form handler array, to handle our add and edit functionalities. Create `SiteAnnouncementForm.php` in the `src` directory to provide the `SiteAnnouncementForm` class that extends the `\Drupal\Core\Entity\EntityForm` class:

```php
<?php

namespace Drupal\mymodule;

use Drupal\Component\Utility\Unicode;
use Drupal\Core\Entity\EntityForm;
use Drupal\Core\Form\FormStateInterface;
use Drupal\Core\Language\LanguageInterface;

class SiteAnnouncementForm extends EntityForm {
  /**
   * {@inheritdoc}
   */
  public function form(array $form, FormStateInterface $form_state)
  {
    $form = parent::form($form, $form_state);

    $form['label'] = [
      '#type' => 'textfield',
      '#title' => t('Label'),
      '#required' => TRUE,
      '#default_value' => $entity->label(),
    ];
    $form['message'] = [
      '#type' => 'textarea',
      '#title' => t('Message'),
      '#required' => TRUE,
      '#default_value' => $entity->getMessage(),
    ];

    return $form;
  }

  /**
   * {@inheritdoc}
   */
  public function save(array $form, FormStateInterface $form_state)
  {
    $entity = $this->entity;
    $is_new = !$entity->getOriginalId();

    if ($is_new) {
```

```
      // Configuration entities need an ID manually set.
      $machine_name = \Drupal::transliteration()
        ->transliterate($entity->label(),
LanguageInterface::LANGCODE_DEFAULT, '_');
      $entity->set('id', Unicode::strtolower($machine_name));

      drupal_set_message(t('The %label announcement has been
created.', array('%label' => $entity->label())));
    }
    else {
      drupal_set_message(t('Updated the %label announcement.',
array('%label' => $entity->label())));
    }

    $entity->save();

    // Redirect to edit form so we can populate colors.
$form_state->setRedirectUrl($this->entity->toUrl('collection'));
  }
}
```

We override the `form` method to add Form API elements to our `label` and
`message` properties. We also override the `save` method to provide user messages
about the changes that are made. We utilize the entity's `toUrl` method to redirect
it to the `collection` (list) page. We use the transliteration service to generate a
machine name based on the label for our entity's identifier.

10. Next, we will create a `mymodule.links.action.yml` file in our module's
    directory. This will allow us to define action links on a route. We will be adding
    an `Add announcement` link to our entity's add form on its collection route:

```
announcement.add:
  route_name: entity.announcement.add_form
  title: 'Add announcement'
  appears_on:
    - entity.announcement.collection
```

This will instruct Drupal to render the `entity.announcement.add_form` link on
the specified routes in the `appears_on` value.

11. To have our site announcement's accessible from the main administrative pages, we will need to create a `mymodule.links.menu.yml` file in our module's directory:

```
mymodule.site_announcements:
  title: 'Site announcements'
  parent: system.admin_config_system
  description: 'Manage site announcements.'
  route_name: entity.announcement.collection
```

12. Our module structure should look like the following screenshot:

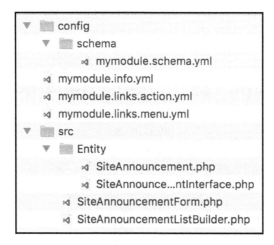

13. Install the module and check out the **Configuration** page. You can now manage the `Site Announcement` entries from the **Site Announcement** link.

How it works...

When creating a configuration schema definition, one of the first properties used for the configuration namespace is `type`. This value can be `config_object` or `config_entity`. When the type is `config_entity`, the definition will be used to create a database table rather than to structure the serialized data for the `config` table.

Entities are powered by the plugin system in Drupal, which means that there is a plugin manager. The default `\Drupal\Core\Entity\EntityTypeManager` provides discovery and handling of entities. The `ConfigEntityType` class for the entity type's plugin class will force the setting of the `uuid` and `langcode` in the `entity_keys` definition. The storage handler for configuration entities defaults to `\Drupal\Core\Config\Entity\ConfigEntityStorage`. The `ConfigEntityStorage` class interacts with the configuration management system to load, save, and delete custom configuration entities.

There's more...

Drupal 8 introduces a typed data system that configuration entities and fields use.

Available data types for schema definitions

Drupal core provides its own configuration information. There is a `core.data_types.schema.yml` file located at `core/config/schema`. These are the base types of data that the core provides and can be used when making configuration schema. The file contains YAML definitions of data types and the class that represents them:

```
boolean:
  label: 'Boolean'
  class: '\Drupal\Core\TypedData\Plugin\DataType\BooleanData'
email:
  label: 'Email'
  class: '\Drupal\Core\TypedData\Plugin\DataType\Email'
string:
  label: 'String'
  class: '\Drupal\Core\TypedData\Plugin\DataType\StringData'
```

When a configuration schema definition specifies an attribute that has an email for its type, that value is then handled by the `\Drupal\Core\TypedData\Plugin\DataType\Email` class. Data types are a form of plugins, and each plugin's annotation specifies constraints for validation. This is built around the Symfony **Validator** component.

See also

- Refer to Chapter 6, *Creating Forms with the Form API*
- Refer to Chapter 4, *Extending Drupal*
- Refer to Chapter 9, *Confiuration Management - Deploying in Drupal 8*
- Refer to configuration schema/metadata
  at https://www.drupal.org/node/1905070

Creating a content entity type

Content entities provide base field definitions and configurable fields through the Field module. There is also support for revisions and translations with content entities. Display modes, both form and view, are available for content entities to control how the fields are edited and displayed. When an entity does not specify bundles, there is automatically one bundle instance with the same name as the entity.

In this recipe, we will create a custom content entity that does not specify a bundle. We will create a Message entity that can serve as a content entity for generic messages.

Getting ready

You will need a custom module to place code into to implement a configuration entity type. Create an src directory for your classes. Refer to the *Creating a module* recipe of Chapter 4, *Extending Drupal*, for information on creating a custom module.

Do not use a module which is currently installed, otherwise Drupal will not install your new entity type.

How to do it...

1. Let's create an `Entity` directory in our module's `src` folder. First, we will create an interface for our entity by creating a `MessageInterface.php` file:

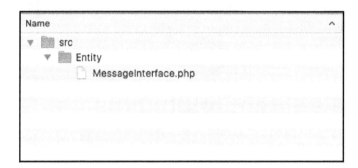

2. The `MessageInterface` will extend `\Drupal\Core\Entity\ContentEntityInterface`:

```php
<?php

namespace Drupal\mymodule\Entity;

use Drupal\Core\Entity\ContentEntityInterface;

interface MessageInterface extends ContentEntityInterface {

  /**
   * Gets the message value.
   *
   * @return string
   */
  public function getMessage();

}
```

This will be implemented by our entity and will provide the method requirements. It is best practice to provide an interface for entities. This allows you to provide required methods if another developer extends your entity or if you are doing advanced testing and need to mock an object. We also provide a method to return our main base field definition (to be defined).

3. Then, let's create `Message.php` in our `Entity` directory in `src`. This file will contain the `Message` class, which extends `\Drupal\Core\Entity\ContentEntityBase` and implements our entity's interface:

```php
<?php

namespace Drupal\mymodule\Entity;

use Drupal\Core\Entity\ContentEntityBase;

class Message extends ContentEntityBase implements MessageInterface
{

}
```

4. We will need to create an annotation document block on our class to provide information about our entity, such as its `id`, `label`, and `entity` keys:

```php
<?php

namespace Drupal\mymodule\Entity;

use Drupal\Core\Entity\ContentEntityBase;

/**
 * Defines the message entity class.
 *
 * @ContentEntityType(
 *   id = "message",
 *   label = @Translation("Message"),
 *   base_table = "message",
 *   fieldable = TRUE,
 *   entity_keys = {
 *     "id" = "message_id",
 *     "label" = "title",
 *     "langcode" = "langcode",
 *     "uuid" = "uuid"
 *   },
 * )
 */
class Message extends ContentEntityBase implements MessageInterface
{

}
```

The id is the internal machine name identifier for the entity type, and the `label` is its human-readable version. The entity keys definition tells Drupal the attributes that represent our identifier and label.

The `base_table` defines the database table in which the entity will be stored, and `fieldable` allows custom fields to be configured through the Field UI module.

5. Next, we will add `handlers` to our entity. We will use the default handlers provided by Drupal:

```
/**
 * Defines the message entity class.
 *
 * @ContentEntityType(
 *   id = "message",
 *   label = @Translation("Message"),
 *   handlers = {
 *     "list_builder" = "Drupal\mymodule\MessageListBuilder",
 *     "form" = {
 *       "default" = "Drupal\Core\Entity\EntityForm",
 *       "add" = "Drupal\Core\Entity\EntityForm",
 *       "edit" = "Drupal\Core\Entity\EntityForm",
 *       "delete" = "Drupal\Core\Entity\ContentEntityDeleteForm",
 *     },
 *   },
 *   base_table = "message",
 *   fieldable = TRUE,
 *   entity_keys = {
 *     "id" = "message_id",
 *     "label" = "title",
 *     "langcode" = "langcode",
 *     "uuid" = "uuid"
 *   },
 * )
 */
```

The `handlers` array specifies classes that provide the interaction functionality with our entity. The list builder class will be created to show you a table of our entities. The form array provides classes for forms to be used when creating, editing, or deleting our content entity.

6. An additional `handler`, the `route_provider`, can be added to dynamically generate our canonical (view), `edit`, `add`, `delete`, and `collection` (list) routes:

```
/**
 * Defines the message entity class.
 *
 * @ContentEntityType(
 *   id = "message",
 *   label = @Translation("Message"),
 *   handlers = {
 *     "list_builder" = "Drupal\mymodule\MessageListBuilder",
 *     "form" = {
 *       "default" = "Drupal\Core\Entity\EntityForm",
 *       "add" = "Drupal\Core\Entity\EntityForm",
 *       "edit" = "Drupal\Core\Entity\EntityForm",
 *       "delete" = "Drupal\Core\Entity\ContentEntityDeleteForm",
 *     },
 *     "route_provider" = {
 *       "html" =
"Drupal\Core\Entity\Routing\DefaultHtmlRouteProvider",
 *     },
 *   },
 *   base_table = "message",
 *   fieldable = TRUE,
 *   entity_keys = {
 *     "id" = "message_id",
 *     "label" = "title",
 *     "langcode" = "langcode",
 *     "uuid" = "uuid"
 *   },
 *   links = {
 *     "canonical" = "/messages/{message}",
 *     "edit-form" = "/messages/{message}/edit",
 *     "delete-form" = "/messages/{message}/delete",
 *     "collection" = "/admin/content/messages"
 *   },
 * )
 */
```

There is a routing service for entities that will automatically provide Drupal a route with the proper controllers based on this annotation.

7. We will then define an administration permission property in our entity's annotation, which the system checks, by default, for all create, update, and delete operations:

```
/**
 * Defines the message entity class.
 *
 * @ContentEntityType(
 *   id = "message",
 *   label = @Translation("Message"),
 *   handlers = {
 *     "list_builder" = "Drupal\mymodule\MessageListBuilder",
 *     "form" = {
 *       "default" = "Drupal\Core\Entity\EntityForm",
 *       "add" = "Drupal\Core\Entity\EntityForm",
 *       "edit" = "Drupal\Core\Entity\EntityForm",
 *       "delete" = "Drupal\Core\Entity\ContentEntityDeleteForm",
 *     },
 *     "route_provider" = {
 *       "html" =
"Drupal\Core\Entity\Routing\DefaultHtmlRouteProvider",
 *     },
 *   },
 *   admin_permission = "administer message",
 *   base_table = "message",
 *   fieldable = TRUE,
 *   entity_keys = {
 *     "id" = "message_id",
 *     "label" = "title",
 *     "langcode" = "langcode",
 *     "uuid" = "uuid"
 *   },
 *   links = {
 *     "canonical" = "/messages/{message}",
 *     "add-form" = "/messages/add",
 *     "edit-form" = "/messages/{message}/edit",
 *     "delete-form" = "/messages/{message}/delete",
 *     "collection" = "/admin/content/messages"
 *   },
 * )
 */
```

8. We will need to implement the `baseFieldDefinitions` method to satisfy the `FieldableEntityInterface` interface, which will provide our field definitions to the entity's base table. Add the following method to your class:

```php
/**
 * {@inheritdoc}
 */
public static function baseFieldDefinitions(EntityTypeInterface
$entity_type) {
  $fields = parent::baseFieldDefinitions($entity_type);

  $fields['title'] = BaseFieldDefinition::create('string')
    ->setLabel(t('Title'))
    ->setRequired(TRUE)
    ->setTranslatable(TRUE)
    ->setRevisionable(TRUE)
    ->setSetting('max_length', 255)
    ->setDisplayOptions('view', array(
      'label' => 'hidden',
      'type' => 'string',
      'weight' => -5,
    ))
    ->setDisplayOptions('form', array(
      'type' => 'string_textfield',
      'weight' => -5,
    ))
    ->setDisplayConfigurable('form', TRUE);

  $fields['content'] = BaseFieldDefinition::create('text_long')
    ->setLabel(t('Content'))
    ->setDescription(t('Content of the message'))
    ->setTranslatable(TRUE)
    ->setDisplayOptions('view', array(
      'label' => 'hidden',
      'type' => 'text_default',
      'weight' => 0,
    ))
    ->setDisplayConfigurable('view', TRUE)
    ->setDisplayOptions('form', array(
      'type' => 'text_textfield',
      'weight' => 0,
    ))
    ->setDisplayConfigurable('form', TRUE);

  return $fields;
}
```

The `FieldableEntityInterface` is implemented by the `ContentEntityBase` class using the `ContentEntityInterface`. The method needs to return an array of `BaseFieldDefinitions` for typed data definitions. The parent class provides field definitions for most of the `entity_keys` value in our entity's annotation. We must provide the label field and any specific fields for our implementation.

The `content` base field definition will hold the actual text of the message.

9. Next, we will implement the `getMessage` method in our class to satisfy our interface and provide a means to retrieve our message's text value:

```
/**
 * {@inheritdoc}
 */
public function getMessage() {
  return $this->get('content')->value;
}
```

This method provides a wrapper around the defined base field's value and returns it.

10. Create the `MessageListBuilder` class defined in our `list_builder` handler by creating a `MessageListBuilder.php` file and extending `\Drupal\Core\Entity\EntityListBuilder`. We will need to override the default implementation to display our base field definitions:

```php
<?php

namespace Drupal\mymodule;

use Drupal\Core\Entity\EntityInterface;
use Drupal\Core\Entity\EntityListBuilder;

class MessageListBuilder extends EntityListBuilder {
  public function buildHeader() {
    $header['title'] = t('Title');
    return $header + parent::buildHeader();
  }

  public function buildRow(EntityInterface $entity) {
    $row['title'] = $entity->label();
    return $row + parent::buildRow($entity);
  }

}
```

In our list builder handler, we override the `buildHeader` and `builderRow` methods so that we can add our configuration entity's properties to the table.

11. Before we move on, we must create a `mymodule.permissions.yml` file in the module's root directory. We will need to provide the permission definition for `administer message`, as provided in our annotation:

```
administer message:
    title: 'Administer messages'
```

12. Our module's structure should resemble the following screenshot:

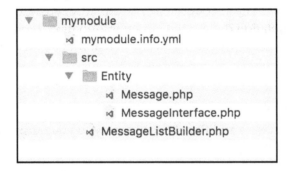

13. Install the module. Go to `/messages/add` to create our first custom content entity entry and then view it on `/admin/content/messages`:

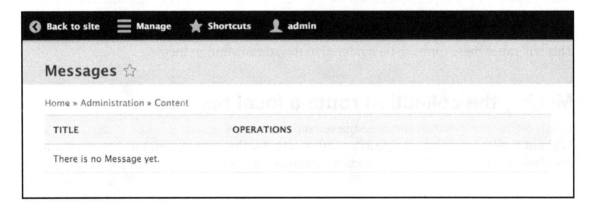

How it works...

Content entities are a version of the `EntityType` plugin. When you define a content entity type, the annotation block begins with `@ContentEntityType`. This declaration and the properties in it represent the definition to initiate an instance of the `\Drupal\Core\Entity\ContentEntityType`, class just like all other plugin annotations. The `ContentEntityType` plugin class implements a constructor to provide default `storage` and `view_builder` handlers, forcing us to implement the `list_builder` and `form` handler arrays.

The plugin manager for entity types lives under the `entity_type.manager` service name and is provided through `\Drupal\Core\Entity\EntityTypeManager` by default. However, while the annotation defines the plugin information, our `Message` class that extends `ContentEntityBase` provides a means to manipulate the data it represents.

There's more...

We will discuss how to add an additional functionality to your entity and use the Entity module to simplify the developer expedience.

Using the AdminHtmlRouteProvider provider

Our `Message` entity type implements the `DefaultHtmlRouteProvider` class. There is also the `\Drupal\Core\Entity\Routing\AdminHtmlRouteProvider` class. This overrides the `getEditFormRoute` and `getDeleteFormRoute` and marks them with `_admin_route`. This will cause these forms to be rendered in the administration theme.

Making the collection route a local task tab

In this recipe, we specified the message collection route as `/admin/content/messages`. Without implementing this route as a local task under the `/admin/content` route, it will not show up as a tab. This can be done by creating a `links.task.yml` file for the module.

In `mymodule.links.task.yml`, add the following YAML content:

```
entity.message.collection_tab:
  route_name: entity.message.collection
  base_route: system.admin_content
  title: 'Messages'
```

This instructs Drupal to use the `entity.message.collection` route, defined in our `routing.yml` file, to be based under the `system.admin_content` route:

See also

- Refer to *Chapter 4, Extending Drupal*

Creating a bundle for a content entity type

Bundles allow you to have different variations of a content entity. All bundles share the same base field definitions but not configured fields. This allows each bundle to have its own custom fields. Display modes are also dependent on a specific bundle. This allows each bundle to have its own configuration for the form mode and view mode.

Using the custom entity from the preceding recipe, we will add a configuration entity to act as the bundle. This will allow you to have different message types for multiple custom field configurations.

Getting ready

We will need a custom module to place the code into to implement a configuration entity type. Create an `src` directory for your classes. We need a custom content entity type to be implemented, such as the one in the *Creating a content entity type* recipe of this chapter.

How to do it...

1. Since content entity bundles are configuration entities, we will need to define our configuration entity schema. Create a `config/schema` directory and `mymodule.schema.yml` file that will contain the configuration entity's schema:

```
mymodule.message_type.*:
  type: config_entity
  label: 'Message type settings'
  mapping:
    id:
      type: string
      label: 'Machine-readable name'
    uuid:
      type: string
      label: 'UUID'
    label:
      type: label
      label: 'Label'
    langcode:
      type: string
      label: 'Default language'
```

We will define the configuration entity's config prefix as `message_type`, which we will provide to Drupal in the entity's annotation block. We will tell Drupal that this is a `config_entity` and provide a label for the schema.

With the mapping array, we provide the attributes that make up our entity and the data that will be stored.

2. In our module's `src/Entity` directory, let's create an interface for our bundle by creating a `MessageTypeInterface.php` file. The `MessageTypeInterface` will extend the `\Drupal\Core\Config\Entity\ConfigEntityInterface`:

```php
<?php

namespace Drupal\mymodule\Entity;

use Drupal\Core\Config\Entity\ConfigEntityInterface;

interface MessageTypeInterface extends ConfigEntityInterface {
  // Empty for future enhancements.
}
```

This will be implemented by our entity and will provide the method requirements. It is best practice to provide an interface for entities. This allows you to provide required methods if another developer extends your entity or if you are doing advanced testing and need to mock an object.

We will be implementing a very basic bundle. It is still wise to provide an interface in the event of future enhancements and mocking ability in tests.

3. Create a `MessageType.php` file in `src/Entity`. This will hold the `MessageType` class, which will extend `\Drupal\Core\Config\Entity\ConfigEntityBundleBase` and implement our bundle's interface:

```php
<?php

namespace Drupal\mymodule\Entity;

use Drupal\Core\Config\Entity\ConfigEntityBundleBase;

class MessageType extends ConfigEntityBundleBase implements
MessageTypeInterface {

}
```

In most use cases, the bundle entity class can be an empty class that does not provide any properties or methods. If a bundle provides additional attributes in its schema definition, they would also be provided here, like any other configuration entity.

4. Entities need to be annotated. Create a base annotation for the `id`, `label`, `entity` keys, and `config_export` keys:

```php
<?php

namespace Drupal\mymodule\Entity;

use Drupal\Core\Config\Entity\ConfigEntityBundleBase;

/**
 * Defines the message type entity class.
 *
 * @ConfigEntityType(
 *   id = "message_type",
 *   label = @Translation("Message type"),
 *   config_prefix = "message_type",
 *   bundle_of = "message",
 *   entity_keys = {
 *     "id" = "id",
 *     "label" = "label"
 *   },
 *   config_export = {
 *     "id",
 *     "label",
 *   },
 * )
 */
class MessageType extends ConfigEntityBundleBase implements
MessageTypeInterface {

}
```

The annotation document block tells Drupal that this is an instance of the `ConfigEntityType` plugin. The `id` is the internal machine name identifier for the entity type and the `label` is its human-readable version. The `config_prefix` matches how we defined our schema using `mymodule.message_type`. The entity keys definition tells Drupal which attributes represent our identifiers and labels.

When specifying `config_export`, we are telling the configuration management system what properties are to be exported when exporting our entity.

5. We will then add handlers, which will interact with our entity:

```
/**
 * Defines the message type entity class.
 *
 * @ConfigEntityType(
 *   id = "message_type",
 *   label = @Translation("Message type"),
 *   handlers = {
 *     "list_builder" = "Drupal\mymodule\MessageTypeListBuilder",
 *     "form" = {
 *       "default" = "Drupal\Core\Entity\EntityForm",
 *       "add" = "Drupal\Core\Entity\EntityForm",
 *       "edit" = "Drupal\Core\Entity\EntityForm",
 *       "delete" = "Drupal\Core\Entity\EntityDeleteForm"
 *     },
 *   },
 *   config_prefix = "message_type",
 *   bundle_of = "message",
 *   entity_keys = {
 *     "id" = "id",
 *     "label" = "label"
 *   },
 *   config_export = {
 *     "id",
 *     "label",
 *   },
 * )
 */
```

The `handlers` array specifies classes that provide the interaction functionality with our entity. The list builder class will be created to show you a table of our entities. The form array provides classes for forms to be used when creating, editing, or deleting our configuration entity.

6. An additional handler, the `route_provider`, can be added to dynamically generate our canonical (view), `edit`, `delete`, and `collection` (list) routes:

```
/**
 * Defines the message type entity class.
 *
 * @ConfigEntityType(
 *   id = "message_type",
 *   label = @Translation("Message type"),
 *   handlers = {
 *     "list_builder" = "Drupal\mymodule\MessageTypeListBuilder",
 *     "form" = {
```

```
 *          "default" = "Drupal\Core\Entity\EntityForm",
 *          "add" = "Drupal\Core\Entity\EntityForm",
 *          "edit" = "Drupal\Core\Entity\EntityForm",
 *          "delete" = "Drupal\Core\Entity\EntityDeleteForm"
 *        },
 *        "route_provider" = {
 *          "html" =
"Drupal\Core\Entity\Routing\DefaultHtmlRouteProvider",
 *        },
 *      },
 *    config_prefix = "message_type",
 *    bundle_of = "message",
 *    entity_keys = {
 *      "id" = "id",
 *      "label" = "label"
 *    },
 *    config_export = {
 *      "id",
 *      "label",
 *    },
 *    links = {
 *      "add-form" = "/admin/structure/message-types/add",
 *      "delete-form" = "/admin/structure/message-
types/{message_type}/delete",
 *      "edit-form" = "/admin/structure/message-
types/{message_type}",
 *      "admin-form" = "/admin/structure/message-
types/{message_type}",
 *      "collection" = "/admin/structure/message-types"
 *    }
 *  )
 */
```

There is a routing service for entities that will automatically provide Drupal a route with the proper controllers based on this annotation. The add form route is not yet supported and needs to be manually added.

7. We will need to modify our content entity to use the bundle configuration entity that we defined. Edit the `src/Entity/Message.php` file and adjust the entity annotation:

```
/**
 * Defines the message entity class.
 *
 * @ContentEntityType(
 *   id = "message",
 *   label = @Translation("Message"),
```

```
 *    handlers = {...},
 *    base_table = "message",
 *    fieldable = TRUE,
 *    bundle_entity_type = "message_type",
 *    field_ui_base_route = "entity.message_type.edit_form",
 *    entity_keys = {
 *      "id" = "message_id",
 *      "label" = "title",
 *      "langcode" = "langcode",
 *      "bundle" = "type",
 *      "uuid" = "uuid"
 *    },
 *    links = {...},
 * )
 */
```

The bundle_entity_type key specifies the entity type used as the bundle. The plugin validates this as an actual entity type and marks it for configuration dependencies. With the field_ui_base_route key pointed to the bundle's main edit form, it will generate the Manage Fields, Manage Form Display, and Manage Display tabs on the bundles. Finally, the bundle entity key instructs Drupal on the field definition to be used to identify the entity's bundle, which is created in the next step.

With the bundle entity key added, the ContentEntityBase class will automatically add an entity reference base field called type to our entity, referencing the bundle configuration entity type.

8. Create the MessageTypeListBuilder class defined in our list_builder handler in a MessageTypeListBuilder.php file and extend \Drupal\Core\Config\Entity\ConfigEntityListBuilder. We will need to override the default implementation to display our configuration entity properties:

```php
<?php

namespace Drupal\mymodule;

use Drupal\Core\Entity\EntityInterface;
use Drupal\Core\Config\Entity\ConfigEntityListBuilder;

class MessageTypeListBuilder extends EntityListBuilder {
  public function buildHeader() {
    $header['label'] = t('Label');
    return $header + parent::buildHeader();
```

```
    }

    public function buildRow(EntityInterface $entity) {
      $row['label'] = $entity->label();
      return $row + parent::buildRow($entity);
    }

  }
```

9. In our list builder handler, we will override the `buildHeader` and `builderRow` methods so that we can add our configuration entity's properties to the table:

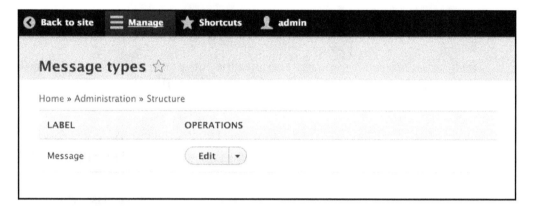

10. Our module's structure should resemble the following screenshot:

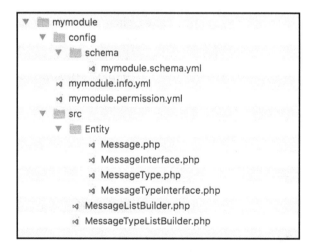

How it works...

Bundles are most utilized in the configured field levels via the `Field` and `Field UI` modules. When you create a new field, it has a base storage item for its global settings. Once a field is added to a bundle, there is a new field configuration that is created and assigned to the bundle. Fields can then have their own settings for a specific bundle along with form and view display configurations.

Content entity bundles work just like any other configuration entity implementation, but they extend the usability of the Field API for your content entity types.

There's more...

We will discuss how to add additional functionality to our entity bundle and use the Entity module to simplify the developer expedience.

Provide action links for adding new bundles

There are special links called **action links** in Drupal. These appear at the top of the page and are generally used for links that allow the creation of an item by creating a `links.action.yml` file.

In your `mymodule.links.action.yml`, each action link defines the route it will link to, titles, and the routes it appears on:

```
message_type_add:
  route_name: entity.message_type.add_form
  title: 'Add message type'
  appears_on:
    - entity.message_type.collection
```

The `appears_on` key accepts multiple values that will allow this route link to appear on multiple pages:

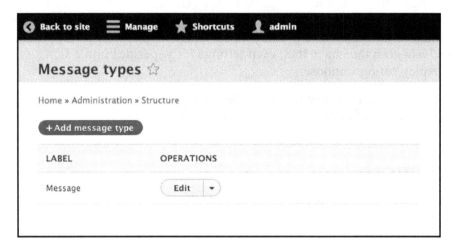

See also

- Refer to `Chapter 4`, *Extending Drupal*
- Refer to `Chapter 9`, *Configuration Management - Deploying in Drupal 8*
- Refer to the *Creating a Configuration Entity type* recipe in `Chapter 10`, *The Entity API*

Implementing custom access control for an entity

All entities have a set of handlers that control specific pieces of functionalities. One handler handles access control. When the access handler is not specified, the base `\Drupal\Core\Entity\EntityType` module will implement `\Drupal\Core\Entity\EntityAccessControlHandler` as the access handler. By default, this will check whether any modules have implemented `hook_entity_create_access` or `hook_entity_type_create_access` and use their opinions. Otherwise, it defaults to the admin permission for the entity type, if implemented.

In this recipe, we will provide an admin permission for our entity and implement the access handler and permission provider available through the Entity API module. We will base this on an entity called **Message**.

 This recipe specifically uses the functionality from the Entity API module because it has been tested and thoroughly reviewed and reduces boilerplate code. Ideally, this will be part of an upcoming minor release of Drupal core.

Getting ready

We will need a custom module to place the code into to implement a configuration entity type. Let's create an `src` directory for our PSR-4 style classes. We will need to implement a custom content entity type, such as the one in the *Creating a content entity type* recipe of this chapter.

How to do it...

1. First, we will need to define an administration permission for the entity. This is done by ensuring that the `admin_permission` key is present in the entity's annotation document block:

```
/**
 * Defines the message entity class.
 *
 * @ContentEntityType(
 *   id = "message",
 *   label = @Translation("Message"),
 *   handlers = {...},
 *   base_table = "message",
 *   fieldable = TRUE,
 *   admin_permission = "administer messages",
 *   entity_keys = {
 *     "id" = "message_id",
 *     "label" = "title",
 *     "langcode" = "langcode",
 *     "uuid" = "uuid"
 *   },
 *   links = {...},
 * )
 */
```

The entity access handler provided by the core will check whether entities implement this option. If it is provided, it will be used as the basis for access checks.

2. Next, we will want to specify permissions that are granular per bundle:

```
/**
 * Defines the message entity class.
 *
 * @ContentEntityType(
 *   id = "message",
 *   label = @Translation("Message"),
 *   handlers = {...},
 *   base_table = "message",
 *   fieldable = TRUE,
 *   admin_permission = "administer messages",
 *   permission_granularity = "bundle",
 *   bundle_entity_type = "message_type",
 *   field_ui_base_route = "entity.message_type.edit_form",
 *   entity_keys = {
 *     "id" = "message_id",
 *     "label" = "title",
 *     "langcode" = "langcode",
 *     "bundle" = "type",
 *     "uuid" = "uuid"
 *   },
 *   links = {...},
 * )
 */
```

The `permission_granularity` key will tell the system what permissions should be generated and how the access should be checked. This way, one user could create *Announcement* messages but not *Bulletin* messages.

3. Then, we define the `permission_provider` handler, which will generate our permissions:

```
/**
 * Defines the message entity class.
 *
 * @ContentEntityType(
 *   id = "message",
 *   label = @Translation("Message"),
 *   handlers = {
 *     "list_builder" = "Drupal\mymodule\MessageListBuilder",
 *     "permission_provider" =
"\Drupal\entity\EntityPermissionProvider",
```

```
 *      "form" = {...},
 *      "route_provider" = {...},
 *    },
 *    base_table = "message",
 *    fieldable = TRUE,
 *    admin_permission = "administer messages",
 *    permission_granularity = "bundle",
 *    bundle_entity_type = "message_type",
 *    field_ui_base_route = "entity.message_type.edit_form",
 *    entity_keys = {...},
 *  links = {...},
 * )
 */
```

4. The final adjustment to our entity annotation is to change the default access handler:

```
/**
 * Defines the message entity class.
 *
 * @ContentEntityType(
 *   id = "message",
 *   label = @Translation("Message"),
 *   handlers = {
 *     "list_builder" = "Drupal\mymodule\MessageListBuilder",
 *     "access" = "\Drupal\entity\EntityAccessControlHandler",
 *     "permission_provider" =
"\Drupal\entity\EntityPermissionProvider",
 *       "form" = {...},
 *       "route_provider" = {...},
 *     },
 *   base_table = "message",
 *   fieldable = TRUE,
 *   admin_permission = "administer messages",
 *   permission_granularity = "bundle",
 *   bundle_entity_type = "message_type",
 *   field_ui_base_route = "entity.message_type.edit_form",
 *   entity_keys = {...},
 *  links = {...},
 * )
 */
```

5. Rebuild Drupal's caches, or install the module if it is not yet installed.

6. Verify that the permissions are available on the permission's overview page:

PERMISSION	ANONYMOUS USER	AUTHENTICATED USER	ADMINISTRATOR
My Module			
Administer messages *Warning: Give to trusted roles only; this permission has security implications.*	☐	☐	☑
Message: Add message	☐	☐	☑
Message: Delete message	☐	☐	☑
Message: Edit message	☐	☐	☑
Message: View message	☐	☐	☑

How it works...

Entities are powered by the plugin system in Drupal, which means that there is a plugin manager. The default \Drupal\Core\Entity\EntityTypeManager provides the discovery and handling of entities. Both the ContentEntityType and ConfigEntityType entity types and classes extend the base \Drupal\Core\Entity\EntityType class.

The EntityType class constructor provides a default access handler if it is not provided through the \Drupal\Core\Entity\EntityAccessControlHandler class. Every core module that provides an entity type implements this to override at least checkAccess and checkCreateAccess. Meanwhile, the Entity API access handler extends this to support bundle granular permissions and owner-based permissions if an entity implements EntityOwnerInterface in a reusable fashion.

The \Drupal\Core\Access\AccessibleInterface defines an access method, and all the entities inherit this interface. The default implementation in \Drupal\Core\Entity\Entity will invoke checkCreateAccess if the operation is create; otherwise, it invokes the generic access method of the access controller, which will invoke entity access hooks and the class' checkAccess method.

When Drupal generates available permissions, the Entity API module finds entity definitions that define the `permission_provider` handler and then invokes that class to generate permissions.

There's more...

We will discuss how to implement custom access control for an entity and use the Entity to simplify the controlling access.

Controlling access to entity fields

The `checkFieldAccess` method in the core's entity access control handler can be overridden to control access to specific entity fields when modifying an entity. Without being overridden by a child class, the `\Drupal\Core\Entity\EntityAccessControlHandler::checkFieldAccess` will always return an allowed access result. The method receives the following parameters:

- The view and edit operations
- The current field's definition
- The user session to check access against
- A possible list of field item values

Entity types can implement their own access control handlers and override this method to provide granular control over the modification of their base fields. A good example would be the `User` module and its `\Drupal\user\UserAccessControlHandler`.

User entities have a `pass` field that is used for the user's current password. There is also a `created` field that records when the user was added to the site.

For the `pass` field, it returns `denied` if the operation is `view`, but allows access if the operation is `edit`:

```
case 'pass':
  // Allow editing the password, but not viewing it.
  return ($operation == 'edit') ? AccessResult::allowed() :
AccessResult::forbidden();
```

The `created` field uses the opposite logic. When a user logs in, the site can be viewed but cannot be edited:

```
case 'created':
  // Allow viewing the created date, but not editing it.
  return ($operation == 'view') ? AccessResult::allowed() :
AccessResult::forbidden();
```

See also

- Refer to `Chapter 4`, *Extending Drupal*

Providing a custom storage handler

Storage handlers control the loading, saving, and deleting of an entity. The `\Drupal\Core\Entity\ContentEntityType` provides the base entity type definition for all content entity types. If it is not specified, then the default storage handler is `\Drupal\Core\Entity\Sql\SqlContentEntityStorage`. This class can be extended to implement alternative `load` methods or adjustments on saving.

In this recipe, we will implement a method that supports loading an entity by a specific property instead of having to write a specific `loadByProperties` method call.

Getting ready

You will need a custom module to place the code into to implement a configuration entity type. Create an `src` directory for your PSR-4 style classes. A custom content entity type needs to be implemented, such as the one in the *Creating a content entity type* recipe of this chapter.

How to do it...

1. Create a `MessageStorage` class in the module's `src` directory. This class will extend the default `\Drupal\Core\Entity\Sql\SqlContentEntityStorage` class:

```php
<?php

namespace Drupal\mymodule;

use Drupal\Core\Entity\Sql\SqlContentEntityStorage;

/**
 * Defines the entity storage for messages.
 */
class MessageStorage extends SqlContentEntityStorage {

}
```

   By extending the default storage class for our entity type, we can simply add new methods that are relevant to our requirements rather than implementing the extra business logic.

2. Create a `loadMultipleByType` method; using this method, we will provide a simple way to load all messages of a specific bundle:

```php
/**
 * Load multiple messages by bundle type.
 *
 * @param string $message_type
 *    The message type.
 *
 * @return array|\Drupal\Core\Entity\EntityInterface[]
 *    An array of loaded message entities.
 */
public function loadMultipleByType($message_type) {
  return $this->loadByProperties([
    'type' => $message_type,
  ]);
}
```

   We pass the `type` property so that we can query it based on the message bundle and return all matching message entities.

3. Update the entity's annotation block to have the new storage handler defined:

```
handlers = {
  "list_builder" = "Drupal\mymodule\MessageListBuilder",
  "access" = "\Drupal\entity\EntityAccessControlHandler",
  "permission_provider" =
"\Drupal\entity\EntityPermissionProvider",
  "storage" = "Drupal\mymodule\MessageStorage",
  "form" = {
    "default" = "Drupal\Core\Entity\EntityForm",
    "add" = "Drupal\Core\Entity\EntityForm",
    "edit" = "Drupal\Core\Entity\EntityForm",
    "delete" = "Drupal\Core\Entity\EntityDeleteForm"
  },
  "route_provider" = {
    "html" = "Drupal\Core\Entity\Routing\DefaultHtmlRouteProvider",
  },
},
```

4. You can now programmatically interact with your message entities using the following code:

```
// Get the entity type manager from the container.
\Drupal::entityTypeManager()

// Access the storage handler.
->getStorage('message')

// Invoke the new method on custom storage class.
->loadMultipleByType('message');
```

How it works...

When defining a content entity type, the annotation block begins with @ContentEntityType. This declaration, and the properties in it represents the definition to initiate an instance of the \Drupal\Core\Entity\ContentEntityType class just like all other plugin annotations.

In the class constructor, there is a merge to provide default handlers for the storage handler if it is not provided. This will always default to \Drupal\Core\Entity\Sql\SqlContentEntityStorage, as it provides methods and logic to help its parent class, ContentEntityStorageBase, interact with the SQL-based storage.

Configuration entities can have their default
`\Drupal\Core\Config\Entity\ConfigEntityStorage` as well.
However, for configuration entities, the configuration management
utilizes the `\Drupal\Core\Config\StorageInterface`
implementations for storage rather than classes, which extend
`ConfigEntityStorage`. This logic resides in the configuration factory
service.

Extending `SqlContentEntityStorage` reuses methods required for default Drupal
implementations and provides an easy method to create custom methods to interact with
loading, saving, and so on.

There's more...

We will discuss the custom storage handler and utilization of different storage backends.

Utilizing a different storage backend for an entity

Drupal provides mechanisms to support different database storage backends that are not
provided by the Drupal core, such as MongoDB. Although it is not stable for Drupal 8 at the
time of writing this book, there is a MongoDB module that provides storage interaction.

The module provides `\Drupal\mongodb\Entity\ContentEntityStorage`, which
extends `\Drupal\Core\Entity\ContentEntityStorageBase`. This class overrides the
methods used to create, save, and delete, to write them to a MongoDB collection.

The project can be found at `https://www.drupal.org/project/mongodb`.

While there are much more steps to provide a custom storage backend for content entities
and their fields, this serves as an example for how you can choose to place a custom entity
in different storage backends.

See also

- Refer to *Chapter 4*, *Extending Drupal*
- Refer to *Chapter 7*, *Plug and Play with Plugins*

Creating a route provider

Entities can implement a route provider that will create the route definitions for the entity's canonical (view), edit, delete, and collection (list) routes. As of Drupal 8.3.0, all the normally required routes are generated (this was not the case in 8.0.0). The provider takes the path for a specific link definition and turns that into a route and accessible path.

In this recipe, we will extend the default
\Drupal\Core\Entity\Routing\DefaultHtmlRouteProvider and override the canonical route to be the same as the edit route, because we assume that messages will always be embedded.

 This is related to a bug that is fixed in 8.4, where the Content Translation module caused errors by assuming that all entities have a canonical link, when they may only support edit--refer to https://www.drupal.org/node/2479377.

Getting ready

You will need a custom module to place the code into to implement a configuration entity type. Create an src directory for your classes. A custom content entity type needs to be implemented, such as the one in the *Creating a content entity type* recipe of this chapter.

How to do it...

1. Create a MessageHtmlRouteProvider class in the src directory that extends \Drupal\Core\Entity\Routing\DefaultHtmlRouteProvider:

```php
<?php

namespace Drupal\mymodule;

use Drupal\Core\Entity\Routing\DefaultHtmlRouteProvider;

/**
 * Provides HTML routes for the message entity type.
 */
class MessageHtmlRouteProvider extends DefaultHtmlRouteProvider {

}
```

2. Override the provided `getCanonicalRoute` method and return the value from `getEditFormRoute`:

```php
<?php

namespace Drupal\mymodule;

use Drupal\Core\Entity\EntityTypeInterface;
use Drupal\Core\Entity\Routing\DefaultHtmlRouteProvider;

/**
 * Provides HTML routes for the message entity type.
 */
class MessageHtmlRouteProvider extends DefaultHtmlRouteProvider {

  /**
   * {@inheritdoc}
   */
  protected function getCanonicalRoute(EntityTypeInterface
$entity_type) {
    // Messages use the edit-form route as the canonical route.
    // @todo Remove this when #2479377 gets fixed.
    return $this->getEditFormRoute($entity_type);
  }

}
```

3. Rebuild Drupal's caches for the change to take effect and routes to be rebuilt.

4. Navigating to `/message/{message}` will now load the edit form, just as `/message/{message}/edit`.

How it works...

Entities are powered by the plugin system in Drupal, which means that there is a plugin manager. The default `\Drupal\Core\Entity\EntityTypeManager` provides discovery and handling of entities. The `\Drupal\Core\Entity\EntityTypeManagerInterface` specifies a `getRouteProviders` method that is expected to return an array of strings that provide the fully qualified class name of an implementation of the `\Drupal\Core\Entity\Routing\EntityRouteProviderInterface` interface.

There is an event subscriber defined in `core.services.yml` called the `entity_route_subscriber`. This service subscribes to the dynamic route event. When this happens, it uses the entity type manager to retrieve all entity type implementations, which provide route subscribers. It then aggregates all the `\Symfony\Component\Routing\RouteCollection` instances received and merges them into the main route collection for the system.

There's more...

Drupal 8 introduces router types and provide the add routes for our entity.

The Entity API module provides additional providers

The Entity module provides two new route providers aimed specifically for entities that support revisions and a bulk delete form option.

If you have an entity that implements the `RevisionLogInterface` interface, the revision route provider generates a user interface for managing revisions. You then add a `revision` entry for the `router_providers` array pointing to the new route provider:

```
    *       "route_provider" = {
    *         "html" = "Drupal\Core\Entity\Routing\DefaultHtmlRouteProvider",
    *         "revision" = "Drupal\entity\Routing\RevisionRouteProvider",
    *       },
```

Then, you just need to define additional items in your entity's `links` definition:

```
    *    links = {
    *        "revision" = "/messages/{message}/revisions/{message_revision}/view",
    *        "revision-revert-form" =
    "/messages/{message_enhanced}/revisions/{message_revision}/revert",
    *        "version-history" = "/messages/{message}/revisions",
    *      "canonical" = "/messages/{message}",
    *      "edit-form" = "/messages/{message}/edit",
    *      "delete-form" = "/messages/{message}/delete",
    *      "collection" = "/admin/content/messages"
    *    }
```

This reduces the amount of boilerplate code required to implement an `Entity`. For an implementation example, refer to the `EnhancedEntity` class in the Entity API's test module `entity_module_test`.

See also

- Refer to Chapter 4, *Extending Drupal*
- Refer to the routing system in Drupal 8 at
  https://www.drupal.org/developing/api/8/routing

11
Off the Drupalicon Island

In this chapter, we will see how to use third-party libraries, such as JavaScript, CSS, and PHP in detail:

- Implementing and using a third-party JavaScript library
- Implementing and using a third-party CSS library
- Implementing and using a third-party PHP library

Introduction

Drupal 8 comes with a *Proudly Built Elsewhere* attitude. There has been an effort made to use more components created by the PHP community at large and other communities. Drupal 8 is built with Symfony. It includes Twig as its templating system, the provided WYSIWYG editor as its CKEditor, and PHPUnit for testing.

How does Drupal 8 promote using libraries made elsewhere? The new asset management system in Drupal 8 makes it easier to use frontend libraries. Drupal implements PSR-0 and PSR-4 from the **PHP Framework Interoperability Group (PHP-FIG)**, and **PHP Standards Recommendations (PSRs)** are suggested standards used to increase interoperability between PHP applications. This has streamlined integrating third-party PHP libraries.

Both areas will be constantly improved with each minor release of Drupal 8. These areas will be mentioned throughout the chapter.

Implementing and using a third-party JavaScript library

In the past, Drupal has only shipped with jQuery and a few jQuery plugins used by Drupal core for the JavaScript API. This has changed with Drupal 8. **Underscore.js** and **Backbone.js** are now included in Drupal, bringing two popular JavaScript frameworks to its developers.

However, there are many JavaScript frameworks that can be used. In *Chapter 5, Frontend for the Win*, we covered the asset management system and libraries. In this recipe, we will create a module that provides **Angular.js** as a library and a custom Angular application; the demo is available on the AngularJS home page.

Getting ready

In this example, we will use Bower to manage our third-party `Angular.js` library components. If you are not familiar with Bower, it is simply a package manager for frontend components. Instead of using Bower, you can just manually download and place the required files.

If you do not have Bower, you can follow the instructions to install it from `bower.io` at `http://bower.io/#install-bower`. If you do not want to install Bower, we will provide links to manually download libraries.

Having a background in AngularJS is not required but is beneficial. This recipe implements the example from the home page of the library.

How to do it...

1. Create a custom module named `mymodule` that will serve the AngularJS library and its implementation:

    ```
    name: My Module!
    type: module
    description: Provides an AngularJS app.
    core: 8.x
    ```

2. Run the `bower init` command to create a Bower project in our module's directory. We will use most of the default values for the prompted questions:

```
$ bower init
? name mymodule
? description Example module with AngularJS
? main file
? what types of modules does this package expose?
? keywords
? authors Matt Glaman <nmd.matt@gmail.com>
? license GPL
? homepage
? set currently installed components as dependencies? Yes
? would you like to mark this package as private which prevents it
from being accidentally published to the registry? No
{
  name: 'mymodule',
  authors: [
    'Matt Glaman <nmd.matt@gmail.com>'
  ],
  description: 'Example module with AngularJS',
  main: '',
  moduleType: [],
  license: 'GPL',
  homepage: '',
  ignore: [
    '**/.*',
    'node_modules',
    'bower_components',
    'test',
    'tests'
  ]
}

? Looks good? Yes
```

3. Next, we will install the AngularJS library using `bower install`:

```
$ bower install --save angular
bower angular#*                  cached
git://github.com/angular/bower-angular.git#1.5.0
bower angular#*                  validate 1.5.0 against
git://github.com/angular/bower-angular.git#*
bower angular#^1.5.0             install angular#1.5.0
angular#1.5.0 bower_components/angular
```

The `--save` option will ensure that the package's dependency is saved in the created `bower.json`. If you do not have Bower, you can download AngularJS from `https://angularjs.org/` and place it in the `bower_components` folder.

4. Create `mymodule.libraries.yml`. We will define AngularJS as its own library:

```
angular:
  js:
    'bower_components/angular/angular.js: {}
  css:
    component:
      'bower_components/angular/angular-csp.css': {}
```

When the `angular` library is attached, it will add the AngularJS library file and attach the CSS style sheet.

5. Next, create a `mymodule.module` file. We will use the theme layer's preprocess functions to add an `ng-app` attribute to the root HTML element:

```php
<?php

/**
 * Implements hook_preprocess_html().
 */
function mymodule_preprocess_html(&$variables) {
    $variables['html_attributes']['ng-app'] = '';
}
```

AngularJS uses the `ng-app` attribute as a directive for bootstrapping an AngularJS application. It marks the root of the application.

6. We will use a custom block to implement the HTML required for the AngularJS example. Create an `src/Plugin/Block` directory and an `AngularBlock.php` file.

7. Extend the `BlockBase` class and implement the `build` method to return our Angular app's HTML:

```php
<?php

namespace Drupal\mymodule\Plugin\Block;

use Drupal\Core\Block\BlockBase;

/**
 * Provides a block for AngularJS example.
```

```
 *
 * @Block(
 *   id = "mymodule_angular_block",
 *   admin_label = @Translation("AngularJS Block")
 * )
 */
class AngularBlock extends BlockBase {

  public function build() {
    return [
      'input' => [
        '#type' => 'textfield',
        '#title' => $this->t('Name'),
        '#placeholder' => $this->t('Enter a name here'),
        '#attributes' => [
          'ng-model' => 'yourName',
        ],
      ],
      'name' => [
        '#markup' => '<hr><h1>Hello {{yourName}}!</h1>',
      ],
      '#attached' => [
        'library' => [
          'mymodule/angular',
        ],
      ],
    ];
  }

}
```

We return a render array that contains the input, name, and our library attachments. The input array returns the Form API render information for a text field. The name returns a regular markup that will bind Angular's changes to the yourName scope variable.

8. Install your custom module, or rebuild Drupal's cache if the module is already installed.
9. Go to the block layout form from the **Structure** page and place your block within a region, such as the **Sidebar first** region.

10. View your Drupal site and interact with your block, which is powered by AngularJS:

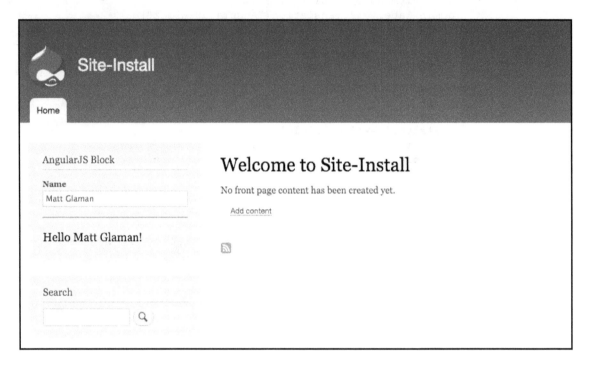

How it works...

The simplicity of integrating with a JavaScript framework is provided by the new asset management system in Drupal 8. The usage of **Bower** is optional, but it is usually a preferred method used to manage frontend dependencies. Using Bower, we can place `bower_components` in an `ignore` file that can be used to keep third-party libraries out of version control.

There's more...

Drupal 8 uses Composer for handling PHP dependencies, but frontend libraries are still being sorted out for best practices.

Best practices for handling external libraries

In our recipe, we added the third-party library through a local copy of the code, inside the module. This approach, however, makes it difficult to reuse the same library in another module. The other module would have to declare a dependency on the module providing the library or define its own copy, and two versions of AngularJS would have been loaded on the page.

 There is currently a discussion in the Drupal core issue queue by the community on how to best tackle this issue--refer to `https://www.drupal.org/node/2605130`.

A leading practice is to place a `libraries` directory in the Drupal docroot (alongside `modules` and `themes`.) An example can be found in the DropzoneJS integration module:

```
dropzonejs:
  title: 'Dropzonejs'
  website: http://www.dropzonejs.com
  version: 4.0.1
  license:
    name: MIT
    url: https://github.com/enyo/dropzone/blob/master/LICENSE
    gpl-compatible: true
  js:
    /libraries/dropzone/dist/min/dropzone.min.js: {}
  css:
    component:
      /libraries/dropzone/dist/min/dropzone.min.css: {}
```

This pattern would allow any module to load the library through this path. Its author recommends that you have a base module that defines the library and simple integration and always make that a dependency.

See also

- Refer to the core issue to add Backbone.js and Underscore.js at `https://www.drupal.org/node/1149866`
- Refer to the *Using the new asset management system* recipe of `Chapter 5`, *Frontend for the Win*
- Refer to the *Creating a Module* recipe of `Chapter 4`, *Extending Drupal*

Implementing and using a third-party CSS library

Drupal provides many things. However, one thing that it does not provide is any kind of CSS component library. In the *Using the new asset management system* recipe of `Chapter 5, Frontend for the Win`, we added `FontAwesome` as a library. CSS frameworks implement robust user interface design components, and they can be quite large if you use a compiled version with everything bundled. The asset management system can be used to define each component as its own library to only deliver the exact files required for a strong frontend performance.

In this recipe, we will implement the Semantic UI framework, using the CSS-only distribution, which provides each individual component's CSS file. We will register the `form`, `button`, `label`, and `input` components as libraries. Our custom theme will then alter the Drupal elements for `buttons`, `labels`, and `inputs` to have the Semantic UI classes and load the proper library.

Getting ready

In this example, we will use Bower to manage our third-party components. If you are not familiar with Bower, it is simply a package manager used for frontend components. Instead of using Bower, you can just manually download and place the required files.

How to do it...

1. For this recipe, create a new custom theme named `mytheme` using Classy as a base theme. This way, you can reuse some existing styling. If you are unfamiliar with creating a base theme, refer to the *Creating a custom theme based on Classy* recipe of `Chapter 5, Frontend for the Win`.

2. Using your terminal, navigate to your theme's directory. Run `bower init` to create a `bower` project:

```
$ bower init
? name mytheme
? description Example theme with Semantic UI
? main file
? what types of modules does this package expose?
? keywords
? authors Matt Glaman <nmd.matt@gmail.com>
```

```
? license GPL
? homepage
? set currently installed components as dependencies? Yes
? would you like to mark this package as private which prevents it
from being accidentally published to the registry? No
{
  name: 'mytheme',
  authors: [
    'Matt Glaman <nmd.matt@gmail.com>'
  ],
  description: 'Example theme with Semantic UI,
  main: '',
  moduleType: [],
  license: 'GPL',
  homepage: '',
  ignore: [
    '**/.*',
    'node_modules',
    'bower_components',
    'test',
   'tests'
  ]
}


? Looks good? Yes
```

3. Next, use `bower install` to save the Semantic UI library:

```
$ bower install --save semantic-ui
bower semantic-ui#*            not-cached git://github.com/Semantic-
Org/Semantic-UI.git#*
bower semantic-ui#*              resolve git://github.com/Semantic-
Org/Semantic-UI.git#*
bower semantic-ui#*            download
https://github.com/Semantic-Org/Semantic-UI/archive/2.1.8.tar.gz
bower semantic-ui#*             extract archive.tar.gz
bower semantic-ui#*            resolved git://github.com/Semantic-
Org/Semantic-UI.git#2.1.8
bower jquery#>=1.8            not-cached
git://github.com/jquery/jquery-dist.git#>=1.8
bower jquery#>=1.8            resolve
git://github.com/jquery/jquery-dist.git#>=1.8
bower jquery#>=1.8            download
https://github.com/jquery/jquery-dist/archive/2.2.0.tar.gz
bower jquery#>=1.8             extract archive.tar.gz
bower jquery#>=1.8            resolved
git://github.com/jquery/jquery-dist.git#2.2.0
bower semantic#^2.1.8          install semantic#2.1.8
```

```
bower jquery#>=1.8                     install jquery#2.2.0
```

The `--save` option will ensure that the package's dependency is saved in the created `bower.json`. If you do not have Bower, you can download Semantic UI from `https://github.com/semantic-org/semantic-ui/` and place it in a `bower_components` folder.

4. Create `mytheme.libraries.yml` in your theme's base directory. This will hold your main Semantic UI definition along with specific component library definitions.

5. You will then add a new library to the `form` component:

```
semantic_ui.form:
  js:
    bower_components/semantic/dist/components/form.js: {}
  css:
    component:
      bower_components/semantic/dist/components/form.css: {}
```

The `form` component for Semantic UI has a style sheet and JavaScript file. Your library ensures that both are loaded when the library is attached.

6. The `button`, `input`, and `label` components do not have any JavaScript files. Add a library for each component:

```
semantic_ui.button:
  css:
    component:
      bower_components/semantic/dist/components/button.css: {}
semantic_ui.input:
  css:
    component:
      bower_components/semantic/dist/components/input.css: {}
semantic_ui.label:
  css:
    component:
      bower_components/semantic/dist/components/label.css: {}
```

7. Now that the libraries are defined, you can use the `attach_library` Twig function to add your libraries to the appropriate templates when you add the Semantic UI classes.

8. Copy the `form.html.twig` file from the Classy theme's `templates` folder and paste it into your theme's templates folder. Then, attach `mytheme/semantic_ui.form` and add the `ui` and `form` classes:

```
{{ attach_library('mytheme/semantic_ui.form') }}
  <form{{ attributes.addClass(['ui', 'form']) }}>
{{ children }}
</form>
```

The `attach_library` function will attach the specified library. Use the `addClass` method from Twig to add the `ui` and `form` classes. Semantic UI requires all elements to have the matching `ui` class.

9. Next, copy the `input.html.twig` file from the Classy theme and paste it into your theme's `template` folder. Then, attach `mytheme/semantic_ui.input` and add the `ui` and `input` classes:

```
{{ attach_library('mytheme/semantic_ui.input') }}
<input{{ attributes.addClass(['ui', 'input']) }} />{{ children }}
```

10. Copy the `input.html.twig` file that you just created and use it to make `input-submit.html.twig`. This template file will be used for `submit` and other buttons:

```
{{ attach_library('mytheme/semantic_ui.button') }}
<input{{ attributes.addClass(['ui', 'button', 'primary']) }} />{{
children }}
```

11. Finally, copy the `form-element-label.html.twig` file from Classy to your theme and add the label library and appropriate class, along with the defaults that Classy has defined:

```
{{ attach_library('mytheme/semantic_ui.label') }}

{%
  set classes = [
    title_display == 'after' ? 'option',
    title_display == 'invisible' ? 'visually-hidden',
    required ? 'js-form-required',
    required ? 'form-required',
    'ui',
    'label',
  ]
%}
{% if title is not empty or required -%}
```

```
    <label{{ attributes.addClass(classes) }}>{{ title }}</label>
    {%- endif %}
```

12. View a form and check whether it has been styled by the Semantic UI CSS framework:

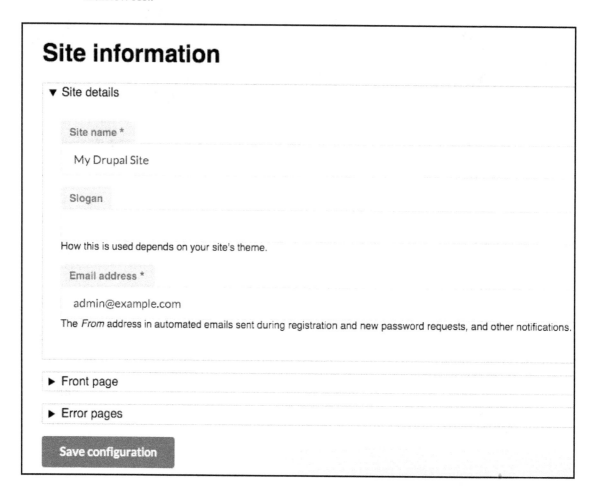

How it works...

The simplicity of integrating with a CSS framework is provided by the new template system, Twig, and the asset management system in Drupal 8. The usage of Bower is optional, but it is usually a preferred method for managing frontend dependencies and can be used to keep third-party libraries out of version control.

Although it may be a task to add each component as its own library and attach when specifically needed, it ensures optimal asset delivery. With CSS and JavaScript aggregation enabled, each page will only have the minimal resources that are needed. This is an advantage when the entire Semantic UI minified is still 524 KB.

See also

- Refer to Semantic UI at `http://semantic-ui.com/`
- Refer to the *Creating a custom theme based on Classy* recipe of `Chapter 5, Frontend for the Win`
- Refer to the *Using the new asset management system* recipe of `Chapter 5, Frontend for the Win`
- Refer to the *Twig templating* recipe of `Chapter 5, Frontend for the Win`

Implementing and using a third-party PHP library

Drupal 8 uses Composer for package dependencies and `autoloading` classes based on PSR standards. This allows us to use any available PHP library much more easily than in previous versions of Drupal.

In this recipe, we will add the `IpRestrict Stack Middleware` library to add the functionality to whitelist access to the Drupal site based on allowed IP addresses.

Getting ready

You need to have Composer installed in order to use the Composer manager workflow. You can follow the *Getting Started* documentation at `https://getcomposer.org/doc/00-intro.md`. We will add the `alsar/stack-ip-restrict` library as a dependency to our Drupal installation.

How to do it...

1. Using your terminal, navigate to your Drupal site's root directory.
2. Use the `require` command from Composer to add the library:

   ```
   composer require alsar/stack-ip-restrict
   ```

3. Composer will then add the library to the `composer.json` file and install the library along with any dependencies. Its namespace will now be registered.
4. Now, you will need to implement a module that registers the library as a middleware service. We'll call the module `ip_restrict`. Add the following code to the `ip_restrict.info.yml` file:

   ```
   name: IP Restrict
   type: module
   description: Restricts access to the Drupal site based on allowed
   IP addresses
   core: 8.x
   ```

5. Create `ip_restrict.services.yml`. This will register the library with Drupal's service container:

   ```
   parameters:
     ip_restrict:
       enabled: true
       ipAddresses: ['127.0.0.1', 'fe80::1', '::1']
   services:
     ip_restrict.middleware:
       class: Alsar\Stack\IpRestrict
       arguments: ['%ip_restrict%']
       tags:
         - { name: http_middleware }
   ```

   The `parameters` section defines configuration values, which can be overridden in the site's `services.yml` file. The `services` section defines the service's machine name, class file, its constructor arguments, and any tags.

6. Next, you will need to implement a compiler pass injection. This will allow us to alter our service in the container definition when it is compiled. Create a `src/Compiler` directory and make `IpRestrictPass.php`.

When making a compiler pass class, the class and filename must be formatted in a specific way. It is the camel case version of the module name followed by `Pass`.

7. The `IpRestrictPass.php` will provide the `IpRestrictPass` class, which implements
`\Symfony\Component\DependencyInjection\Compiler\CompilerPassInterface`:

```php
<?php

namespace Drupal\ip_restrict\Compiler;

use Symfony\Component\DependencyInjection\ContainerBuilder;
use Symfony\Component\DependencyInjection\Compiler\CompilerPassInterface;

/**
 * Adds the IP Restrict middleware if enabled.
 */
class IpRestrictPass implements CompilerPassInterface {

  /**
   * {@inheritdoc}
   */
  public function process(ContainerBuilder $container) {
    if (FALSE ===
$container->hasDefinition('ip_restrict.middleware')) {
      return;
    }

    $ip_restrict_config = $container->getParameter('ip_restrict');

    if (!$ip_restrict_config['enabled']) {
      $container->removeDefinition('ip_restrict.middleware');
    }
  }

}
```

In our compiler pass, we check the `enabled` parameter and remove our middleware if it has been disabled (so that it does not restrict allowed IPs).

8. Enable the module. The stack middleware service will be registered and now supporting restrict access from local IP addresses.

How it works...

Drupal 8 utilizes Symfony components. One of them is the service container and the services it has registered. During the building of the container, there is a compiler pass process that allows alterations of the container's services.

First, we will need to register the service in the module's `services.yml` file. The `\Drupal\Core\DependencyInjection\Compiler\StackedKernelPass` class provided by the core will automatically load all the services tagged with `http_middleware`, such as our `ip_restrict.middleware` service.

Our `arguments` definition loads items defined in the `parameters.ip_restrict` that are used for the class's constructor.

With our provided `IpRestrictPass` class, we are also tapping into the container's compile cycle. We will take a look at the parameter values for the `ip_restrict` section to check whether they are enabled. If the enabled setting is set to `false`, we remove our service from the container.

See also

- Refer to Services and dependency injection in the Drupal 8 documentation at https://www.drupal.org/docs/8/api/services-and-dependency-injection/services-and-dependency-injection-in-drupal-8
- Refer to the Symfony service container documentation at http://symfony.com/doc/current/book/service_container.html
- Refer to the Symfony Dependency Injection component documentation at http://symfony.com/doc/current/components/dependency_injection/introduction.html

12
Web Services

Drupal 8 ships with the RESTful web servers functionality to implement web services to interact with your application. This chapter shows you how to enable these features and build your API, covering the following topics:

- Enabling RESTful interfaces
- Using POST to create data
- Using PATCH to update data
- Using Views to provide custom data sources
- Authentication
- Using JSON API

Introduction

There are several modules provided by Drupal 8 that enable the ability to turn it into a web service provider. The Serialization module provides a means of serializing data to or deserializing from formats such as JSON and XML. The RESTful web services module then exposes entities and other APIs through Web APIs. Operations done through RESTful resource endpoints use the same create, edit, delete, and view permissions that would be used in a non-API format.

The HAL module serializes entities using the **Hypertext Application Language** (**HAL**) format. HAL is an Internet Draft standard convention used to hyperlink between resources in an API. HAL+JSON is required when working with POST and PATCH methods. For authentication, the HTTP Basic Authentication module provides a simple authentication via HTTP headers.

There is a community-lead effort to implement the JSON API specification with Drupal, using the JSON API module, covered in the *Using JSON API* recipe of this chapter. Like HAL, it provides specifications not only on how data should be represented, but also on how it should be sorted and filtered via request parameters.

This chapter covers how to work with the RESTful Web Services module and the supporting modules around developing a RESTful API powered by Drupal 8. We will cover how to use the GET, POST, and PATCH HTTP methods to manipulate content on the website. Additionally, we will cover how to use views to provide custom content that lists endpoints. Finally, we will cover how to handle custom authentication for our API.

In an article, *Putting off PUT*, the team behind the Web services initiative chose not to implement PUT and only support PATCH. For more information, refer to the original article at `https://groups.drupal.org/ node/284948`.

However, the API is open for contributed modules to add the PUT support for core resources or their own.

Enabling RESTful interfaces

The RESTful Web Services module provides routes that expose endpoints for your RESTful API. It utilizes the Serialization module to handle the normalization to a response and denormalization of data from requests. Endpoints support specific formats and authentication providers. Upon installation, the RESTful Web Services module does not provide any default configured endpoints.

There is one caveat: RESTful Web Services does not provide a user interface to configure available endpoints. Enabling resource endpoints can be done by manually editing configuration or the **REST UI** module. We will use the REST UI module in this recipe.

In this recipe, we will install RESTful Web Services and enable the proper permissions to allow the retrieval of nodes via REST to receive our formatted JSON.

We will cover using GET, POST, PATCH, and DELETE in later recipes. This recipe covers the installation and configuration of the base modules to enable Web services.

Getting ready

There is a configuration change that might be required if you are running PHP 5.6: the `always_populate_raw_post_data` setting. If you try to enable the RESTful Web Services module without changing the default setting, you will see the following error message on installation:

The `always_populate_raw_post_data` PHP setting should be set to `-1` in PHP version 5.6. Please check the PHP manual for information on how to correct this. (Currently using `always_populate_raw_post_data` PHP setting version not set to -1.)

How to do it...

1. First, we must add the REST UI module to our Drupal site so that we can easily configure our endpoints:

   ```
   cd /path/to/drupal8
   composer require drupal/restui
   ```

2. Go to **Extend** from the administrative toolbar and install the following Web services modules: **Serialization, RESTful Web Services**, and **REST UI**:

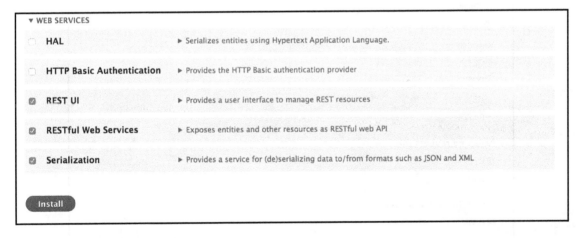

3. Go to **Configuration** and click on **REST** under **Web Services** to configure the available endpoints.

4. Click on the **Enable** button for the **Content** row:

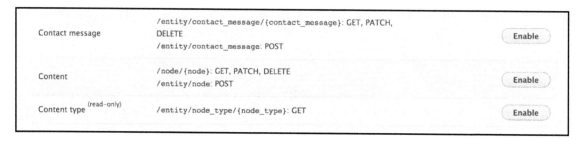

5. With the endpoint enabled, it must be configured. Check the **GET** method checkbox to allow GET requests. Then, check the **json** checkbox so that data can be returned as JSON. All endpoints require a selected authentication provider. Check the **cookie** checkbox, and then save it:

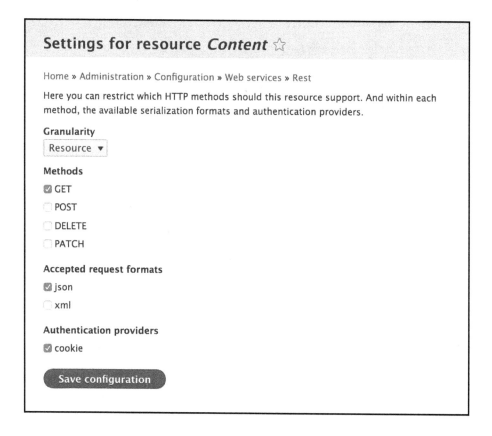

6. Any RESTful resource endpoint enabled will use the same create, update, delete, and view permissions that have been already configured for the entity type. In order to allow anonymous access over GET for content, ensure that anonymous users have the **View published content permission**.

7. Using cURL on the command line, a piece of content can now be retrieved using the RESTful endpoint. You must pass `?_format=json` to ensure that the proper format is returned:

```
curl http://127.0.0.1:8888/node/1?_format=json
```

```
{"nid":[{"value":1}],"uuid":[{"value":"9a473f09-fa61-42c9-b4ad-
f24b857d04f6"}],"vid":[{"value":51}],"langcode":[{"value":"en"}],"t
ype":[{"target_id":"page","target_type":"node_type","target_uuid":"
8a8ad160-69dc-453f-
bc11-86775040465e"}],"status":[{"value":true}],"title":[{"value":"E
xample
node"}],"uid":[{"target_id":0,"target_type":"user","target_uuid":"e
31b3de2-2195-48c6-9a5e-
ab0553461c93","url":"\/user\/0"}],"created":[{"value":1500650071}],
"changed":[{"value":1500650374}],"promote":[{"value":true}],"sticky
":[{"value":false}],"revision_timestamp":[{"value":1500650374}],"re
vision_uid":[{"target_id":1,"target_type":"user","target_uuid":"2d7
ee3ef-6f8a-4feb-
a99a-4af8cfd24402","url":"\/user\/1"}],"revision_log":[],"revision_
translation_affected":[{"value":true}],"default_langcode":[{"value"
:true}],"path":[],"body":[{"value":"Defui dolor elit jus luptatum.
Ad augue causa hos loquor luctus minim singularis sino utinam.
","format":"plain_text","summary":""}]}
```

The RESTful Web Services module will return the entire entity object with each field the user has access to view.

How it works...

The **RESTful Web Services** module works by implementing an event subscriber service, `rest.resource_routes`, that adds routes to Drupal based on implementations of its `RestResource` plugin. Each plugin returns the available routes based on HTTP methods that are enabled for the resource.

When routes are built, the `\Drupal\rest\Routing\ResourceRoutes` class uses the `RestResource` plugin manager to retrieve all the available definitions. The endpoint configuration objects are loaded and inspected. If the resource plugin provides an HTTP method that is enabled in the configuration definitions, it begins to build a new route. Verification is done against the defined supported formats and supported auth definitions. If the basic validation passes, the new route is added to the `RouteCollection` and returned.

If you provide a `supported_formats` or `supported_auth` value that is not available, the endpoint will still be created. There will be an error, however, if you attempt to use the route with the invalid plugin. This cannot occur when using the REST UI module, but manually providing and managing the configuration.

The default routes provided by the base class for resource plugins, `\Drupal\rest\Plugin\ResourceBase` class, set `\Drupal\rest\RequestHandler::handle` as the controller and method for the route. This method checks the passed `_format` parameter against the configured plugin. If the format is valid, the data is passed to the appropriate serializer. The serialized data is then returned in the request with appropriate content headers.

There's more...

The RESTful Web Services module provides a robust API that has some additional items to make a note of. We will explore these in the next recipe.

Using _format instead of the Accept header

Earlier in the Drupal 8 life cycle, up until 8.0.0-beta12, Drupal supported the use of the `Accept` header instead of the `_format` parameter. Unfortunately, there were issues with external caches. Drupal was serving HTML and other formats on the same path, only using different `Accept` headers. CDNs and reverse proxies do not invalidate cache based on this header alone. The only solution to prevent cache poisoning on these external caches, such as `Varnish`, was to ensure the implementation of the `Vary: Accept` header. There were, however, too many issues regarding CDNs and variance of implementation, so the `_format` parameter was introduced instead of appending extensions (`.json` and `.xml`) to paths.

A detail of the problem can be found on the following core issues:

- Refer to external caches mix up response formats on URLs where content negotiation is in use at `https://www.drupal.org/node/2364011`
- Check how to implement query parameter-based content negotiation as an alternative to extensions at `https://www.drupal.org/node/2481453`

RestResource plugin to expose data through RESTful Web Services

The RESTful Web Services module defines a `RestResource` plugin. This plugin is used to define resource endpoints. They are discovered in a module's `Plugin/rest/resource` namespace and need to implement the `\Drupal\rest\Plugin\ResourceInterface` interface. Drupal 8 provides two implementations of the `RestResource` plugin. The first is the `EntityResource` class that is provided by the RESTful Web Services module. It implements a driver class that allows it to represent each entity type. The second is the **Database Logging** module that provides its own `RestResource` plugin, as well. It allows you to retrieve logged messages by IDs. The `\Drupal\rest\Plugin\ResourceBase` class provides an abstract base class that can be extended for the `RestResource` plugin implementations. If the child class provides a method that matches the available HTTP methods, it will support them. For example, if a class has only a GET method, you can only interact with that endpoint through HTTP `GET` requests. On the other hand, you can provide a trace method that allows an endpoint to support HTTP `TRACE` requests.

Drupal 8 provides two implementations of the `RestResource` plugin. The first is the `EntityResource` class that is provided by the RESTful Web Services module. It implements a `deriver` class that allows it to represent each entity type. The second is the Database Logging module that provides its own `RestResource` plugin. It allows you to retrieve logged messages by IDs.

Rate limiting your API

Many APIs implement a rate limit to prevent abuse of public APIs. When you have publicly exposed APIs, you will need to control the amount of traffic hitting the service and prevent abusers from slowing down or stopping your service.

The **Rate Limiter** module implements multiple ways to control access to your public APIs. There is an option to control the rate limit on specific requests, IP address-based limiting, and IP whitelisting.

You can find the Rate Limiter module at `https://www.drupal.org/project/rate_limiter`.

Using the HAL format

When installed, the HAL module can format the entity returned to provide links to related entities, such as the user or revision or any other entity reference field. When the HAL module is installed, you can add it as a supported format, then do a request with `_format=hal_json`. The response from the recipe would come back with a `_links` parameter:

```
"_links" : {
    "http://127.0.0.1:8888/rest/relation/node/page/revision_uid" : [
        {
            "href" : "http://127.0.0.1:8888/user/1?_format=hal_json"
        }
    ],
    "self" : {
        "href" : "http://127.0.0.1:8888/node/1?_format=hal_json"
    },
    "http://127.0.0.1:8888/rest/relation/node/page/uid" : [
        {
            "lang" : "en",
            "href" : "http://127.0.0.1:8888/user/0?_format=hal_json"
        }
    ],
    "type" : {
        "href" : "http://127.0.0.1:8888/rest/type/node/page"
    }
},
```

See also

- Refer to the Drupal.org documentation for the RESTful Web Services module at `https://www.drupal.org/documentation/modules/rest`
- Refer to *Change record: Accept header based routing got replaced by a query parameter*, `https://www.drupal.org/node/2501221`
- Refer to *Chapter 7, Plug and Play with Plugins*
- Refer to the *Rate Limiter module* at `https://www.drupal.org/project/rate_limiter`
- Refer to the *REST UI module* at `https://www.drupal.org/project/restui`

Using POST to create data

When working with RESTful Web Services, the HTTP POST method is used to create new entities. We will use the **HTTP Basic Authentication** to authenticate a user and create a new node.

In this recipe, we will use the exposed node endpoint to create a new piece of article content through the RESTful Web Services module. We will use the `json` format. In the *There's more...* section, we will discuss how to use the HAL module for the `hal_json` format.

Getting ready

You will use the `Article` content type provided by the standard installation. Following the preceding recipe, *Enabling RESTful interfaces*, you should have the **REST UI** module added to your Drupal installation using Composer. This can be done with the following command:

```
cd /path/to/drupal8
composer require drupal/restui
```

In this recipe, the Drupal 8 installation is accessible through `http://127.0.0.1:8888`. Use the appropriate URL for your Drupal 8 site.

How to do it...

1. Go to **Extend** from the administrative toolbar and install the following Web Services modules: **Serialization**, **RESTful Web Services**, **REST UI**, and **HTTP Basic Authentication**:

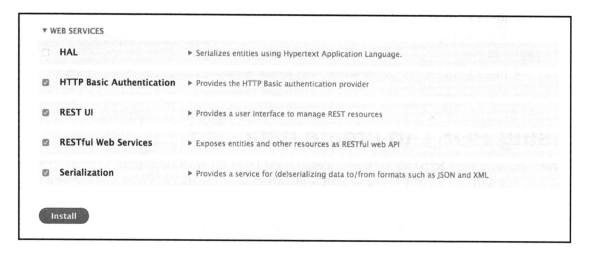

2. Go to **Configuration** and click on **REST** under **Web Services** to configure the available endpoints.

3. Click on the **Enable** button for the **Content** row:

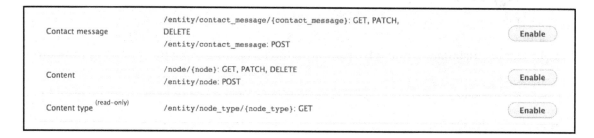

4. With the endpoint enabled, it must be configured. Check the **GET** and **POST** methods checkbox to allow GET and POST requests. Then, check the **json** checkbox so that data can be returned as JSON. Check the **basic_auth** checkbox, and then save it:

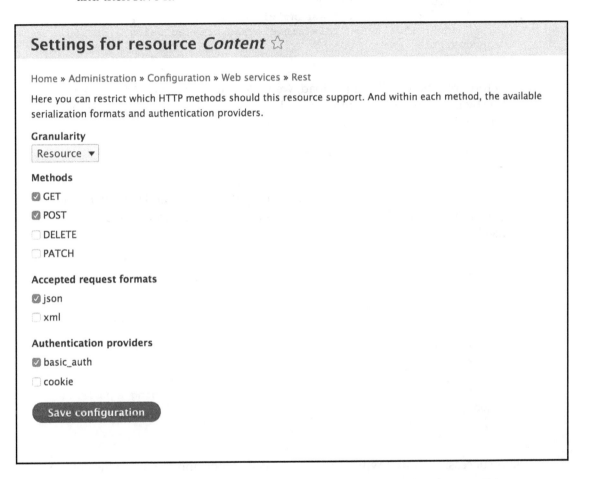

5. We create our JSON payload to match the field structure expected by Drupal:

```
{
  "type": "article",
  "status": {"value": true},
  "title": {"value": "Testing via REST!"},
  "body": {"value": "This article was created using a RESTful
endpoint"}
}
```

6. Before we send our JSON payload, we will need to retrieve a CSRF token. We do this by performing a GET request against /session/token. We'll use the returned value in our POST request header:

```
curl -X GET http://127.0.0.1:8888/session/token
```

7. We can send the request containing our body payload to the /entity/node?_format=json endpoint path through an HTTP POST request to create our node. Ensure that you pass a valid user login where admin:admin is used:

```
curl -X POST \
  'http://127.0.0.1:8888/entity/node?_format=json' \
  -u admin:admin \
  -H 'content-type: application/json' \
  -H 'x-csrf-token: K5UW756_nWJxjX8Lt5NXXrE0xYSAqCn8MPKLbgE6Gps' \
  -d '{
  "type": "article",
  "status": {"value": true},
  "title": {"value": "Testing via REST!"},
  "body": {"value": "This article was created using a RESTful
endpoint"}
}
'
```

8. A successful request will return a 201 header code and the full values of the created node, including its identifier.

9. View your Drupal site and verify that the node was created, by going to /node/{nid}, using the node ID from the request response:

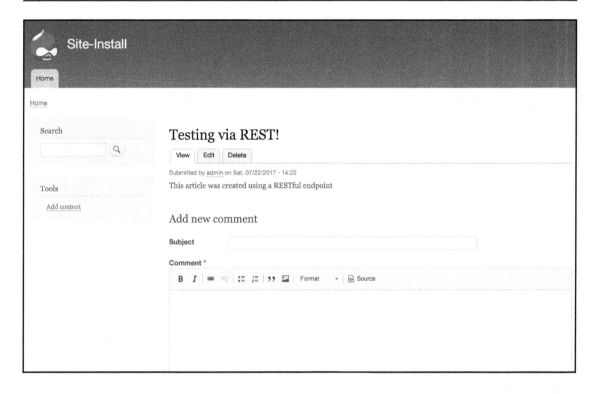

How it works...

When working with content entities and the POST method, the endpoint is different to the one used for GET requests. The `\Drupal\rest\Plugin\rest\resource\EntityResource` class extends the `\Drupal\rest\Plugin\ResourceBase` base class, which provides a route method. If a resource plugin provides an `https://www.drupal.org/link-relations/create` link template, then that path will be used for the POST path.

The `EntityResource` class defines `/entity/{entity_type}` as the create link template. It then overrides the `getBaseRoute` method to ensure that the `entity_type` parameter is properly populated from the definition.

The `EntityResource` class will run a set of conditions for the request. First, it will validate the POST request by checking whether the entity is `null`. Then, the current user is authorized to create the entity type if the current user also has access to edit all fields provided, and finally, it checks whether an identifier was passed or not. The last condition is important, as updates are only to be made through a PATCH request.

If the entity is validated, it will be saved. On a successful save, an empty HTTP 201 response will be returned.

There's more...

Working with POST requests requires some specific formatting that will be explained in the next recipe.

Using HAL and understanding _links requirements

When using the HAL module and the `hal_json` format, you must provide relationships for the entity. This is done through the `_links` parameter in the request. This is done to ensure that the entity is properly created with any relationships it requires, such as the entity type for a content entities bundle. Another example will be to create a comment over a RESTful interface. You will need to provide a `_links` entry for the user owning the comment.

The `rest.link_manager` service uses the `rest.link_manager.type` and `rest.link_manager.relation` and is responsible for returning the URIs for types and relations. By default, a bundle will have a path that resembles `/rest/type/{entity_type}/{bundle}` and its relations will resemble `/rest/relation/{entity_type}/{bundle}/{field_name}`.

Taking a user reference as an example, we will have to populate a `uid` field, as follows:

```
{
  "_links": {
    "type": {
      "href": "http://127.0.0.1:8888/rest/type/node/page"
    },
    "http://127.0.0.1:8888/rest/relation/node/article/uid": [
      {
        "href": "http://127.0.0.1:8888/user/1?_format=hal_json",
        "lang": "en"
      }
    ]
  }
}
```

Unfortunately, the documentation is sparse, and the best way to learn what `_links` are required is to perform a GET request and study the returned `_links` from the HAL JSON.

Working with images

Most RESTful APIs utilize `base64` encoding of files to support POST operations to upload an image. Unfortunately, this is not supported in the Drupal core. Although there is a `serializer.normalizer.file_entity.hal` service that serializes file entities into HAL JSON, it does not currently work as of 8.3, but is hopefully slated for 8.4.

The `\Drupal\hal\Normalizer\FileEntityNormalizer` class supports denormalization; however, it does not handle `base64` and expects binary data.

There is a Drupal core issue for this problem, which is available at `https://www.drupal.org/node/1927648`.

Using Cross-Site Request Forgery tokens

When working with a POST request, you will need to pass a **Cross-Site Request Forgery (CSRF)** token if you are authenticating with a session cookie. The X-CSRF-Token header is required when using a session cookie to prevent accidental API requests.

If you are using the cookie provider for authentication, you will need to request a CSRF token from the `/session/token` route:

```
curl -X GET http://127.0.0.1:8888/session/token
```

See also

- Refer to how to serialize file content (`base64`) to support REST GET/POST/PATCH
  on file entity at `https://www.drupal.org/node/1927648`

Using PATCH to update data

When working with RESTful Web Services, the HTTP PATCH method is used to update entities. We will use the HTTP Basic Authentication to authenticate our user and update a node.

In this recipe, we will use the exposed node endpoint to create a new piece of article content through the RESTful Web Services module.

Getting ready

We will use the `Article` content type provided by the standard installation. Following the *Enabling RESTful interfaces* recipe, you should have the REST UI module added to your Drupal installation using Composer. This can be done with the following command:

```
cd /path/to/drupal8
composer require drupal/restui
```

How to do it...

1. Go to **Extend** from the administrative toolbar and install the following Web Services modules: **Serialization**, **RESTful Web Services**, **REST UI**, and **HTTP Basic Authentication**:

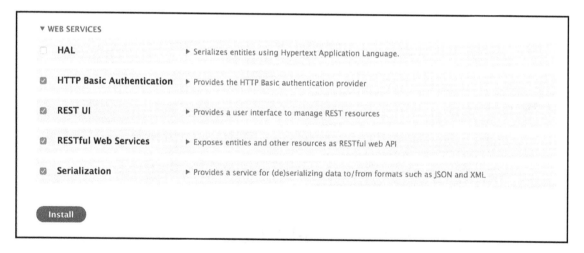

2. Go to **Configuration** and click on **REST** under **Web Services** to configure the available endpoints.

3. Click on the **Enable** button for the **Content** row:

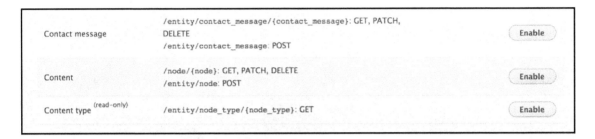

4. With the endpoint enabled, it must be configured. Check the **GET**, **POST**, and **PATCH** methods checkbox to allow the GET, POST, and PATCH requests. Then, check the **json** checkbox so that data can be sent as JSON. Check the **basic_auth** checkbox and then save it:

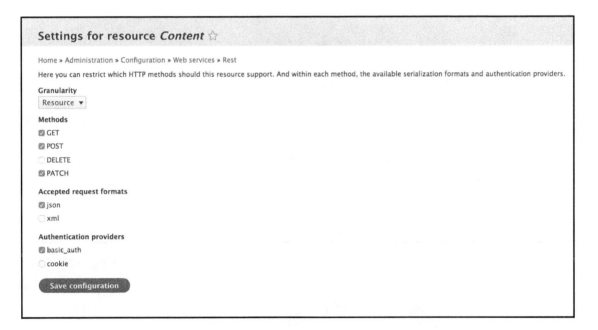

5. Create a sample `Article` node on your Drupal site that you will modify using the REST endpoint. Ensure that you note its path. You will use the same path later in our request (for example, `/node/4`). This will also show you the node's ID:

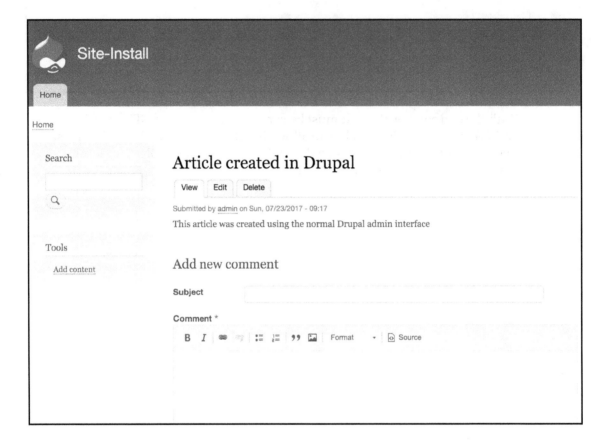

6. Then, start building your JSON payload. You must provide the identifier (nid) value for the existing node and the content type (type) value. Ensure that you provide the value of nid, which matches your current node:

```
{
    "nid" : {
        "value" : 4
    },
    "body" : {
        "value" : "This article was updated using the RESTful API
endpoint!"
    },
    "type" : "article"
}
```

7. Before you send your JSON payload, you will need to retrieve a CSRF token. You can do this by performing a GET request against /session/token. Then, use the returned value in your POST request header:

```
curl -X GET http://127.0.0.1:8888/session/token
```

8. You can send the request that contains your body payload to the /node/4?_format=json, where /node/4 matches the path of the node you would like to edit, path through an HTTP PATCH request to create our node:

```
curl -X PATCH \
  'http://127.0.0.1:8888/node/4?_format=json' \
  -u admin:admin \
  -H 'x-csrf-token: MAjbBsIUmzrwHQGN1XxvGMZQJzQCDZbmtecstzbk5UQ' \
  -d '{
  "type": "article",
  "nid": {"value": 4},
  "body": {"value": "This article was updated using the RESTful API
endpoint!!"}
}
'
```

9. A successful request will return a 200 header code and the full values of the updated node.

10. View your Drupal site and verify that the node was created, by going to `/node/{nid}`, using the node ID from the request response:

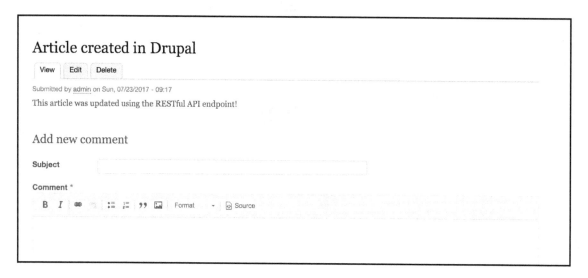

How it works...

When working with content entities and the PATCH method, the endpoint is the same as the GET method path. The current user's access is checked to see whether they have the permission to update the entity type and each of the submitted fields provided in the request body.

Each field provided will be updated on the entity and then validated. If the entity is validated, it will be saved. On a successful save, an HTTP 200 response will be returned with the entire updated entity's content.

Using Views to provide custom data sources

The RESTful Web Services module provides Views plugins that allow you to expose data over Views for your RESTful API. This allows you to create a view that has a path and outputs data using a serializer plugin. You can use this to output entities, such as JSON, HAL JSON, or XML, and it can be sent with appropriate headers.

In this recipe, we will create a view that outputs the users of the Drupal site, providing their username, email, and picture if provided.

How to do it...

1. Got o **Extend** from the administrative toolbar and install the following Web Services modules: **Serialization** and **RESTful Web Services**:

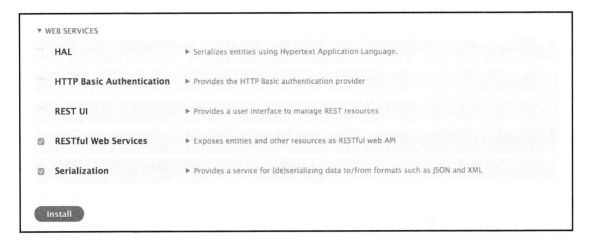

2. Go to **Structure** and then to **Views**. Click on **Add view**. Name the view **API Users** and make it show **Users**.
3. Check the **Provide a REST export** checkbox, and type in the `api/users` path. This is where requests will be made:

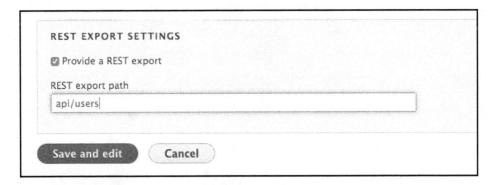

4. Click on **Save and edit**.

5. Change the format of the row plugin from **Entity** to **Fields** instead so that we can control the specific output.

6. Ensure that your view has the following user entity fields: **Name, Email**, and **Picture**.

7. Change the **User: Name** field to a plain text formatter and do not link it to the user, so the response does not contain any HTML.

8. Change the **User: Picture** field to use URL to image formatter so that only a URL is returned and not HTML.

9. Save your view.

10. Access your view by visiting `/api/users`; you will receive a JSON response containing the user information:

```json
[
  {
    "name": "spuvest",
    "mail": "spuvest@example.com",
    "user_picture":
"\/sites\/default\/files\/pictures\/2017-07\/generateImage_xIQkfx.j
pg"
  },
  {
    "name": "crepathuslus",
    "mail": "crepathuslus@example.com",
    "user_picture":
"\/sites\/default\/files\/pictures\/2017-07\/generateImage_eauTko.g
if"
  },
  {
    "name": "veradabufrup",
    "mail": "veradabufrup@example.com",
    "user_picture":
"\/sites\/default\/files\/pictures\/2017-07\/generateImage_HsEjKW.p
ng"
  }
]
```

How it works

The RESTful Web Services module provides display, row, and format plugins that allows you to export content entities to a serialized format. The REST Export display plugin allows you to specify a path to access the RESTful endpoint and properly assigns the Content-Type header for the requested format.

The Serializer style is provided as the only supported style plugin for the REST export display. This style plugin only supports row plugins that identify themselves as data display types. It expects data from the row plugin to be raw so that it can be passed to the appropriate serializer.

You then have the option of using the data entity or data field row plugins. Instead of returning a render array from their render method, they return raw data that will be serialized into the proper format.

With the row plugins returning raw format data and the data serialized by the style plugin, the display plugin will then return the response that is converted into the proper format via the Serialization module.

There's more...

Views provide a way to deliver specific RESTful endpoints. We will explore some additional features in the next recipe.

Controlling the key name in JSON output

The Data fields row plugin allows you to configure field aliases. When the data is returned to the view, it will have Drupal's machine names. This means that custom fields will look something like `field_my_field`, which may not make sense to the consumer.

By clicking on **Settings** next to **Fields**, you can set aliases in the modal form:

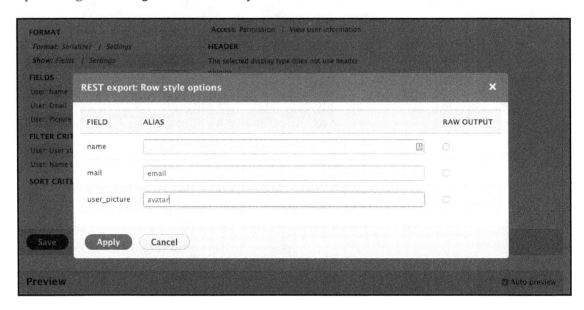

When you provide an alias, the fields will match. For example, `user_picture` can be changed to `avatar` and the mail key can be changed to `email`:

```
[{
  "name": "veradabufrup",
  "email": "veradabufrup@example.com",
  "avatar":
"\/sites\/default\/files\/pictures\/2017-07\/generateImage_HsEjKW.png"
}]
```

Controlling access to RESTful Views

When you create a RESTful endpoint with Views, you are not using the same permissions created by the RESTful Web Services module. You will need to define the route permissions within the view, allowing you to specify specific roles or permissions for the request.

The default GET method provided by the `EntityResource` plugin does not provide a way to list entities and allows any entity to be retrieved by an ID. Using Views, you can provide a list of entities, limiting them to specific bundles.

Using Views, you can even provide a new endpoint to retrieve a specific entity. Using Contextual filters, you can add route parameters and filters to limit and validate entity IDs. For example, you may want to expose the article content over the API, but not pages.

Authentication

Using the RESTful Web Services module, we define specific supported authentication providers for an endpoint. The Drupal core provides a cookie provider, which authenticates through a valid cookie, such as your regular login experience. Then, there is the HTTP Basic Authentication module to support HTTP authentication headers.

There are alternatives that provide more robust authentication methods. With cookie-based authentication, you will need to use CSRF tokens to prevent unrequested page loads by an unauthorized party. When you use the HTTP authentication, you are sending a password for each request in the request header.

OAuth is a popular and open authorization framework. It is a proper authentication method that uses tokens and not passwords. In this recipe, we will implement the Simple OAuth module to provide OAuth 2.0 authentication for GET and POST requests.

Getting ready

If you are not familiar with OAuth or OAuth 2.0, it is a standard for authorization. The implementation of OAuth revolves around the usage of tokens sent in HTTP headers. Refer to the OAuth home page for more information at `http://oauth.net/`.

By following the *Enabling RESTful interfaces* recipe, you should have the **REST UI** module added to your Drupal installation using Composer. This can be done with the following command:

```
cd /path/to/drupal8
composer require drupal/restui
```

How to do it

1. First, we must add the Simple OAuth module to our Drupal site:

   ```
   cd /path/to/drupal8
   composer require drupal/simple_oauth
   ```

2. Go to **Extend** from the administrative toolbar and install the following Web Services modules: **Serialization**, **RESTful Web Services**, **REST UI**, and **Simple OAuth**:

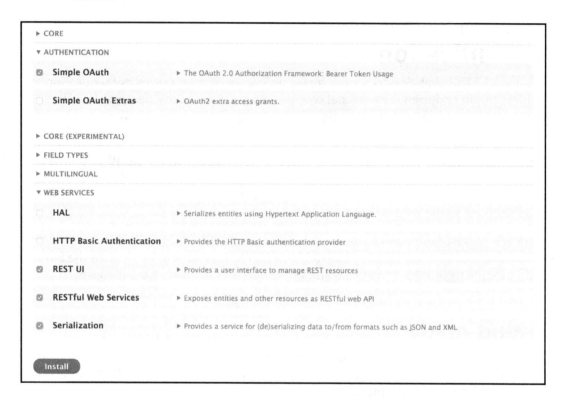

3. Go to **Configuration** and click on **REST** under **Web Services** to configure the available endpoints.

4. Click on the **Enable** button for the **Content** row:

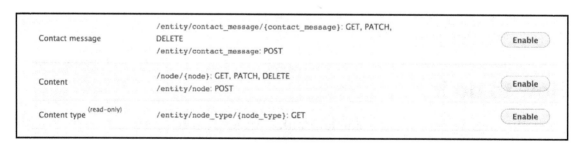

5. With the endpoint enabled, it must be configured. Check the **GET** and **POST** methods checkbox to allow GET and POST requests. Then, check the **json** checkbox so that data can be returned as JSON. Check the **oauth2** checkbox and then save it.

6. Before we can configure the Simple OAuth module, we have to generate a pair of keys to encrypt the OAuth tokens. Generate these in a path accessible to Drupal, but not available through the web server:

```
openssl genrsa -out private.key 2048
openssl rsa -in private.key -pubout > public.key
```

7. With the keys generated, go to the **Configuration** page and then to **Simple OAuth**. Enter in the paths to your private and public key that were just generated and click on **Save configuration**:

8. From the Simple OAuth configuration form, click on **Add client**. Provide a label for the client and select the **Administrator** scope. Click on **Save** to create the client.

9. Next, we will generate a token through the `/oauth/token` endpoint. You will need the ID from the client you just created. We must pass `grant_type`, `client_id`, `username`, and `password`. The `grant_type` is `password`, the `client_id` is the ID from the created client, and then the `username` and `password` of the account you wish to use:

```
curl -X POST \
  http://127.0.0.1:8888/oauth/token \
  -H 'content-type: application/x-www-form-urlencoded' \
  -d
'grant_type=password&client_id=3ec55f70-18cd-422f-9abd-2223f6ca3636
&username=admin&password=admin'
```

 At the time of writing this book, the endpoint did not accept a JSON body, but only form-encoded values.

10. The response will contain an `access_token` property. This is to be used as your token when making API requests.

11. Request a node over REST with the `Authorization: Bearer [token]` header:

```
curl -X GET \
    'http://127.0.0.1:8888/node/1?_format=json' \
    -H 'accept: application/json' \
    -H 'authorization: Bearer JT9zgBgMEDlk2QIF0ecpZEOcsYC7-
x649Bovo83HXQM'
```

How it works

The Simple OAuth module is built using the `League\OAuth2` PHP library, a community de facto library for OAuth2 implementation.

In a typical authentication request, there is an authentication manager that uses the `authentication_collector` service to collect all the tagged authentication provider servers. Based on the provider's set priority, each service is invoked to check whether it applies to the current request. Each applied authentication provider then gets invoked to see whether the authentication is invalid.

For the RESTful Web Services module, the process is more explicit. The providers identified in the `supported_auth` definition for the endpoint are the only services that run through the *applies* and *authenticates* process.

There's more...

We will explore more information on working with authentication providers and the RESTful Web Services module in the next section.

Authentication provider services

When working with the RESTful Web Services module endpoints, the `supported_auth` values reference services tagged with `authentication_provider`. Out of the box, Drupal supports cookie authentication. The following code is provided by the `basic_auth` module to support the HTTP header authentication:

```
services:
  basic_auth.authentication.basic_auth:
    class: Drupal\basic_auth\Authentication\Provider\BasicAuth
    arguments: ['@config.factory', '@user.auth', '@flood',
'@entity.manager']
    tags:
      - { name: authentication_provider, provider_id: 'basic_auth',
priority: 100 }
```

An authentication provider can be created by creating a class in your module's `Authentication\Provider` namespace and implementing the `\Drupal\Core\Authentication\AuthenticationProviderInterface` interface. Then, register the class as a service in your module's `services.yml`.

Page cache request policies and authenticated Web service requests

When working with data that expects authenticated users, the authentication service provider should also provide a page cache service handler. Services that are tagged with `page_cache_request_policy` have the ability to check whether the content is cached or not. This prevents authorization requests from being cached.

The following code is taken from the `basic_auth` module:

```
basic_auth.page_cache_request_policy.disallow_basic_auth_requests:
    class: Drupal\basic_auth\PageCache\DisallowBasicAuthRequests
    public: false
    tags:
      - { name: page_cache_request_policy }
```

The `\Drupal\basic_auth\PageCache\DisallowBasicAuthRequests` class implements the `\Drupal\Core\PageCache\RequestPolicyInterface` interface. The check method allows the page cache policy to explicitly deny or remain neutral on a page's ability to be cached. The `basic_auth` module checks whether the default authentication headers are present. For the `simple_oauth` module, it checks whether a valid token is present.

This is an important security measure if you are implementing your own authentication services.

A page cache policy service can be implemented by creating a class in your module's `PageCache` namespace and implementing the `\Drupal\Core\PageCache\ResponsePolicyInterface` interface. Then, we need to register the class as a service in your module's `services.yml`.

The IP Authentication provider

Some APIs that implement server-to-server communication will authenticate using IP address whitelists. For this use case, we have the IP Consumer Auth module. Whitelisted IP addresses are controlled by a form that saves a configuration value.

If an IP address is whitelisted, the user is authenticated as an anonymous user. While this may not be recommended for POST, PATCH, and DELETE requests, it can provide a simple way to control specific GET endpoints in a private network.

You can download IP Consumer Auth from its project page at `https://www.drupal.org/project/ip_consumer_auth`.

See also

- Refer to the OAuth Community Site at `http://oauth.net/`
- Refer to the OAuth module for OAuth 1.0 support at `https://www.drupal.org/project/oauth`
- Refer to the simple OAuth module for OAuth 2.0 support at `https://www.drupal.org/project/simple_oauth`
- Refer to the IP Consumer Auth module at `https://www.drupal.org/project/ip_consumer_auth`

Using JSON API

When developing a backend API for frontend consumers, there is often much debate on naming conventions and returned value structures. In comes {json:api}, an open source specification set to standardize and simplify the building of APIs, which consume and return JSON payloads. The specification and documentation can be found at `http://jsonapi.org/`.

For Drupal, there is a community-lead effort to provide a robust JSON API specification implementation to turn Drupal into a streamlined API server. This recipe will install the JSON API module and show how to enable resources.

Just like the RESTful Web Services module provided by Drupal core, the JSON API module does not provide a user interface. It also enables all content to be available over the API automatically (given that users have permissions configured to access the endpoint.) The JSON API Extra module changes that, and this will be covered in the *There's more...* section of this recipe.

The JSON API module can be found at `https://www.drupal.org/project/jsonapi`

Getting ready

Create sample content using the `Article` content type provided by the standard Drupal installation. This will make testing the GET methods much easier.

When making requests, all endpoint paths are prefixed with `jsonapi`.

How to do it

1. First, we must add the JSON API module to our Drupal site:

```
cd /path/to/drupal8
composer require drupal/jsonapi
```

2. Install the **JSON API** and **Serialization** module. Once the module is installed, the API endpoints will be active.:

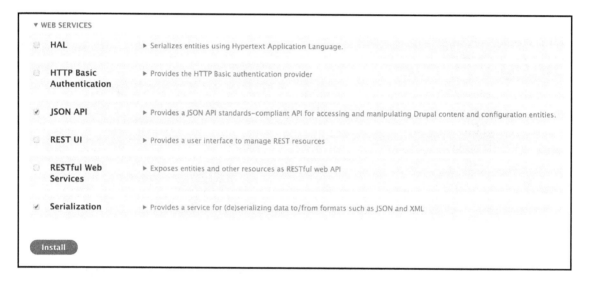

3. To perform a request, you must pass an Accept header with the value `application/vnd.api+json`.

4. For the JSON API specification, every resource must have a unique type name, and JSON API derives this from the entity type and its bundle. The endpoint for retrieving Article nodes will be:

```
http://127.0.0.1:8888/jsonapi/node/article
```

5. The entire request can be executed with the following command:

```
curl -X GET \
  http://127.0.0.1:8888/jsonapi/node/article \
  -H 'accept: application/vnd.api+json'
```

6. The response will resemble the following. The content values will be in the attributes property:

```
{
  "data": [
    {
      "type": "node--article",
      "id": "c897acba-eb81-454a-94ed-13107fd205cf",
      "attributes": {...},
      "relationships": {...},
      "links": {
        "self":
"http://127.0.0.1:8888/jsonapi/node/article/c897acba-eb81-454a-94ed
-13107fd205cf"
      }
    }
  ],
  "links": {
    "self": "http://127.0.0.1:8888/jsonapi/node/article",
  }
}
```

How it works...

The JSON API module implements the `{json:api}` specification. Like the RESTful Web Services module provided by Drupal core, it exposes data over various endpoints. It builds on top of Drupal's existing routing system to work with non-HTML formats. The major difference is it follows a community-driven specification on how the data should be formatted, linked, filtered, sorted, and more.

There's more...

Next, we'll cover filtering, paging, sorting, and the JSON API Extras module.

Paginating, filtering, and sorting requests

The request in the recipe will return all available Article nodes in the system. These can be paginated, filtered, and sorted. Each of these operations is done through query parameters, which contain an array of values.

Pagination is done by appending a `page` query parameter. To limit the request to 10 nodes, we would append `?page[limit]=10`. To access the next set of results, we would also pass `page[offset]=10`.

The following is an example of returning the first and second pages of results:

```
http://127.0.0.1:8888/jsonapi/node/article?page[limit]=10
http://127.0.0.1:8888/jsonapi/node/article?page[offset]=10&page[limit]=10
```

Each request contains a links property; this will also contain the next and previous links when using a paginated result.

Filtering is done by appending a `filter` query parameter. The following is an example for requesting all nodes that have been promoted to the front page:

```
http://127.0.0.1:8888/jsonapi/node/article?filter[promoted][path]=promote&f
ilter[promoted][value]=1&filter[promoted][operator]==
```

Each filter is defined by a name--in the preceding example, it is `promoted`. The filter then takes `path`, which is the field to filter on. The `value` and `operator` decide how to filter.

Sorting is the simplest operation. A sort query parameter is added. The field name value is the field to sort by, and to sort in descending order, you add a minute symbol in front of the field name. The following examples show how to sort by the `nid` in ascending and descending order, respectively:

```
http://127.0.0.1:8888/jsonapi/node/article?sort=nid
http://127.0.0.1:8888/jsonapi/node/article?sort=-nid
```

Installing the JSON API Extras module

The JSON API Extras module provides a user interface for additional customization. The JSON API Extras module should be added to your Drupal installation like all other modules, using Composer:

```
cd /path/to/drupal8
composer require drupal/jsonapi_extras
```

Once the module is installed in Drupal, you will have the ability to enable or disable endpoints, change resource names, alter resource paths, disable fields, alias field names, and enhance field outputs.

Changing the API path prefix

The API path prefix can be changed from `jsonapi` to `api` or any other prefix using the extras module.

From the administrative toolbar, navigate to **Configuration**. Under the **Web services** section, click on **JSON API Overwrites** to customize the JSON API implementation. The **Settings** tab allows modification of the API path prefix:

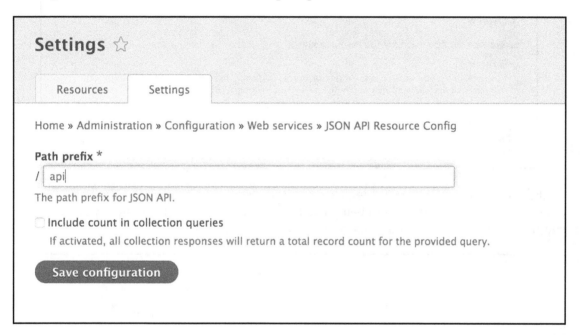

Disabling and enhancing returned entity fields

The JSON API Extras module allows overwriting endpoints automatically exposed by the JSON API module. This allows disabling fields from being returned. It also allows using enhancers to simplify the structure of a field property.

From the administrative toolbar, go to **Configuration**. Under the **Web services** section, click on **JSON API Overwrites** to customize the JSON API implementation.

To disable an endpoint, click on **Overwrite** on any endpoint. Check the **Disabled** checkbox to turn off that specific endpoint:

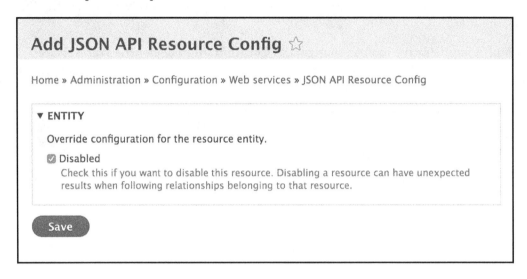

To disable, alias, or use an enhancer, click on **Overwrite** on any endpoint. The checkbox will allow you to prevent a field from being used in the API. The enhancers allow you to simplify fields when returned or used in POST/PATCH requests:

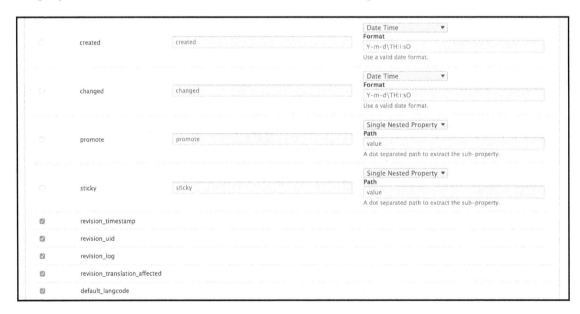

In this example, the `created` and `changed` fields will no longer return Unix timestamps, but RFC ISO8601-formatted timestamps. The `promote` and `sticky` fields will return their value directly, not nested under a `value` property. Finally, no revision information fields will be returned.

Contenta CMS

Contenta CMS is a decoupled, API-driven Drupal distribution built using the JSON API. It is being built through the same community initiative pushing forward the JSON API module. The project's home page can be found at `http://www.contentacms.org/`.

It provides many preconfigured options, including customizations to default endpoints. It also provides Simple OAuth to set up decoupled authentication with your frontend consumer and the API backend.

On top of delivering a distribution, the community contributors have developed various frontend consumers as examples:

- **Angular**: `https://github.com/contentacms/contenta_angular`
- **Vue/Nuxt**: `https://github.com/contentacms/contenta_vue_nuxt`
- **Ember.js**: `https://github.com/contentacms/contenta_ember`
- **Ionic**: `https://github.com/contentacms/contenta_ionic`
- **React**: `https://github.com/contentacms/contenta_react`

See also

- JSON API project page at `https://www.drupal.org/project/jsonapi`
- JSON API Extras page at `https://www.drupal.org/project/jsonapi_extras`
- JSON API module documentation at `https://www.drupal.org/docs/8/modules/json-api/json-api`
- JSON API module video tutorials at `https://www.youtube.com/playlist?list=PLZOQ_ZMpYrZsyO-3IstImK1okrpfAjuMZ`
- The `{json:api}` specification documentation at `http://jsonapi.org/`

13
The Drupal CLI

There are two command-line tools for Drupal 8: **Drupal Console** and **Drush**. In this chapter, we will discuss how they make working with Drupal easier by covering the following recipes:

- Rebuilding cache in Drupal Console or Drush
- Using Drush to interact with the database
- Debugging Drupal using Drupal Console
- Scaffolding code through Drupal Console
- Making a Drush command
- Making a Drupal Console command

Introduction

In the previous chapters of this book, there have been recipes that provide ways of using command-line tools to simplify working with Drupal. There are two contributed projects that provide Drupal with a command-line interface experience.

First, there is Drush. Drush was first created for Drupal 4.7 and has become an integral tool used for day-to-day Drupal operations. However, with Drupal 8 and its integration with Symfony, there came Drupal Console. Drupal Console is a Symfony Console-based application that allows it to reuse more components and integrate more easily with contributed modules.

This chapter contains recipes that will highlight operations that can be simplified using Drush or Console. By the end of this chapter, you will be able to work with your Drupal sites through the command line.

At the time of writing this book, Drush was still the primary tool of choice for Drupal 8; however, Drupal Console is earning more market share. Drupal Console is rapidly being developed. Due to this rapid development, the commands will still exist, but the output may differ.

Both Drush and Drupal Console support global installation, but both projects are migrating to per-project installation using Composer. To get started, refer to the following installation guides for each tool for up-to-date installation information:

- **Drush**: http://docs.drush.org/en/master/install/
- **Drupal Console**: https://docs.drupalconsole.com/en/getting/project.html

Rebuilding cache in Drupal Console or Drush

Drupal utilizes caching to store plugin definitions, routes, and so on. When you add a new plugin definition or a new route, you need to rebuild Drupal's cache for it to be recognized.

Rebuilding the cache over the command line is also more performant than using the user interface since it does not use web server resources to execute the cache rebuild.

In this recipe, we will walk you through using both Drush and Drupal Console to clear various cache bins in Drupal. It is important to know how to clear specific cache bins so that you do not need to rebuild everything, if possible.

How to do it...

1. Open a terminal and navigate to an installed Drupal directory.
2. We use the `cache-rebuild` command in Drush to rebuild all of Drupal's caches, including routes:

```
$ drush cache-rebuild
Cache rebuild complete.
```

3. In Drupal Console, we use the `cache:rebuild` command to clear specific cache bins. The input uses autocomplete to help specify a specific cache bin to clear. In this example, we clear the render cache:

```
$ drupal cache:rebuild all
 Select cache. [all]:
 > render
 Rebuilding cache(s), wait a moment please.
 [OK] Done clearing cache(s).
```

4. If we only need to rebuild our routes in Drupal, we can use the `router:rebuild` command in Console. This will keep render, discovery, and other caches, but expose new routes:

```
$ drupal router:rebuild
 Rebuilding routes, wait a moment please
 [OK] Done rebuilding route(s).
```

5. Drush provides `twig-compile` to rebuild templates. Passing the verbose option displays templates being compiled:

```
$ drush twig-compile --verbose
```

How it works...

Both Drush and Drupal Console will load files from the Drupal installation and bootstrap the application. This allows the commands to invoke functions and methods found in Drupal.

For Drush 8.x, Drush does not implement the dependency injection container and still needs to rely on procedural functions in Drupal.

Drupal Console, however, harnesses the dependency injection container, allowing it to reuse Drupal's container and services.

The *Making a Drush command* and *Making a Drupal Console command* recipes will describe the differences in more detail.

See also

- The Drush documentation at `http://docs.drush.org/en/master/`
- The Drupal Console documentation at `https://docs.drupalconsole.com/`
- The Drush command cheat sheet at `https://drushcommands.com/`
- The Drupal Console command cheat sheet at `http://drupalconsole.com/cheatsheet/`

Using Drush to interact with the database

When working with any application that utilizes a database, there are times when you will need to export a database and import it elsewhere. Most often, you would do this with a production site to work on it locally. This way, you can create a new configuration that can be exported and pushed to production, as discussed in `Chapter 9`, *Configuration Management – Deploying in Drupal 8*.

In this recipe, we will export a database dump from a production site in order to set up the local development. The database dump will be imported over the command line and sanitized. We will then execute an SQL query through Drush to verify sanitization.

Getting ready

Drush has the ability to use site aliases. Site aliases are configuration items that allow you to interact with a remote Drupal site. In this recipe, we will use the following alias to interact with a fictional remote site to show how a typical workflow will go to fetch a remote database.

Note that you do not need to use a Drush alias to download the database dump created in the recipe; you can use any method you are familiar with (manually from the command line with `mysqldump` or `phpMyAdmin`):

```
$aliases['drupal.production'] = [
  'uri' => 'example.com',
  'remote-host' => 'example.com',
  'remote-user' => 'someuser',
  'ssh-options' => '-p 2222',
];
```

Read the Drush documentation for more information on site aliases at
`http://docs.drush.org/en/master/usage/#site-aliases`. Site aliases
allow you to interact with remote Drupal installations.

We will also assume that the local development site has not yet been configured to connect
it to the database.

How to do it...

1. We will use the `sql-dump` command to export the database into a file. The
   command returns the output that needs to be redirected to a file:

   ```
   $ drush @drupal.production sql-dump > ~/prod-dump.sql
   ```

2. Navigate to your local Drupal site's directory and copy
   `sites/default/default.settings.php` to `sites/default/settings.php`.

3. Edit the new `settings.php` file and add a database configuration array at the
   end of the file; this will be the database used by Drupal:

   ```php
   // Database configuration.
   $databases['default']['default'] = [
     'driver' => 'mysql',
     'host' => 'localhost',
     'username' => 'mysql',
     'password' => 'mysql',
     'database' => 'data',
     'prefix' => '',
     'port' => 3306,
     'namespace' => 'Drupal\\Core\\Database\\Driver\\mysql',
   ];
   ```

4. Using the `sql-cli` command, we can import the database dump that we created:

   ```
   $ drush sql-cli < ~/prod-dump.sql
   ```

5. The `sql-sanitize` command allows you to obfuscate user emails and
   passwords in the database:

   ```
   $ drush sql-sanitize
   ```

6. To verify that our information is imported sanitized, we will use the `sql-query` command to run a query against the database:

```
$ drush sql-query "SELECT uid, name, mail FROM users_field_data;"
```

How it works...

When working with Drush, we have the ability to use Drush aliases. A Drush alias contains a configuration that allows the tool to connect to a remote server and interact with that server's installation of Drush.

> You need to have Drush installed on your remote server in order to use a site alias for it.

The `sql-dump` command executes the proper dump command for the database driver, which is typically MySQL and the `mysqldump` command. It streams to the terminal and must be piped to a destination. When piped to a local SQL file, we can import it and execute the create commands to import our database schema and data.

> The `sql-dump` command supports a `--result-file` option; however, that saves the file relative to the Drupal installation.

With the `sql-cli` command, we will be able to execute SQL commands to the database through Drush. This allows us to redirect the file contents to the `sql-cli` command and run the set of SQL commands. With the data imported, the `sql-sanitize` command replaces usernames and passwords.

Finally, the `sql-query` command allows us to pass an SQL command directly to the database and return its results. In our recipe, we will query the `users_field_data` to verify that we imported our users and that emails have been sanitized.

There's more...

Working with Drupal over the command line simplifies working with the database. We will explore this in more detail in the following sections.

Using gzip with sql-dump

Sometimes, databases can be quite large. The `sql-dump` command has a `gzip` option that will output the SQL dump using the `gzip` command. In order to run the command, you would simply:

```
$ drush sql-dump --gzip dump.sql.gz
```

The end result provides a reduction in the dump file:

```
-rw-r--r--   1 user  group  3058522 Jan 14 16:10 dump.sql
-rw-r--r--   1 user  group   285880 Jan 14 16:10 dump.sql.gz
```

> If you create a gzipped database dump, ensure that you unarchive it before attempting an import with the `sql-cli` command.

Using Console to interact with the database

At the time of writing this book, Console does not provide a command for sanitizing the database. The feature is currently documented in this issue; refer to `https://github.com/hechoendrupal/drupal-console/issues/3192`.

The `database:connect` and `database:client` commands will launch a database client. This allows you to be logged into the database's command-line interface:

```
$ drupal database:client
$ drupal database:connect
```

These commands are similar to the `sql-cli` and `sql-connect` commands from Drush. The client command will bring you to the database's command-line tool, where connect shows the connection string.

Drupal Console also provides the `database:dump` command. Unlike Drush, this will write the database dump for you in the Drupal directory:

```
$ drupal database:dump
  [OK] Database exported to: /path/to/drupal/www/data.sql
```

Using Drush to manage users

When you need to add an account to Drupal, you will visit the `People` page and manually add a new user. Drush provides the complete user management for Drupal, from creation to role assignment, password recovery, and deletion. This workflow allows you to create users easily and provides them with a login without having to enter your Drupal site.

In this recipe, we will create a `staff` role with a `staffmember` user and log in as that user through Drush.

How to do it...

1. Use the `role-create` command to create a new role labeled `staff`:

   ```
   $ drush role-create staff
    Created "staff"
   ```

2. Use the `role-lists` command to verify that the role was created in Drupal:

   ```
   $ drush role-list
   ID Role Label
   anonymous Anonymous user
   authenticated Authenticated user
   administrator Administrator
   staff Staff
   ```

3. The `user-create` command will create our user:

   ```
   $ drush user-create staffmember
   User ID : 2
   User name : staffmember
   User roles : authenticated
   User status : 1
   ```

4. In order to add the role, we will need to use the `user-add-role` command:

   ```
   $ drush user-add-role staff staffmember
   Added role staff role to staffmember
   ```

5. We will now log in as the `staffmember` user using the `user-login` command:

```
$ drush user-login staffmember --uri=http://example.com
http://example.com/user/reset/2/1452810532/Ia1nJvbr2UQ3Pi_QnmIT1Vgc
CWzDtnKmHxf-I2eAqPE
```

6. Copy the link and paste it in your browser to log in as that user:

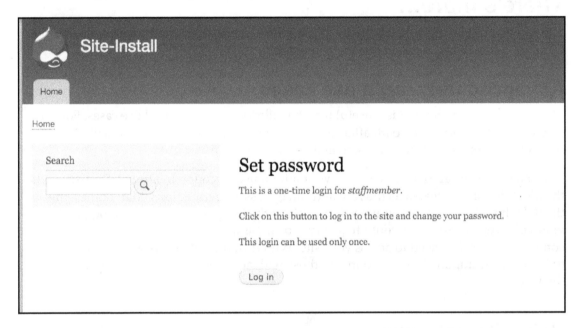

How it works...

When you reset a password in Drupal, a special one-time login link is generated. The login link is based on a generated hash. The Drush command validates the given user, which exists in the Drupal site, and then passes it to the `user_pass_reset_url` function from the User module.

The URL is made up of the user's ID, the timestamp when the link was generated, and a hash based on the user's last login time, link generation, and email. When the link is loaded, this hash is rebuilt and verified. For example, if the user has logged in since the time it was generated, the link will become invalid.

When used on a machine that has a web browser installed, Drush will make an attempt to launch the link in a web browser for you. The browser option allows you to specify which browser should be launched. Additionally, you can use no-browser to prevent one from being launched.

There's more...

The command line offers the ability to simplify user management and user administration. Next, we will explore more on this topic in detail.

Advanced user-login use cases

The user-login command is a useful tool that allows some advanced use cases. For instance, you can append a path after the username and be launched to that path. You can pass a UID or email instead of a username in order to log in as a user.

You can use the user-login to secure your admin user account. In Drupal, the user with the identifier of 1 is treated as the root and can bypass all permissions. Many times, this is the default maintenance account used to work on the Drupal site. Instead of logging in manually, you can set the account to a very robust passphrase and use the user-login command when you need to access your site. With this, the only users who should be able to log in as the administrator account are those with access to run the Drush commands on the website.

Using Drupal Console

Drupal Console also provide commands to interact with users. Although they do not allow the creation of users or roles, they provide a basic user management.

The user:login:url command will generate a one-time login link for the specified user ID. This uses the same methods as the Drush command:

```
$ drupal user:login:url 2
```

The user:password:reset command allows you to reset a user's password to the new provided password. You can provide the user ID and new password as arguments, but if missing, the values will be prompted for interactively:

```
$ drupal user:password:reset 2 newpassword
```

The `create:users` command provides an interactive way to generate bulk users, which are useful for debugging. However, it cannot create individual users with specific passwords like Drush.

Scaffolding code through Console

When Drupal Console was first introduced, one of the biggest highlights was its ability to scaffold code. The project has turned into a much larger Drupal runner over the command-line interface, but much of its resourcefulness is code generation.

As you may have noted in the previous chapters and recipes, there can be a few mundane tasks and a bit of boilerplate code. Drupal Console enables Drupal developers to create various components without having to write all of the boilerplate code.

In `Chapter 10`, *The Entity API*, we covered the creation of a custom entity type. In this recipe, we will automate most of that process using Drupal Console to generate our content entity.

Getting ready

For this recipe, you will need to have Drupal Console installed. The tool will generate everything else for us. You will need to have a Drupal 8 site installed. Many of Console's commands will not work (or be listed) unless they can access an installed Drupal site. This is because of the way it interacts with Drupal's service container.

How to do it...

1. From the root of your Drupal site, generate a module with the `generate:module` command and follow the interactive process. Use the defaults prompted as well as giving it a module name:

   ```
   $ drupal generate:module
   // Welcome to the Drupal module generator
   Enter the new module name:
   > Content Entity Provider

   Enter the module machine name [content_entity_provider]:
   >

   Enter the module Path [/modules/custom]:
   ```

```
>

Enter module description [My Awesome Module]:
>

Enter package name [Custom]:
>

Enter Drupal Core version [8.x]:
>

Do you want to generate a .module file (yes/no) [yes]:
>

Define module as feature (yes/no) [no]:
>

Do you want to add a composer.json file to your module (yes/no)
[yes]:
>

Would you like to add module dependencies (yes/no) [no]:
>

Do you want to generate a unit test class (yes/no) [yes]:
>

Do you want to generate a themeable template (yes/no) [yes]:
>

Do you confirm generation? (yes/no) [yes]:
>

Generated or updated files
 1 -
modules/custom/content_entity_provider/content_entity_provider.info
.yml
 2 -
modules/custom/content_entity_provider/content_entity_provider.modu
le
 3 - modules/custom/content_entity_provider/composer.json
 4 -
modules/custom/content_entity_provider/tests/src/Functional/LoadTes
t.php
 5 -
modules/custom/content_entity_provider/content_entity_provider.modu
le
 6 - modules/custom/content_entity_provider/templates/content-
```

```
entity-provider.html.twig
```

2. Next, we will generate our content entity. Specify the module name that will provide the entity:

```
$ drupal generate:entity:content
Enter the module name [devel]:
> content_entity_provider

Enter the class of your new content entity [DefaultEntity]:
> CustomContentEntity

Enter the machine name of your new content entity
[custom_content_entity]:
>

Enter the label of your new content entity [Custom content entity]:
>

Enter the base-path for the content entity routes
[/admin/structure]:
>

Do you want this (content) entity to have bundles (yes/no) [no]:
>

Is your entity translatable (yes/no) [yes]:
>

Is your entity revisionable (yes/no) [yes]:
>

Generated or updated files
1 -
modules/custom/content_entity_provider/content_entity_provider.perm
issions.yml
2 -
modules/custom/content_entity_provider/content_entity_provider.link
s.menu.yml
3 -
modules/custom/content_entity_provider/content_entity_provider.link
s.task.yml
4 -
modules/custom/content_entity_provider/content_entity_provider.link
s.action.yml
5 -
modules/custom/content_entity_provider/src/CustomContentEntityAcces
sControlHandler.php
```

```
6 -
modules/custom/content_entity_provider/src/CustomContentEntityTrans
lationHandler.php
7 -
modules/custom/content_entity_provider/src/Entity/CustomContentEnti
tyInterface.php
8 -
modules/custom/content_entity_provider/src/Entity/CustomContentEnti
ty.php
9 -
modules/custom/content_entity_provider/src/CustomContentEntityHtmlR
outeProvider.php
10 -
modules/custom/content_entity_provider/src/Entity/CustomContentEnti
tyViewsData.php
11 -
modules/custom/content_entity_provider/src/CustomContentEntityListB
uilder.php
12 -
modules/custom/content_entity_provider/src/Form/CustomContentEntity
SettingsForm.php
13 -
modules/custom/content_entity_provider/src/Form/CustomContentEntity
Form.php
14 -
modules/custom/content_entity_provider/src/Form/CustomContentEntity
DeleteForm.php
15 -
modules/custom/content_entity_provider/custom_content_entity.page.i
nc
16 -
modules/custom/content_entity_provider/templates/custom_content_ent
ity.html.twig
17 -
modules/custom/content_entity_provider/src/Form/CustomContentEntity
RevisionDeleteForm.php
18 -
modules/custom/content_entity_provider/src/Form/CustomContentEntity
RevisionRevertTranslationForm.php
19 -
modules/custom/content_entity_provider/src/Form/CustomContentEntity
RevisionRevertForm.php
20 -
modules/custom/content_entity_provider/src/CustomContentEntityStora
ge.php
21 -
modules/custom/content_entity_provider/src/CustomContentEntityStora
geInterface.php
```

```
22 -
modules/custom/content_entity_provider/src/Controller/CustomContent
EntityController.php
```

3. Install your module using Drupal Console:

```
$ drupal module:install content_entity_provider
 Installing module(s) "content_entity_provider"

 [OK] The following module(s) were installed successfully:
"content_entity_provider"
                                                              //
cache:rebuild
Rebuilding cache(s), wait a moment please.
 [OK] Done clearing cache(s).
```

4. View Structure and find your **Custom content entity settings**:

How it works...

One of the biggest features of Console is its ability to reduce the time spent by developers to create code for Drupal 8. Console utilizes the Twig templating engine to provide code generation. These Twig templates contain variables and logic that are compiled into the end result code.

A set of generator classes receives specific parameters, which are received through the appropriate command, and pass them to Twig for rendering. This allows Console to easily stay up to date with changes in Drupal core and still provide valuable code generation.

Making a Drush command

Drush provides an API that allows developers to write their own commands. These commands can be part of a module and loaded through a Drupal installation, or they can be placed in the local user's Drush folder for general purposes.

Often, contributed modules create commands to automate user interface operations. However, creating a custom Drush command can be useful for specific operations. In this recipe, we will create a command that loads all the users who have not logged in in the last 10 days and resets their password.

Getting ready

For this recipe, you will need Drush available. We will be creating a command in a local user directory.

How to do it...

1. Create a file named `disable_users.drush.inc` in the `~/.drush` folder for your user:

```php
<?php

/**
 * @file
 * Loads all users who have not logged in within 10 days and
disables them.
 */
```

2. Add the Drush command hook that will allow Drush to discover our commands provided by the file:

```
/**
 * Implements hook_drush_command().
 */
function disable_users_drush_command() {
  $items = [];
  $items['disable-users'] = [
    'description' => 'Disables users after 10 days of inactivity',
  ];
  return $items;
}
```

3. Next, we will create the command callback function, which will end up holding all of our logic. Since our filename is `disable_users.drush.inc` and our command is `disable-users`, the hook turns out to be `drush_disable_users_disable_users`:

```
/**
 * Implements drush_hook_COMMAND().
 */
function drush_disable_users_disable_users() {

}
```

4. Update the function to create a `DateTime` object, representing 10 days ago. We will use this to generate a timestamp for our query:

```
/**
 * Implements drush_hook_COMMAND().
 */
function drush_disable_users_disable_users() {
  // Get the default timezone and make a DateTime object for 10
days ago.
  $system_date = \Drupal::config('system.date');
  $default_timezone = $system_date->get('timezone.default') ?:
date_default_timezone_get();
  $now = new DateTime('now', new DateTimeZone($default_timezone));
  $now->modify('-10 days');
}
```

5. Now, we will add our query, which will query all the user entities who have a login timestamp greater than 10 days:

```
/**
```

```
 * Implements drush_hook_COMMAND().
 */
function drush_disable_users_disable_users() {
  // Get the default timezone and make a DateTime object for 10
days ago.
  $system_date = \Drupal::config('system.date');
  $default_timezone = $system_date->get('timezone.default') ?:
date_default_timezone_get();
  $now = new DateTime('now', new DateTimeZone($default_timezone));
  $now->modify('-10 days');

  $query = \Drupal::entityQuery('user')->condition('login',
$now->getTimestamp(), '>');
  $results = $query->execute();
  if (empty($results)) {
    drush_print('No users to disable!');
  }

}
```

6. Next, we will iterate over the results and mark the user as disabled:

```
/**
 * Implements drush_hook_COMMAND().
 */
function drush_disable_users_disable_users() {
  // Get the default timezone and make a DateTime object for 10
days ago.
  $system_date = \Drupal::config('system.date');
  $default_timezone = $system_date->get('timezone.default') ?:
date_default_timezone_get();
  $now = new DateTime('now', new DateTimeZone($default_timezone));
  $now->modify('-10 days');

  $query = \Drupal::entityQuery('user')->condition('login',
$now->getTimestamp(), '>');
  $results = $query->execute();
  if (empty($results)) {
    drush_print('No users to disable!');
  }

  foreach ($results as $uid) {
    /** @var \Drupal\user\Entity\User $user */
    $user = \Drupal\user\Entity\User::load($uid);
    $user->block();
    $user->save();
  }
```

```
        drush_print(dt('Disabled !count users', ['!count' =>
    count($results)]));
    }
```

7. Drush's cache will need to be cleared in order to discover your new command:

   $ drush cache-clear drush

8. Check whether the command exists:

   $ drush disable-users --help
   Disables users after 10 days of inactivity

How it works...

Drush works by scanning specific directories for files that follow the COMMANDFILE.drush.inc pattern. You can think of COMMANDFILE for Drush as a representation of a module name in Drupal's hook system. When implementing a Drush hook, in the HOOK_drush format, you will need to replace HOOK with your COMMANDFILE name, just as you would do in Drupal with a module name.

In this recipe, we created a disable_users.drush.inc file. This means that all hooks and commands in the file need to use disable_users for hook invocations. Drush uses this to load the hook_drush_command hook that returns our command information.

We then provided the functionality of our logic in the drush_hook_command hook. For this hook, we replaced hook with our COMMANDFILE name, which was disable_users, giving us drush_disable_users_command. We replaced command with the command that we defined in hook_drush_command, which was disable-users. We then had our final drush_disable_users_disable_users hook.

There's more...

Drush commands have additional options that can be specified in their definitions. We explore their abilities to control the required level of Drupal integration for a command.

Specifying the level of Drupal's bootstrap

Drush commands have the ability to specify the level of Drupal's bootstrap before being executed. Drupal has several bootstrap levels in which only specific parts of the system are loaded. By default, a command's bootstrap is at DRUSH_BOOTSTRAP_DRUPAL_LOGIN, which is at the same level as accessing Drupal over the Web.

Commands, depending on their purpose, can choose to avoid bootstrapping Drupal at all or only until the database system is loaded. Drush commands that are utilities, such as the Git release notes module, provide a Drush command that does not interact with Drupal. It specifies a bootstrap of DRUSH_BOOTSTRAP_DRUSH, as it only interacts with repositories to generate change logs based on Git tags and commits.

See also

- Refer to how to creating custom Drush commands at http://docs.drush.org/en/master/commands/.
- Refer to how to install Drush at http://docs.drush.org/en/master/install/.
- Refer to the Drush Bootstrap process at http://docs.drush.org/en/master/bootstrap/.

Making a Console command

Drupal Console makes use of the Symfony Console project and other third-party libraries to utilize modern PHP best practices. In doing so, it follows Drupal 8 practices as well. This allows Console to use namespaces for the command detection and interaction with Drupal by reading its class loader.

This allows developers to easily create a Console command by implementing a custom class in a module.

In this recipe, we will create a command that loads all the users who have not logged in in the last 10 days and resets their password. We will generate the base of our command using the scaffolding commands.

Getting ready

For this recipe, you will need to have Drupal Console installed. The tool will generate everything else for us. You will need to have a Drupal 8 site installed.

How to do it...

1. Create a new module that will hold your Drupal Console command, such as console_commands:

   ```
   drupal generate:module

   // Welcome to the Drupal module generator
   Enter the new module name:
    > Console Commands

   Enter the module machine name [console_commands]:
    >

   Enter the module Path [/modules/custom]:
    >

   Enter module description [My Awesome Module]:
    >

   Enter package name [Custom]:
    >

   Enter Drupal Core version [8.x]:
    >

   Do you want to generate a .module file (yes/no) [yes]:
    >

   Define module as feature (yes/no) [no]:
    >

   Do you want to add a composer.json file to your module (yes/no)
   [yes]:
    >
   ```

```
Would you like to add module dependencies (yes/no) [no]:
 >

Do you want to generate a unit test class (yes/no) [yes]:
 >

Do you want to generate a themeable template (yes/no) [yes]:
 >

Do you confirm generation? (yes/no) [yes]:
 >

Generated or updated files
1 - modules/custom/console_commands/console_commands.info.yml
 2 - modules/custom/console_commands/console_commands.module
 3 - modules/custom/console_commands/composer.json
 4
modules/custom/console_commands/tests/src/Functional/LoadTest.php
 5 - modules/custom/console_commands/console_commands.module
 6 - modules/custom/console_commands/templates/console-
commands.html.twig
```

2. Next, we will generate the command's base files using the `generate:command` command. Call it the `disable_users` command:

```
drupal generate:command

// Welcome to the Drupal Command generator
 Enter the extension name [devel]:
 > console_commands

Enter the Command name. [console_commands:default]:
 > console_commands:disable_users

Enter the Command Class. (Must end with the word 'Command').
[DefaultCommand]:
 > DisableUsersCommand

Is the command aware of the drupal site installation when
executed?. (yes/no) [no]:
 > yes

Do you confirm generation? (yes/no) [yes]:
 >

Generated or updated files
 1 -
modules/custom/console_commands/src/Command/DisableUsersCommand.php
```

```
2 - modules/custom/console_commands/console.services.yml
3 -
modules/custom/console_commands/console/translations/en/console_com
mands.disable_users.yml
```

3. Edit the created `DisableUsersCommand.php` file and remove the boilerplate example code from the execute method:

```
/**
 * {@inheritdoc}
 */
protected function execute(InputInterface $input, OutputInterface
$output) {
}
```

4. Update the function to create a `DateTime` object, representing 10 days ago. We will use this to generate a timestamp for our query:

```
/**
 * {@inheritdoc}
 */
protected function execute(InputInterface $input, OutputInterface
$output) {
  // Get the default timezone and make a DateTime object for 10
days ago.
  $system_date = \Drupal::config('system.date');
  $default_timezone = $system_date->get('timezone.default') ?:
date_default_timezone_get();
  $now = new \DateTime('now', new
\DateTimeZone($default_timezone));
  $now->modify('-10 days');
}
```

5. Now, we will add our query, which will query all the user entities who have a login timestamp greater than 10 days:

```
/**
 * {@inheritdoc}
 */
protected function execute(InputInterface $input, OutputInterface
$output) {
  // Get the default timezone and make a DateTime object for 10
days ago.
  $system_date = \Drupal::config('system.date');
  $default_timezone = $system_date->get('timezone.default') ?:
date_default_timezone_get();
  $now = new \DateTime('now', new
```

```
\DateTimeZone($default_timezone));
  $now->modify('-10 days');

  $query = \Drupal::entityQuery('user')->condition('login',
$now->getTimestamp(), '>');
  $results = $query->execute();

  if (empty($results)) {
    $output->writeln('<info>No users to disable!</info>');
  }
}
```

6. Next, we will iterate over the results and mark the user as disabled:

```
/**
 * {@inheritdoc}
 */
protected function execute(InputInterface $input, OutputInterface
$output) {
  // Get the default timezone and make a DateTime object for 10
days ago.
  $system_date = \Drupal::config('system.date');
  $default_timezone = $system_date->get('timezone.default') ?:
date_default_timezone_get();
  $now = new \DateTime('now', new
\DateTimeZone($default_timezone));
  $now->modify('-10 days');

  $query = \Drupal::entityQuery('user')->condition('login',
$now->getTimestamp(), '>');
  $results = $query->execute();

  if (empty($results)) {
    $output->writeln('<info>No users to disable!</info>');
  }

  foreach ($results as $uid) {
    /** @var \Drupal\user\Entity\User $user */
    $user = \Drupal\user\Entity\User::load($uid);
    $user->block();
    $user->save();
  }

  $total = count($results);
  $output->writeln("Disabled $total users");
}
```

7. Enable the module in order to access the following command:

```
$ drupal module:install console_commands
```

How it works...

Drupal Console provides integration with modules using namespace discovery methods. When Console is run in a Drupal installation, it will discover all the available projects. It then discovers any files in the `\Drupal\{ a module }\Command` namespace that implements `\Drupal\Console\Command\Command`.

Drupal Console will rescan the Drupal directory for available commands every time it is invoked, as it does not keep a cache of available commands.

There's more...

Drupal Console provides a much more intuitive developer experience as it follows Drupal core's coding formats. We will touch on how Console can be used to create entities.

Using a Console command to create entities

A benefit of Console is its ability to utilize Symfony Console's question helpers for a robust interactive experience. Drupal Commerce utilizes Console to provide a `commerce:create:store` command to generate stores. The purpose of the command is to simplify the creation of a specific entity.

The `\Drupal\commerce_store\Command\CreateStoreCommand` class overrides the default interact method that is executed to prompt data from the user. It will prompt users to enter the store's name, email, country, and currency.

Developers can implement similar commands to give advanced users a simpler way to work with modules and configuration.

See also

- Refer to how to create custom commands at https://docs.drupalconsole.com/en/extending/creating-custom-commands.html

Index

_links
requirements 348

A

Acqua
reference 19
Acquia Dev Desktop
reference 31
administrative interfaces
language files, manual installation 229
text language, detecting 232
translating 226, 229
translation permissions 231
translation status, checking 231
translation, using for default English string
customization 232
translations, exporting 231
translations, providing for custom module 233
Angular.js 320
annotations-based plugins
reference 198
asset management system
CDN or external resource, using as library 146
CSS groups 143
JavaScript, placing inheader 147
libraries, manipulating from hooks 147
library asset options 144
library dependencies 144
other libraries, extending 145
other libraries, overriding 145
using 140
authentication
about 359
authenticated Web service requests 364
page cache request policies 363
provider services 363

B

Backbone.js 320
reference 325
block
access, defining 197
altering 194
creating, from View 77
creating, plugins used 190
exposed form, placing 80
setting forms 195
Bower 324
Breakpoint module
accessing programmatically 155
caveat, for providing breakpoints from themes
155
multipliers 156
reference 156
using 153
bundle
creating, for content entity type 295, 303

C

cat, entity type 106
CKEditor plugin
reference 42
command-line workflow processes
and version control, using 267
configuration, editing from command line 266
Drupal Console, using 265
Drush config-pull 265
single configuration item, exporting 267
using 262
Composer
installation links 8
reference 16

used, for creating Drupal site 15
configuration development
  reference 272
configuration entity type
  creating 274, 279, 283
  data types, for schema definitions 284
configuration management
  existing configuration, modifying on installation 119
  subdirectories 118
configuration translation module
  info definitions, altering 237
  using 234, 237
  views, translating 237
Configuration Update Base 271
Configuration Update Manager
  about 126, 268
  reference 272
Configuration Update Reports 271
configuration YAML
  providing, on installation or update 114
configurations
  dependencies 255
  exporting 250, 254
  importing 250, 254
  schemas 256
  YAML file, saving for module configuration installation 256
Console command
  creating 392
  used, for creating entities 397
Console
  about 266
  code, scaffolding through 383
  using, for interaction with database 379
content entity type
  action links, providing for new bundle addition 303
  AdminHtmlRouteProvider provider, using 294
  bundle, creating 295
  collection route, making as local task tab 294
  creating 285, 294
content
  adding 42
  bulk actions, performing 46

editing 42
linking, to menu 46
links, translating 241
listing 68
menu link, managing from form 49
Pathauto 45
saving, as draft 45
translating 238, 240
translation handlers for entities, defining 242
translations, flagging as outdated 241
Contenta CMS
  reference 371
  Vue/Nuxt, reference 371
contextual filters
  about 81
  displaying, as tab on user page 83
  multiple and exclusion option 85
  page title, altering 84
  used, for previewing 83
  validation 84
Contextual links 51
Core themes documentation
  reference 139
Create, Read, Update, and Delete (CRUD) 274
Cross-Site Request Forgery (CSRF) tokens
  using 349
cross-site scripting (XSS) 151
custom access control
  implementing, for entity 304
  providing, to entity fields 309
custom commands
  reference 397
custom content type
  creating 52
custom field formatter
  creating 210
  formatter setting 214
custom field type
  creating 198
  empty field, defining 204
  field types, altering 204
custom field widget
  creating 205, 209
  setting and summary 209
custom module

creating 96
dependencies, defining 99
discovery locations 98
namespaces 98
package group, defining 99
version, specifying 100
custom page
defining 101
routes, parameters 105
custom plugin type
alter hook, specifying 222
cache backend, using 222
creating 215, 221
plugins, accessing through manager 223
custom storage handler
different storage backend, utilizing for entity 313
providing 310
custom theme based on Classy
base themes 138
CKEditor style sheets 139
creating 134
favicons 137
logos 137
screenshots 137
shared resources 138
theme settings 137

D

Database Logging module 341
default admin inter
filter identifiers 76
routes, overriding with Views 77
default admin interfaces
editing 73, 76
exposed, versus non-exposed 76
dependencies, DrupalVM
Vagrant 29
VirtualBox, reference 29
development environment
Acquia Dev Desktop 31
Kaklabox 31
XAMPP+ Bitnami 31
display output, node
customizing 64
distribution

Composer, using 19
installing, with Drush 18
makefiles 18
reference 17
using, with Drupal 8 17
Drupal 7
requirements, reference 9
Drupal 8 core field types
applying 55
Date field 57
Email field 57
Entity Reference field 58
Link field 56
Telephone field 57
Drupal 8 subtheme
reference 139
Drupal 8
database 13
database prefixes 14
database user, creating 13
distribution, using 17
downloading, Drush used 15
installation 9, 12
installing, with Drush 15
multisites, using 26
reference 8, 9
requirements, link 8
requirements, reference 9
security updates 16
Drupal Commerce
reference 36
Drupal Console
cache, rebuilding 374
reference 374
using 382
Drupal PHPUnit
reference 36
Drupal project
reference 16
Drupal.org API documentation
reference 125, 172
Drupal.org
handbook, reference 52
modules, reference 101
Drupal

about 7
feature 95
DrupalCI
reference 36
DrupalVM
reference 29
Drush command
creating 388
level of Drupal's bootstrap, specifying 392
reference 392
Drush
about 266
advanced user-login use cases 382
cache, rebuilding 374
reference 16, 374, 376
used, for installing Drupal 8 15
used, for installing module 25
used, for interacting with database 376
used, for managing users 380
dynamic arguments
utilizing 81

E

Embed display, Views module
using 72
Entity API 274
Entity Reference field
upcoming updates 60
Views and Entity Reference 60
Entity Reference result View
providing 90
entity
custom access control, implementing 304
event subscriber
creating 120, 123
dependency injection, using 123
external libraries
handling, best practices 325

F

Features 3.0
bundles 130
configuration state, managing 131
reference 131
suggested feature modules 128

using 125, 128
Form API
reference 173
form data
multidimensional array values, accessing 177
multiple validation handlers 176
validating 173
form display, node
customizing 60
default to hidden form items, providing 64
form display modes, managing 64
form elements
reference 167
form
additional submit handlers, adding 188
additional validate handlers, adding 188
altering 184
cache 168
creating 162, 167
elements 167
state 167
frontend 133
frontend consumers
Angular, reference 371
Ember.js, reference 371
Ionic, reference 371
React, reference 371

G

GeoIP API module 215
gzip
using, with sql-dump 379

H

HAL module
using 348
hook
reference 147
HTML5 elements
new elements, creating 173
specific element properties 172
using 168
HTTP Basic Authentication 343
HTTP POST
used, for creating data 343

Hypertext Application Language (HAL) 335

I

images
  working with 349
info.yml file
  reference 139
inline editing
  outside-in approach 52
  providing 49
IP Authentication provider 364
IP Consumer Auth
  reference 364

J

JSON API
  contenta CMS 371
  extras module, installing 368
  path prefix, changing 369
  reference 365, 371
  requests, filtering 368
  requests, paginating 367
  requests, sorting 368
  returned entity fields, disabling 369
  returned entity fields, enhancing 369
  using 365
JSON output
  key name, controlling 357

L

local development environment
  setting up, tools 29

M

Menu UI module 49
menu
  creating 46
Message entity 305
Mink PHP library
  reference 32
module configurations
  Configuration Development module 271
  installing 268
  updating 268

modules
  discovering 23
  installation 24
  installation, Composer used 24
  installing 20
  installing, with Drush 25
  uninstalling 25
Mozilla Developer Network (MDN) 160
multilingual module
  configuration translation 226
  content translation 226
  interface translation 225
  language 225
  page display menu items, translating 247
multilingual views
  display and row format items, translating 247
  creating 242, 246
  exposed form items and filters, translating 246
multisites
  domain aliases 28
  reference 29
  security concerns 28
  using, in Drupal 8 26

O

OAuth
  about 359
  references 365

P

PATCH
  used, for updating data 349
permissions
  defining, programmatically 113
  restrict access flag, using 113
  user permissions, checking 114
PhantomJS
  reference 32
PHP Framework Interoperability Group (PHP-FIG)
  98, 319
PHP library
  reference 32
PHP Standards Recommendations (PSRs) 319
PHP Xdebug
  reference 13

phpMyAdmin
  reference 13
PhpStorm
  reference 35
PHPUnit-Functional 34
PHPUnit-FunctionalJavascript 34
PHPUnit-Kernel 34
PHPUnit-Unit 33
PHPUnit
  reference 32, 36
picturefill
  reference 160
plugins
  used, for creating blocks 190
PSR-4
  reference 101

Q

Quick Edit module 49

R

Rate Limiter 342
relationships
  adding, in Views 85
  aggregation and views, using 90
  by entity reference fields 89
  through custom code 89
Responsive Image module
  benefits, performance 159
  picturefill polyfill, removing 159
  using 156
REST UI module 336, 343, 359
RESTful interfaces
  _format, using instead of Accept header 340
  enabling 336, 340
  RestResource plugin, using 341
RESTful Web Services module 340
RestResource plugin
  API, rate limiting 341
  HAL format, using 342
route provider
  by Entity API module 316
  creating 314
routes
  dynamic routes, providing 107

existing routes, altering 109
parameters, validating 106
requirements 107
routing system
  reference 317
run-tests
  as shell script 34

S

Scalable and Modular Architecture for CSS
    (SMACSS)
  reference 143
service and dependency injection
  reference 223
Simpletest
  about 33
  running 32
site configurations
  installing, from new site 261
  synchronization folder 261
  synchronizing 257, 260
  Universally Unique Identifier (UUID) 261
social_template
  reference 19
specific tests
  running 35
style plugins, Views
  row 72
  style 72
submitted form data
  multiple submit handlers 183
  processing 177
Symfony Dependency Injection component
  reference 334
Symfony service container
  reference 334
Symfony
  reference 8

T

tests
  running, without Drupal installed 35
themes
  discovering 23
  installation 20, 24

installation, Composer used 24
third-party CSS library
  implementing 326, 330
  using 326
third-party JavaScript library
  implementing 320, 324
  using 320, 324
third-party PHP library
  implementing 331
  using 331
translation server
  reference 233
Twig template
  hook suggestions, debugging 152
  logic and operators 152
  overriding 148
  reference 152
  security 151
  template file selection, debugging 152

U

Underscore.js
  about 320
  reference 325
Universally Unique Identifier (UUID) 255

V

VDC initiative
  reference 73
View published content permission 339
Views module
  in Drupal core initiative 71
Views plugins
  used, for providing custom data sources 354
Views
  block, creating 77
  display types 71
  relationship, adding 85

W

What You See Is What You Get (WYSIWYG) editor
  CKEditors 42
  configuring 38
  filter module 40
  improved links 41
  reference 40

X

XAMPP
  reference 31